Sebastian Serfas

Cognitive Biases in the Capital Investment Context

GABLER RESEARCH

Sebastian Serfas

Cognitive Biases in the Capital Investment Context

Theoretical Considerations and Empirical Experiments on Violations of Normative Rationality

With a foreword by Prof. Dr. Uwe Götze

GABLER

RESEARCH

Bibliographic information published by the Deutsche Nationalbibliothek
The Deutsche Nationalbibliothek lists this publication in the Deutsche Nationalbibliografie; detailed bibliographic data are available in the Internet at http://dnb.d-nb.de.

Dissertation Chemnitz University of Technology,
Faculty of Economics and Business Administration, 2010

1st Edition 2011

Editorial Office: Stefanie Brich | Anita Wilke

Gabler Verlag is a brand of Springer Fachmedien.
Springer Fachmedien is part of Springer Science+Business Media.
www.gabler.de

Coverdesign: KünkelLopka Medienentwicklung, Heidelberg
Printed on acid-free paper
Printed in Germany

ISBN 978-3-8349-2643-2

Foreword

It is a well-known matter of fact that successful investment activities are of very high importance both to individual companies as well as to the economy as a whole. Consequently, it is vital for the responsible decision makers to take the 'right' decisions, the ones which lead to success. Assuming that rational behavior usually favors the achievement of success, then cognitive biases which violate the principles of rationality are a clear threat to it. The existence of such biases which result from unconsciously applying mental heuristics has repeatedly been demonstrated empirically for financial investments. However, the obviously highly relevant questions whether and how such cognitive biases also affect capital investments, and how they can be tamed, have not been answered yet.

The research presented in this book addresses exactly these questions. Based on the current state of knowledge with regard to cognitive biases and investment theory, it analyses theoretically and empirically whether three typical cognitive biases also influence capital investment decisions. The results are unambiguous: the existence of cognitive biases is clearly demonstrated for the anchoring heuristic, framing, and asymmetric dominance, each at a high level of statistical significance – an insight with tremendous importance for the management of investments, which could also benefit from the approaches to deal with heuristics and biases that are subsequently presented by the author.

This scientific contribution is based on a comprehensive and thorough analysis of the relevant literature which forms the foundation for the author's own coherent and conclusive argumentation as well as for the methodologically impeccably conducted series of empirical analyses. Being the first comprehensive research to address cognitive biases in the context of capital investments, this book constitutes a remarkable 'pioneer work' and is expected to initiate further studies in this multifarious and highly relevant area at the intersection of economics and psychology. At the same time, this book is worth reading not only for scientists and academics, but also for practitioners in the field of investments, as it conveys multiple thought-provoking impulses and suggestions for practical applications and thus deserves a broad audience.

Prof. Dr. Uwe Götze

Table of Contents

List of Illustrations

List of Abbreviations

ARR	Accounting rate of return
BRIC	Brazil, Russia, India, and China
CE	Certainty equivalent
CFO	Chief financial officer
IRR	Internal rate of return
MAUT	Multiple attribute utility theory
NPV	Net present value
PP	Payback period
RADR	Risk adjusted discount rate
ROCE	Return on capital employed
SEU	Subjective expected utility
WTA	Willingness to accept
WTP	Willingness to pay

List of Symbols

n	Sample size
$\hat{p}$	Sample proportion
p	Population proportion
s	Sample standard deviation
μ	Population mean
$\overline{x}$	Sample mean

1 Introduction

In today's business environment, investments in general, and capital investments in particular, are of high importance for the majority of companies. Judgments and decisions regarding these capital investments are usually based on the principles of normative rationality. However, during the past decades, across a large variety of other domains, several effects have been observed which systematically violate normative rationality and distort judgments and decision making: cognitive biases. Given that decision making in a capital investment context is, in essence, similar to decision making in other areas, for which the existence of cognitive biases and their effects have already been demonstrated, it seems likely that these cognitive biases could also exist in a capital investment context and hence negatively influence the respective decisions. This thesis, which adopts both a theoretical as well as an empirical perspective, aims to shed light on that surmise. The target of the intended research is therefore to look for first indications that suggest whether or not cognitive biases potentially exist in a capital investment context and systematically violate normative rationality, and thereby distort decision making.

However, before actually starting to explore capital investments and cognitive biases, this first introductory chapter briefly addresses the origin and the scientific relevance of the above stated research intention and describes the overall structure and the components of this thesis.

1.1 Origin and Academic Relevance of the Research Focus

The starting point for this research was the observation that very often deviations exist between the ideal or predicted outcome and the actual outcome of capital investment decisions.[1] There are many potential explanations for these deviations, for instance changes of internal or external variables compared to the original or expected situation. However, deviations could also be due to distortions in the investment appraisal and decision making process. The source for these distortions can be either conscious behavior – that is acting on purpose, for instance due to gaming the budget, building-in slack, cheating, false reporting, etc. – or it can be unconscious behavior, for example due to cognitive biases[2]. While the former have already received extensive coverage in literature and managerial practice, the latter have to date only been addressed for financial investments, but not for capital investments[3], which are the research focus for this thesis. The following illustration schematically summarizes this derivation:

1 For instance, many large-scale investment projects turn out to be considerably more expensive and need substantially longer to be completed than previously stated and predicted. See for instance Flyvbjerg et al. (2009) for respective examples of large infrastructure projects.

2 Other unconscious factors exist that could potentially also influence decisions, for instance emotions or mood, but the focus for this research is exclusively on cognitive biases: deviations from normative rationality due to the use of simplifying information processing strategies, the so-called heuristics. Further information regarding definitions of cognitive biases is provided in detail in chapter 3.2.1.

3 For a distinction between financial and non-financial investments, which are referred to as capital investments, see for instance Kern (1974: p10ff) or Götze et al. (2008: p4) as well as the respective discussion in chapter 2.1.2.

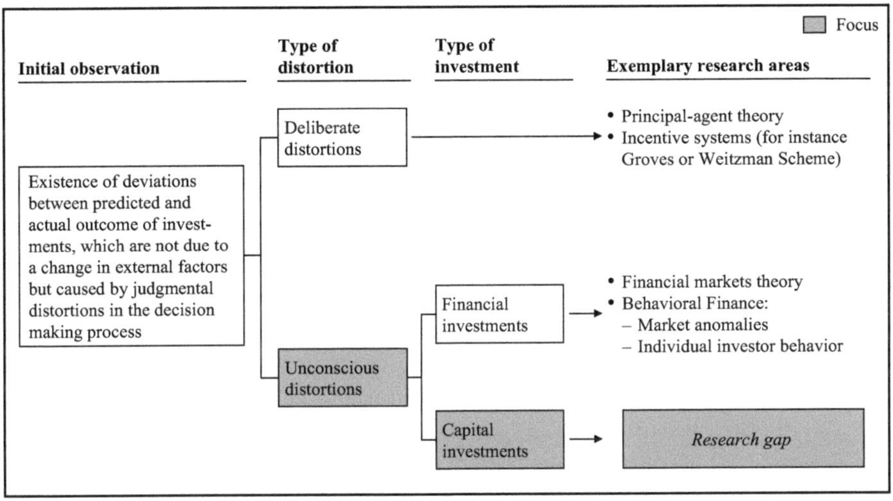

Illustration 1: Origin and academic relevance of the intended research

In addition to clarifying the origin of the intended research in a schematic way, the above diagram also names existing research areas along the selected structure: distortions due to conscious behavior are for instance addressed by the principal-agent theory[4] and by a variety of theories and models on incentive schemes, for instance the Weitzman Scheme[5] or the Groves Scheme[6]. Concerning deviations due to unconscious behavior in the context of financial investments, the transfer of several psychological approaches and theories – including cognitive biases – to financial markets theory[7] and financial investments resulted in a completely new

4 See for example Laffont/Martimort (2002) for a detailed discussion of principal-agent theory.

5 See for instance Weitzman (1976) or Ewert/Wagenhofer (2008: p417ff) for further information on the Weitzman Scheme, which is also often referred to as the 'new Soviet incentive model'.

6 See for example Groves/Loeb (1979) for an early discussion of the Groves Scheme.

7 See for instance Barucci (2003) for a detailed description of financial markets theory.

domain that has received considerable attention during the last years: behavioral finance[8].

Furthermore, the above diagram also classifies and integrates the selected research focus into the above mentioned existing domains, and illustrates that the intended research addresses an area that has not been adequately approached from a scientific perspective yet. This highlights the academic relevance of the intended research, which helps to fill the above illustrated gap.

1.2 Structure of the Thesis

The overall structure of this thesis reflects its argumentative thread and consists of two major parts: the first part introduces the theoretical foundations of capital investments and cognitive biases, and the second part combines those two aspects and discusses in detail theoretical and empirical perspectives on cognitive biases in the context of capital investments. A section covering potential counter-measures against the effects of cognitive biases as well as an overall conclusion and an outlook on potential areas for future research finally complement those two major parts.

However, before addressing the content of each chapter in more detail, it is important to be aware of and therefore highlight the purpose and focus of this thesis. Given that the intended research addresses an area that has not received any noteworthy scientific attention yet, the intention is to look for first indications for – or against – the potential existence of cognitive biases and their effects in capital investment contexts in general. Accordingly, the selected approach addresses, on a basic level, a broad range of cognitive biases and covers a variety

8 See for example Nofsinger (2008), Pompian (2006), or Wärneryd (2001) as well as the detailed discussion in chapter 4.1.2 for further information on behavioral finance and its two major sub-streams: 'market anomalies' and 'individual investor behavior'.

of different capital investment related decision situations, instead of focusing in-depth on one specific bias for a single decision situation. Similarly, it must be clear that the intended research does explicitly not aim to ultimately 'prove' the existence of cognitive biases in the domain of capital investments.[9] Nevertheless, providing solid first indications for their existence would already constitute a significant step for the scientific advancement in this area. Accordingly, in line with this intention, the thesis is structured in the following way:

The *second chapter* addresses the general fundamentals of capital investments and their appraisal, in order to establish a foundation for later parts and ensure a common understanding. Subsequent to a basic introduction of theoretical aspects and key characteristics of capital investments, decision theory and the underlying concept of normative rationality are introduced. Finally, this chapter describes the appraisal of investments in general and outlines the most relevant tools for the evaluation of capital investments.

Analogously, the *third chapter* provides an introduction to cognitive biases and their theoretical foundations. Following a brief description of general psychology and cognitive psychology, it introduces the 'heuristics and biases' approach, defines and characterizes cognitive biases in general, and discusses in detail a large selection of specific biases. Finally, it reviews and critically discusses the most important objections brought up by critics of the 'heuristics and biases' approach.

The *fourth chapter*, which is the core part of this thesis, combines the theoretical aspects discussed in the two previous chapters and analyzes, from a theoretical and an empirical perspective, whether cognitive biases are relevant in the capital investment context. First, it discusses preparatory considerations from a theoretical perspective. Afterwards, two illustrative case examples about

---

9 Because such a proof is considered as impossible given the current situation – and the respective constraints – of not being able to build on prior research. Accordingly, such a proof might be addressed in the future, when significantly more research is conducted, but it is not seen as a scientifically adequate target for the very first research steps in a completely new area.

potential effects of cognitive biases in different capital investment decision situations are presented. Subsequently, it focuses on the design, execution and analysis of a series of empirical experiments that explore the effects of cognitive biases in simplified capital investment situations. Finally, it highlights potential conclusions, addresses the issue of generalizing the observed findings to a broader context and critically discusses potential limitations.

The *fifth chapter* provides an introduction to debiasing and potential countermeasures against cognitive biases. Subsequent to an illustration of the persistency of these distortions, several debiasing techniques are discussed. In the last part, a general framework for developing a counterstrategy in a business environment is presented.

The *sixth chapter* finally presents an overall summary of the theoretical considerations and empirical findings discussed in the previous chapters. Subsequently, several potential areas and foci for future research are suggested.

2 Theoretical Foundations of Capital Investments and Investment Appraisal

This chapter provides a basic understanding of capital investments in general. The first part introduces the fundamentals of capital investments, including their key characteristics and classifications. The second part of this chapter covers decision theory and establishes the basic concept of rationality as foundation for a decision model. The third part finally addresses investment appraisals and discusses major investment appraisal techniques that are used to evaluate capital investments.

The intention of this chapter is to give a brief introduction to capital investments and their appraisal, in order to establish a foundation for later chapters and ensure a common understanding. This chapter does by no means aim to cover all aspects of capital investments or to provide an in-depth discussion of all capital investment related issues, as there is a large body of literature available for both purposes[10]. Instead, the focus is explicitly on introducing the basic concepts and principles that are relevant in later parts of this thesis.

2.1 Fundamentals of Capital Investments

Due to their nature and special characteristics, investments, and in particular capital investments, are of highly important for most companies. The following sections provide some fundamental information on these investments. First of all, the general term 'investment' is introduced and defined. Subsequently, investments are categorized, with capital investments being one of two main types. Following a brief description of their major characteristics and traits, the final section outlines the key phases of a typical capital investment project.

---

10 See for example Götze et al. (2007), McLaney (2009), Drury (2008), or Dayananda et al. (2002) for information on capital investments and investment appraisal in general; regarding recent developments on specific topics and practical applications see for instance Hansen et al. (2009).

2.1.1 Definition of Investments in General

The word 'investment' originally stems from the Latin word 'investire', which means 'to clothe' or 'to accouter'[11]. In today's environment, the term 'investment' is frequently used in all sorts of business context. However, it is important to point out that the term 'investment' is used in two disciplines, economics and business administration, but it is only the business administration concept of 'investments' that is of relevance here and in the remainder of this thesis, not the 'investment' concept used in economics[12]. In the business administration context, "in its simplest form, an investment decision can be defined as one which involves the firm in making a cash outlay with the aim of receiving, in return, future cash inflows" (Lumby, 1988: p22). Atrill/McLaney (2002: p188) present a slightly broader, more general definition of investments: "investment involves making an outlay of something of economic value, usually cash, at one point in time that is expected to yield economic benefits to the investor at some other point in time". Although there is no single, collectively used definition – actually, there is a multitude of slightly different definitions in literature[13] – most definitions in the respective English literature are similar to the two examples mentioned above: they focus on an (intertemporal) exchange of something valuable, usually represented by cash flows, and incorporate time as a central component. However, time is often not only referred to as an essential component of investments[14], but also as a key differentiating and defining characteristic between (short-term)

---

[11] For a detailed discussion of the etymological and linguistic roots of the term 'investment' see for example Heinen (1957).

[12] See for example Mankiw (2009) or Baumol/Blinder (2009) for more information on the concept of 'investments' used in economics.

[13] See for instance Drury (2004: p493), Götze (2006: p3) or Röhrich (2007: p2) for further similar definitions of investments.

[14] One example being Atrill/McLaney (2002: p188) who state that "the essential feature of investment decisions is time".

business decisions and (long-term) investments: "the distinguishing feature between short-term decisions and capital investment (long-term) decisions is time. Generally, we can classify short-term decisions as those that involve a relatively short time horizon, say one year, from the commitment of funds to the receipt of the benefits. On the other hand, capital investment decisions are those decisions where a significant period of time elapses between the outlay and the recoupment of the investment" (Drury, 2004: p493). This contrast between business decisions and investments, and consequently the requirement for a significant period of time to pass between outlay and benefit, is often not expressed as explicitly as above, but it seems to be implicitly inherent in most authors' investment definitions[15].

In addition to the wide-spread use of cash flow focused definitions, there are also other potential foci. Lücke (1991: p151f) proposes four different approaches for the definition of investments: cash flow focus, capital appropriation focus, combination of assets focus, and limitation of freedom of action focus[16]. The first approach, based on sequences of cash inflows and cash outflows, corresponds to the standard definitions presented earlier. The capital appropriation approach focuses on the two-sided concept of a balance sheet and understands investments as the transformation of capital (liabilities side of the balance sheet) into assets (assets side of the balance sheet). The third definition, the combination of assets approach, describes investments as the process of combining assets, especially capital equipment, into new goods, in particular production facilities. In contrast to the three approaches presented so far, which see investments as a process, the limitation of freedom of action approach characterizes investments as a state: an investment is the long-term commitment of financial resources, which in conse-

15 Although 'time' is presented here as integral part of the investment definition, most authors describe time also as one of the key characteristics of investments (see chapter 2.1.2) and implicitly regard time as a kind of defining feature.

16 Author's translation, as original terms are in German: zahlungsbestimmt, vermögensbestimmt, kombinationsbestimmt, dispositionsbestimmt.

quence constrains the freedom of action of the investing company during that particular period.

Although all presented approaches for defining investments have their proponents and eligibility, it is necessary to select one as the guiding principle and base for the forthcoming discussions. Being the most popular and most frequently referred to approach with regard to defining investments, the cash flow based definition and understanding is used as foundation for all discussions throughout the remaining parts of this thesis.

2.1.2 Classifications and Characteristics

Investments can be classified in several ways. A comprehensive overview is provided by Kern (1974: p10ff), who distinguishes between 'peripheral' and 'central' criteria.[17] While 'central' criteria focus on inherent characteristics of an investment – in particular qualitative, quantitative and temporal consequences, as well as interdependencies[18] and degree of uncertainty – and provide support for the selection of the appropriate evaluation method, the classification along 'peripheral' criteria addresses mainly descriptive attributes that are not relevant for determining how beneficial the investment itself is: the asset type of the investment, its underlying reason, and the affected operational function(s).[19] The classification according to asset types distinguishes between financial and capital

17 The classification of investments according to 'peripheral' criteria is considered as more suitable for the purpose of this thesis and the intended research; accordingly, the discussed investment classifications focus primarily on these criteria, and 'central' criteria are only briefly mentioned.

18 See for example Dayananda et al. (2002: p4) for a refined and enhanced categorization of investments along the criterion of interdependency; classifications include 'independent projects', 'mutually exclusive projects' and 'contingent projects'.

19 Kern (1974: p16f) also lists 'size' as central criterion, but acknowledges that a categorization according to size is often ambiguous, for example because it would require relative definitions; as a consequence, 'size' has not been established as a meaningful classification criterion.

investments. Financial investments include all types of securities – for example stocks, bonds, derivatives, equity stakes, etc. – and can be of speculative or non-speculative nature. Capital investments can be divided into physical investments – for example machinery, facilities, real estate property, etc. – and intangible investments, for instance research and development, competitive intelligence or training and education of employees.[20] The following illustration summarizes the described investment types:

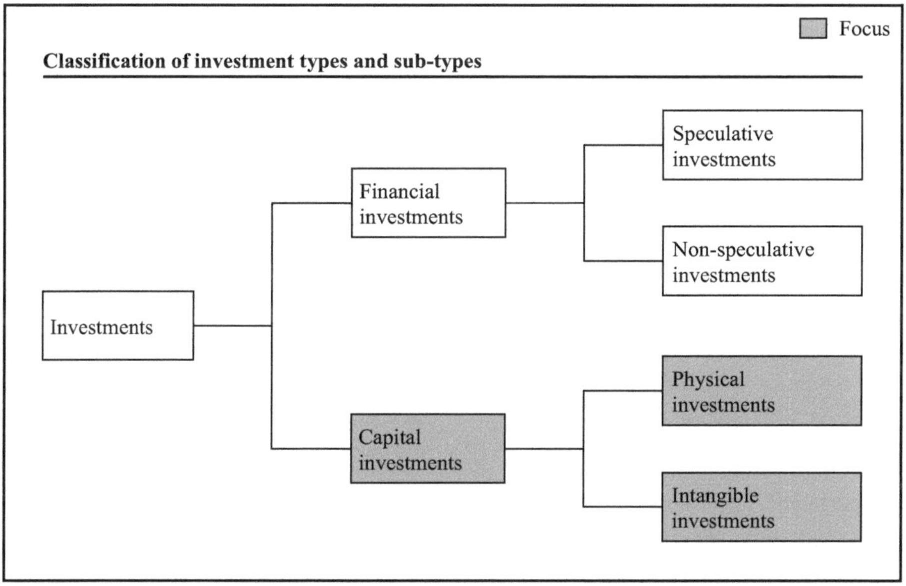

Illustration 2: Classification of investments according to asset type[21]

The second option discussed by Kern (1974: p13ff) is to classify investments according to the underlying reason or motive[22]: foundational investments (for

[20] The mentioned investment (sub-) types can be broken down even further; however, for the purpose of this thesis, the presented level of detail is regarded as sufficient.

[21] Illustration adapted from Kern (1974: p12).

example the initial startup of the business, the expansion into a new market segment, the installation of a production site at a new geographic location, etc.), recurring investments (including replacements and substituting investments as well as large repair and maintenance investments) and supplementary investments. The latter can be further divided into extension investments (for example the expansion of capacity at an existing production facility), alteration investments (for example rationalizations, internal changes and adjustments, etc.) and protective investments to safeguard a company's position or competitiveness. Finally, investment can be classified according to the operational function(s) they affect, for instance production, logistics, procurement, research and development, administration, etc. Although most authors of investment-related literature have slightly different emphases when categorizing investments[23], the classification according to asset type seems to prevail. Following this classification, and incorporating the introductory aspects discussed in the first chapter, only one of the two major types is relevant for the remaining parts of this thesis and its particular research intention: capital investments.

Capital investments are usually regarded as being "of crucial importance to the business" (Atrill/McLaney, 2002: p189). Drury (2004: p493) even claims that "capital investment decisions normally represent the most important decisions that an organization makes". The underlying reason for this attributed high importance is a set of certain distinctive features that characterize capital investments[24]: a substantial initial outlay, resulting in a high level of committed funds, and a generally long-run time horizon. Furthermore, capital investment

22 See also Heinen (1957) for further information on this motive-based classification approach.

23 For example, Röhrich (2007: p3) and Schäfer (2005: p18ff) focus on object and underlying reason, Blohm et al. (2006: p1) address object and operational area, and Götze et al. (2007: p4f) discuss object, underlying reason and operational area.

24 See for instance Dayananda et. al (2002: p1), Blohm et al. (2006: p1), Röhrich (2007: p2), or Atrill/McLaney (2002: p188f) for characteristics of capital investments in general.

decisions are normally not easily reversible, in contrast to most financial investments in securities, for instance because they are usually tailored to the specific needs of a particular company and often include tangible assets like plants or special tools. In addition, capital investments usually result in significant long-term consequences for other parts of the business and create considerable interdependencies[25] that have to be accounted for prior to taking the investment decision. For the special case of extraordinarily large investments, Chadwick (1998: p152) adds that those capital decisions are taken rather infrequently, at least for the majority of companies, resulting in a relatively low level of experience. The combination of all the above mentioned characteristics turns judgments related to capital investments into one of the key challenges for the success of each company, because "costly and far-reaching mistakes can, and probably will, be made unless businesses take great care in making their investment decisions" (McLaney, 2006: p78).

2.1.3 Phases of Capital Investments

The life-cycle of a typical capital investment can be broadly divided into four phases[26]: planning, implementation, utilization and disinvestment[27]. The following illustration summarizes this process and its core activities:

---

25 See for example Kruschwitz (2007: p1) or Dayananda et. al (2002: p1).

26 This approach typically assumes a physical investment, but its major aspects are also applicable to intangible investments (although slight modifications might be necessary).

27 See for example Götze (2006: p14f) for general information regarding the investment process; for an in-depth discussion see for instance Sierke (1990: p93ff) or Adam (1996: p31ff).

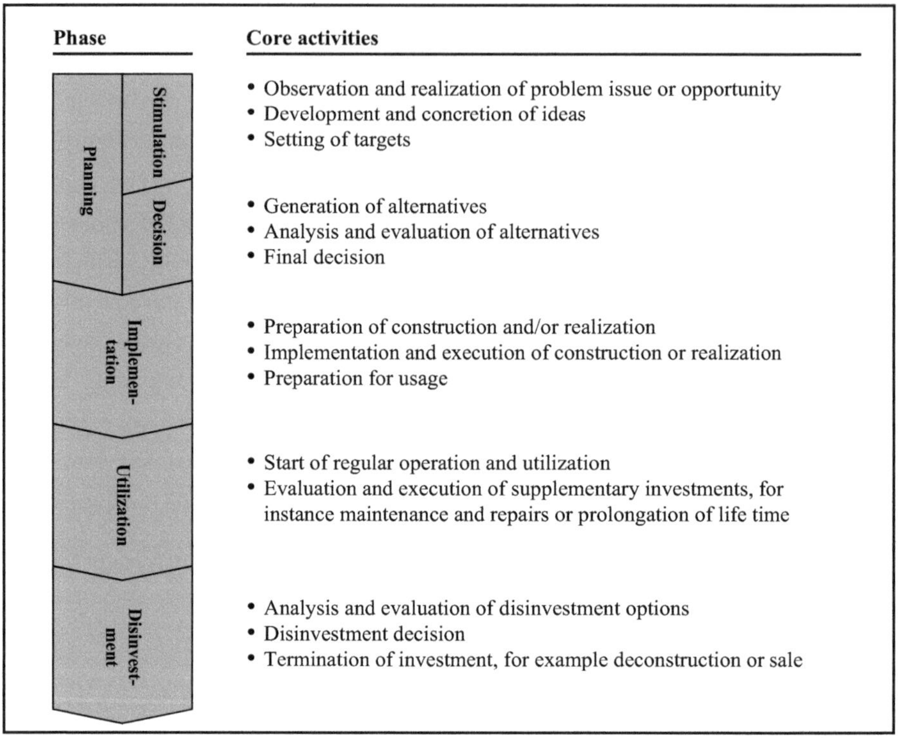

Illustration 3: Capital investment process and related core activities[28]

The planning phase can be decomposed into a stimulation phase, which incorporates all activities from the observation and realization of the problem to the creation of ideas until the general target setting, and a decision phase, which includes all activities from the identification of potential alternatives to the analysis and evaluation of each alternative until the final decision[29]. In the implementation phase, the construction (of physical investments) or realization

[28] Illustration based primarily on the descriptions in Götze (2006: p14f) and Adam (1996: p31ff).

[29] This phase is discussed in more detail in chapter 2.3.1.

(of intangible investments) is executed, and all necessary preparations for its usage are initiated. The utilization phase begins with the start of the regular operation and might include itself several investment activities, for example maintenance and repairs, or additional investments to improve the original investment or prolong its life time. Finally, in the disinvestment phase, the decision to disinvest is taken, and the capital investment is deconstructed, sold or otherwise terminated.

Although the outlined process and the illustration seem to suggest a linear and non-overlapping sequence of activities, it is important to highlight that this is by no means the case. In fact, the capital investment process is characterized by several feedback loops and iterative steps, including a continuous control and (re-) planning cycle. Furthermore, the individual phases frequently overlap and are often interdependent of each other. As a result, the actual capital investment process is rather complex and depends on the specific project and situation.

Having defined and classified investments in general, and having characterized capital investments, the next step is to address how capital investments can be evaluated. Decision theory has been established as a suitable foundation for this purpose. Accordingly, the next sub-chapter focuses on the overall concept of decision theory in general, before investment appraisal and the respective methods are addressed in the subsequent sub-chapter.

2.2 Fundamentals of Decision Theory and Decision Models

Most judgments and decisions in today's economic context are based, at least to a certain extent, on the principles of decision theory. This is especially true for capital investment decisions. The following sections therefore introduce the respective fundamentals, starting with a general introduction of its two major approaches: normative and descriptive decision theory. Subsequently, the basic concept of rationality, that most normative approaches are based on, is discussed. The last section finally addresses the key components and characteristics of decision models. The intention of this sub-chapter is to introduce the basic concept and some selected aspects, not to address decision theory in its full width and depth[30].

2.2.1 Introduction to Decision Theory

In general, "decision theory deals with situations in which one or more actors must make choices among given alternatives" (Rapoport, 1989: p1). Resnik (1987: pxi) specifies more formally that decision theory is "the collection of mathematical, logical, and philosophical theories of decision making by rational individuals – taken alone, in competition, and in groups". Decision theory is usually divided into two types or branches[31]: normative[32] and descriptive. While normative decision theories prescribe "how people *ought* to behave in given decision situations" (Rapoport, 1989: p2) and "aim to tell us how we ideally should [...] reason, make judgments, and take decisions" (Over, 2004: p3), descriptive decision theories comprise "a number of general propositions describing the actual behaviour of individuals or groups of people making some decisions" (Kozielecki, 1981: p2) and aim to figure out how decisions actually *are* made.[33] Based on observations of decisions in particular situations, descriptive approaches aim to understand, infer and establish general patterns of actual behavior. In contrast, normative approaches aim to deduce prescriptive rules for

---

30 See for example Baron (2007) or Jungermann et al. (2005) for detailed discussions of decision theory.

31 See for example Laux (2005: p13ff) for a detailed discussion of the traditional two branches of decision theory.

32 Some authors occasionally make use of the term 'prescriptive' as synonym for 'normative', for example Resnik (1987).

33 See Resnik (1987: p3).

ideal behavior, based on theoretical considerations, concepts and models, for example probability theory or logical reasoning.

Most authors follow this traditional classification of decision theory into two branches. In contrast, Baron (2007: p31ff) distinguishes three models: descriptive, prescriptive and normative. While the descriptive component is in line with the traditional approach, and describes how decisions are actually taken, prescriptive models are described as lists of rules that state how we should think, and the purpose of normative models is finally presented as determining "which prescriptive models are the most useful" (Baron, 2007: p33) ones in order to achieve the thinker's specific goals.[34] However, although this additional split might make sense from a particular, conceptual point of view, for the purpose of the intended research, it seems appropriate and sufficient to stick with the traditional understanding and distinction into normative and descriptive approaches to decision making. Actually, both concepts are of high relevance for this thesis: the research question requires a descriptive approach in order to determine the actual behavior of subjects under the influence of cognitive biases, and normative theories of rationality are necessary to establish a baseline with which the observations can be compared. These theories of rationality are the focus of the following section.

2.2.2 The Basic Concept of Rationality

The concept of 'rationality' is frequently referred to across many areas of economic sciences and business life. However, there is no universal definition. In the context of decision theory, rational behavior – that is behavior that follows the principles of rationality – is often described in a simplifying way as "behavior that maximizes the value of consequences" (Hastie/Dawes, 2001: p249) in a parti-

---

34 For a slightly different characterization of descriptive, prescriptive and normative decision theory and models see Bell et al. (1988: p9ff).

cular decision situation. Accordingly, "rational decision theory specifies optimal methods for the solution of particular decision problems by taking reference to some of the postulates of rational action" (Kozielecki, 1981: p3). It advises, in a normative way, which methods to choose and which procedures to follow, in order to maximize the achievement of particular goals, but it is not concerned about the conclusions or the goals themselves[35]. The focus is on the methods applied, not on the results. Consequently and reversely, "irrationality is not the same as error. We can use good methods and reach erroneous conclusions, or we can use poor methods and be lucky" (Baron, 2007: p63).

As pointed out earlier, there is no universal definition of rationality. Instead, rationality is derived from specific sets[36] of key postulates and axioms, which are usually expressed as mathematical equations that define a normative framework. In the context of rational decision theory, these axioms describe a system of rules for the generation of preferences. A classic example of such an axiomatic system is the expected utility theory: Bernoulli (1738) has already described this theory verbally in the 18th century, but it was only about two hundred years later that von Neumann/Morgenstern (1944) accomplished the formal axiomatization[37]. Savage (1954) further refined and enhanced their work to arrive at the so-called subjective expected utility theory[38] (SEU), which constitutes a key foundation of today's decision theory.

---

35 See for example Kozielecki (1981: p5) or Baron (2007: p63).

36 As the wording already implies, there is not one single set, but many different sets exist; however, their basics are often similar.

37 See for example Hastie/Dawes (2001: p249ff) or Heun (2007: p19ff) for a discussion of Bernoulli's first descriptions of what is today called expected utility theory, and the respective axiomatization by von Neumann and Morgenstern.

38 See for example Garnham/Oakhill (1994: p177ff), Binmore (2009: p117ff), Hastie/Dawes (2001: p249ff), or Jungermann et al. (2005: p203ff) for more detailed discussions of the subjective expected utility theory.

Discussing in detail a full axiomatic system that describes the normative framework of rational decision theory would be far beyond the scope and intention of this thesis. Instead, a selection of three of the most important basic axioms – comparability, transitivity, and invariance – is discussed, which must be satisfied to fulfill the requirement of stable and consistent preferences assumed by normative rationality.

Comparability[39] demands that a pairwise comparison is feasible between any two given alternatives and "that the person is in no doubt as to which is the better one, or that both are equally attractive" (Kozielecki, 1981: p4). More formally expressed, "for any two possible outcomes, A and B, either A is preferred to B, or B to A, or the decision maker is indifferent in the sense of not caring which transpires" (Garnham/Oakhill, 1994: p180). For example, assuming that a person has to make a decision between four alternatives (A, B, C, and D), then the comparability principle demands that he or she can state for each of the six pairs[40] of two alternatives, which respective alternative is favored or if he or she is indifferent between those two alternatives.[41]

"Transitivity means that there is an internal consistency in the person's preferences: if he prefers x to y and y to z, then he must prefer x to z" (Kozielecki, 1981: p4). If that was not the case – for example, if someone prefers A to B, B to C, but C to A[42] – that person's (intransitive) preferences would express a circular pattern, and the person thus theoretically runs the risk of being exploited as 'money pump'[43]: the person should always be willing to pay a very small amount of money to give up his or her current alternative and receive the

39 Some authors, for instance Kozielecki (1981), refer to this principle as 'connectivity' instead of comparability.

40 The pairs of alternatives in this case are A-B, A-C, A-D, B-C, B-D, and C-D.

41 See for example Laux (2005: p31ff) or Jungermann et al. (2005: p209ff) for further information on comparability.

42 Instead of preferring A to C, which would be in line with the transitivity principle.

43 See for example Hastie/Dawes (2001: p263f) or Piatelli-Palmarini (1994: p8ff).

respectively preferred alternative instead. However, due to the circular pattern of his or her preferences, this swapping of alternatives – each at a minimal cost – could go on forever. Consequently, the transitivity axiom usually constitutes a vital part of the axiomatic system of rational decision theory.[44]

The invariance principle demands that a choice between the same options, with the same goals in mind, should always lead to the same outcome. Furthermore, "invariance should apply to both the way the outcomes are described (descriptive invariance) and the way the choice is made (procedural or response mode invariance)" (Garnham/Oakhill, 1994: p186). For example, assuming that a person prefers option A to option B, then the axiom of procedural invariance demands that this person acts in the following way for two decision tasks: if he or she is asked to select one of the two alternatives, he or she selects A (as this is the preferred one), and if he or she is asked to eliminate one of the two alternatives, he or she selects B for elimination (and keeps A, as this is the preferred one).

Although all the three exemplarily presented principles seem at first sight reasonable from a normative point of view, several objections have been raised against their validity in real life decision situations[45], and enhanced theories that additionally incorporate some of those objections into decision theory have been suggested, for example Prospect Theory[46] or Cumulative Prospect Theory[47]. However, all those theories are in the end, at least to a certain extent, based on decision models. Therefore, the following section describes their key components and characteristics.

---

44 See for example Garnham/Oakhill (1994: p180ff), Laux (2005: p32f), Jungermann et al. (2005: p209f) for further information on transitivity.

45 See for example Hastie/Dawes (2001: p275ff), Aumann (1997), Garnham/Oakhill (1994: p183ff), Jungermann et al. (2005: p211ff), or Binmore (2009: p17ff).

46 See for example Kahneman/Tversky (1979).

47 See for example Tversky/Kahneman (1992).

2.2.3 Decision Models

Before addressing decision models in particular, it makes sense to first clarify in general what a model is. A model is a simplifying and simplified illustration of reality that focuses on those aspects that are relevant for the underlying problem and purpose and possesses a structure that is similar to the respective reality[48]. Lilien/Rangaswamy (2004: p7) point out that each model must have a well-defined specific purpose, "which represents the reason for its construction and circumstances its domain of applicability", and a set of assumptions[49], that "provide the context or framework for a model". Models can be classified in several ways[50], for instance according to their structural representation into verbal, graphical, mathematical, and physical models.[51]

A decision model is in essence a particular type of model that has the purpose of supporting decision making, especially in a business-related context. While von Halle/Goldberg (2009: p14) describe it in a more abstract way "as an intellectual template for perceiving, organizing, and managing the business logic behind a business decision", Bhimani et al. (2008: p937) simply define it as a "formal model for making a choice [...], frequently involving quantitative analysis".[52] Using formalized decision models in a business-related context usually improves decision making and delivers several potential benefits for the decision maker and the respective company:[53] they improve the consistency of

48 See Bamberg/Coenenberg (2002: p13f).

49 Assumptions can generally be either explicit or implicit; however, in the particular case of decision models, it is preferrable that all assumptions are made explicit.

50 See for example Adam (1996: p81ff) for a detailed discussion of model classification according to five different criteria.

51 See for example Lilien/Rangaswamy (2004: p8) who differentiate between verbal, graphical and mathematical models, while Adam (1996: p81ff) distinguishes graphical, mathematical and physical models.

52 See for example Laux (2005: p16ff), Adam (1996: p87ff), or Lücke (1991: p71) for further definitions of decision models, and the differentiation from explanatory models.

53 See Lilien/Rangaswamy (2004: p13ff) for a detailed discussion of the mentioned benefits.

decisions, often help to generate additional decision options, assess the relative impact of variables, support the transformation of formerly implicit mental models into explicit models, and facilitate group decision making.

Decision models consist of a 'decision variables component' and an 'objectives component'[54].[55] The former can be divided into acts, states, and outcomes. Acts are simply all potential activities, meaning all optional alternatives that outline what could be done. States, also called states of nature or states of the world, describe the different conditions that the environment[56] can be in or end up. States can include both "non-physical as well as physical conditions" (Resnik, 1987: p7) and "must be mutually exclusive and exhaustive" (Resnik, 1987: p7). Outcomes are all possible results that the combination of acts and states can yield.[57] They are usually derived based on one or more functions and equations, which transform and convert acts and states into outcomes.

An important aspect with regard to the 'decision variables component' concerns the condition under which the decision making takes place: certainty, risk, or ignorance.[58] Certainty means that "all outcomes of any decision are known completely and in advance" (Allsopp, 1995: p54), hence, it is undoubtedly clear what will happen. In the opposite case, referred to as uncertainty, it is not clear what will happen. Uncertainty can be further divided into risk and ignorance. While risk refers to a situation where "it is possible to assign probabilities to all

---

54 Author's translation of the German terms 'Entscheidungsfeld' and 'Zielraum/Zielsystem'.

55 For details regarding the components of decision models see for example Resnik (1987: p6ff), Salinger (1993: p2ff), Laux (2005: p19ff), or Bamberg/Coenenberg (2002: p15ff), whose works constitute the source for the following explanations.

56 This element can also consist of and be split into several sub-components, depending on the degree of complexity of the particular model.

57 The derivation of potential outcomes is independent of the decision maker's preferences. In addition, outcomes must not be confused with goals, which are part of the 'objectives component'.

58 See for example Resnik (1987: p13ff), Allsopp (1995: p53ff), Heun (2007: p11ff), or Laux (2005: p22ff).

the outcomes arising from each act" (Resnik, 1987: p14) – this includes known or given probabilities as well as reasonably estimated probabilities –, ignorance means that there is no suitable indication of any likelihoods and "it makes no sense to assign probabilities to the outcomes emanating from one or more of the acts" (Resnik, 1987: p14). The implications of this distinction between certainty, risk and ignorance must be taken into account when developing a decision model.

The 'objectives component' consists of a system of goals and preferences. It specifies the target variables of the decision maker, the respective type of target achievement – maximization, minimization, or satisficing[59] – and how a potential preference trade-off between conflicting targets is to be done:

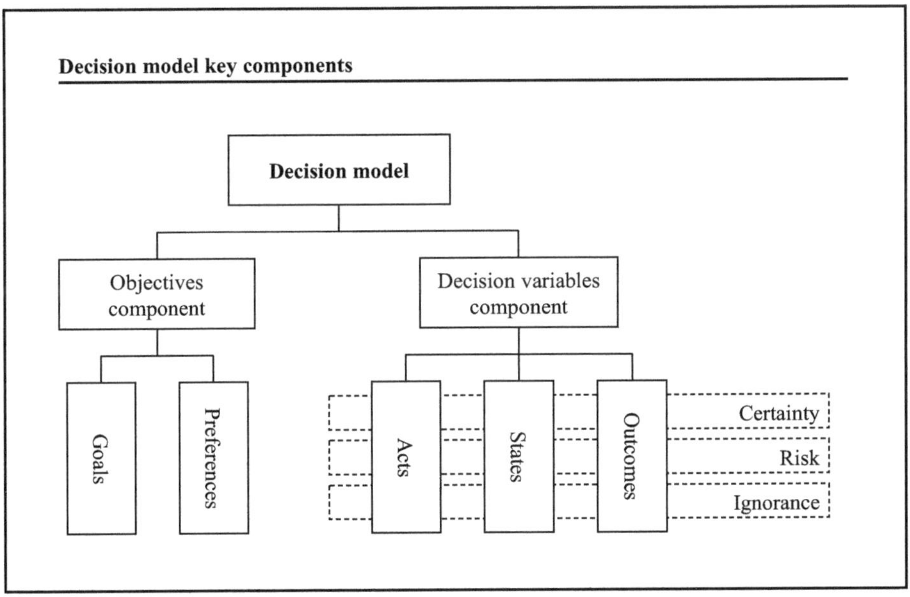

Illustration 4: Key components of a decision model[60]

[59] See for example Salinger (1993: p3).

[60] Illustration adapted from Laux (2005: p20), extended with additional aspects.

The brief introduction to the fundamentals of decision theory in this sub-chapter, including a short discussion of the basic concept of rationality and the key components of decision models, has established the foundation for the evaluation of decision situations in general. The next sub-chapter focuses on a particular type of decisions: the analysis of capital investments.

2.3 Investment Appraisal

Investment appraisal refers to the decision making process applied by businesses for the purpose of deciding which investments to undertake[61]. To do this, taking into account a large variety of possible intentions[62] – for example to choose between several mutually exclusive investments, or to decide whether to pursue or reject a particular investment –, a multitude of different tools and methods have been developed. This sub-chapter addresses a selection of these methods. Following a brief illustration of the investment appraisal process in general, the focus is subsequently on traditional investment methods with only one target variable, divided into static and dynamic models[63]. Afterwards, a selection of further investment appraisal tools is presented, including models for decision situations with multiple targets and for investments under uncertainty. The focus throughout this sub-chapter is on providing a basic understanding of a few selected tools, in order to serve as a common foundation for the discussions in later

---

61 See for example (Proctor, 2006: p177).

62 See for example Götze et al. (2007: p24f) for a list of possible intentions, including for instance questions of absolute and relative profitability, ideal point in time, or investment programs.

63 Dayananda et al. (2002: p91) define static models as tools that do not take into account the time value of money, while dynamic models do incorporate the time value of money.

chapters; the intention is not to cover all possible methods or to discuss any of them in its full depth.[64]

2.3.1 Investment Appraisal Process

Investment appraisal is in essence a decision making process, hence, it is to a large extend based on the general process of taking decisions[65] and adapted to fit the particular circumstances of the business and capital investments contexts. With regard to the phases of capital investments described earlier[66], the focus of investment appraisal is on the second part of the planning phase: the decision phase. However, it is not restricted to this part, some activities overlap with earlier and later stages of the capital investment project life cycle.

The investment appraisal process itself is usually independent of the specific tools that are applied during the process. Therefore, it is helpful to first describe and understand the full process, and only then address the actual techniques and methods. Moreover, although the following description of the investment appraisal process might at first sight evoke the impression of being a linear sequence of steps, the actual process is rather non-linear and flexible, characterized by iterative feedback loops and potential overlaps. Consequently, the components of the presented investment appraisal process should be understood as a set of activities, which do of course adhere to a certain overall logic, but are not bound to precisely follow a constricted layout.

64 See for example Drury (2008), Götze et al. (2007), or Kruschwitz (2007) for detailed discussions of a large number of investment appraisal methods.

65 See for example Laux (2005: p8ff) for a description and discussion of usual activities during the decision making process in general.

66 See chapter 2.1.3.

The investment appraisal process is described with several small variations and differing emphases and levels of detail by different authors[67], but most of the core activities are similar to a certain extent. Atrill/McLaney (2002: p223ff) present a rather simple, but nevertheless appealingly meaningful approach that is suitable for the intended purpose of giving a short overview of the major activities during the investment appraisal process, which consists of five steps:

1. Determine investment funds available
2. Identify profitable project opportunities
3. Evaluate the proposed projects[68]
4. Approve the selected project
5. Monitor and control the project

The author's focus is clearly on phase 3 – the evaluation of the previously identified projects –, which incorporates the major analytical activities as well as the selection decision itself. The above outlined process is quite simplistic and approaches investment appraisal from a rather practical point of view. This becomes evident through the existence of phases 1 (determination of available funds) and 4 (formal approval of selected project): both phases, though important in particular real life business contexts of capital investments, are partly neglected or ignored by authors who approach investment appraisal from a purely theoretical perspective. However, this group of authors usually present and discuss the appraisal process on a more detailed level instead. Dayananda et al. (2002: p5ff) for instance highlight that investment appraisal is based on previously defined corporate or business unit goals and starts with a planning phase that sets the framework for the subsequent identification of potential

67 See for example Dayananda et al. (2002: p5ff), Atrill/McLaney (2002: p223ff), Drury (2008: p332ff), or Kruschwitz (2007: p7ff) for different approaches to the investment appraisal process.

68 This step also includes the project selection decision.

investment opportunities. Furthermore, the evaluation phase is addressed in a more detailed fashion: it includes for example preliminary screenings to quickly reduce the number of initially identified potential opportunities, a qualitative assessment that supports the financial appraisal and the quantitative analysis of pre-screened opportunities, and an explicit decision to accept or reject the investment project. Moreover, the monitor and control phase is explicitly split into activities that take place during the implementation and/or the operational phase of the project on the one hand, and a post-completion audit after the end of the capital investment's life cycle on the other hand. However, despite the described differences in perspective and level of detail, both approaches are in agreement that the actual evaluation of a capital investment project is only one aspect – though an important one – of the whole appraisal process. The techniques and tools that can be used to facilitate this evaluation are the focus of the following sections.

2.3.2 Fundamental Static Methods

Investment appraisal methods are usually classified into two different groups[69]. Approaches that do not take into account the time value of money are referred to as static or non-discounted cash flow tools, and techniques that do take into account the time value of money are called dynamic or discounted cash flow methods. The focus of this sub-chapter is on static methods, which are usually considerably simpler compared to dynamic methods; those are addressed in the subsequent sub-chapter.

A large variety of static investment appraisal tools exist. The two methods that are primarily applied by companies[70], and are also by far the most treated ones in

---

69 See for example Dayananda et al. (2002: p91).

70 See for example Watson/Head (2007: p199ff), McLaney (2006: p96f), or Drury (2004: p512) who quote several empirical studies that illustrate the high dissemination of accounting rate of return and payback period among companies.

the literature, are the 'accounting rate of return' (ARR) method and the 'payback period' (PP) method. Both are very briefly illustrated in the following sections[71].

Accounting Rate of Return Method

Accounting rate of return is a profitability measure that determines "the ratio of average annual profits, after depreciation, to the capital invested" (Lucey, 2003: p409). Capital invested can either refer to the initial outlay at the beginning of the project, or alternatively to the average of all invested funds, that generate the respective profits, during the whole life of the investment project[72]. According to the underlying decision rule of the accounting rate of return method, in a setting with several alternative projects (relative profitability) the investment with the highest percentage return is chosen; in a single project context, the investment is accepted if its ARR exceeds a pre-set minimum percentage return (absolute profitability)[73]. Due to their high resemblance, return on capital employed (ROCE) and accounting rate of return are sometimes used as synonyms. However, while ARR refers to specific investment projects, ROCE is actually used to assess the performance of a whole company or a business unit[74].

The advantages of the accounting rate of return method are that it is simple, quick and intuitively easy to understand, which make this method a widely-used tool among companies. However, in addition to potential problems when comparing investments with different sizes, and its major drawback of ignoring the

---

71 Although the following descriptions are, in line with the intention of this chapter, kept rather short, several references for further information regarding the discussed methods are provided throughout the respective discussions.

72 See for example Atrill/McLaney (2002: p190f), Drury (2004: p511ff), Röhrich (2007: p29), or McLaney (2006: p94f).

73 See for example Götze et al. (2007: p41ff) or Kruschwitz (2007: p35ff).

74 See for example Atrill/McLaney (2002: p192).

time factor, and hence the differing time value of money, another potential issue arises from the fact that there is not a clear, single standard of how to calculate the ARR. Rather, several different variations exist, raising a multitude of questions[75], for instance which profit to take – for example pre-tax or post-tax, before or after interest –, what to include in the capital invested element – for example with or without working capital – or whether to use accounting figures or cash flows. This ambiguity complicates the usage of the ARR method, especially in comparative multi-company contexts, and – together with the other drawbacks – reduces the intuitively perceived suitability of this measure.

Payback Period Method

Payback period refers to "the length of time it takes for an initial investment to be repaid out of the net cash inflows from a project" (Atrill/McLaney, 2002: p194). This measure of how long it takes to recoup the initial investment outlay is usually expressed in years and exists in two different variations[76]: a simpler approach that uses average annual cash flows[77], and a more sophisticated approach that calculates the "period of time over which the accumulated cash flows will equal the initial outlay" (Dayananda et al., 2002: p97).[78] While the former is only adequate under certain conditions[79], the second approach is not limited in such a way. According to the underlying decision rule of the PP method, an investment is accepted if its payback period is shorter than a pre-defined length of time, otherwise it is rejected; in a setting with several alternative

75 See for instance Lucey (2003: p409) or Dayananda et al. (2002: p101).

76 See for example Kruschwitz (2007: p38ff) for a detailed discussion of both alternatives.

77 See for instance Röhrich (2007: p33) or Götze et al. (2007: p44ff).

78 In fact, the simpler variation also accumulates cash flows, but simplifyingly uses average cash flows, while the more sophisticated method employs fluctuating cash flows without averaging.

79 Especially a stable level of net cash inflows with no or only minimal fluctuations over the years.

investment opportunities, the project with the shortest payback period is selected.[80]

The major advantage of the PP method is that "it is quick and easy to calculate and can be easily understood by managers" (Atrill/McLaney, 2002: p195). Moreover, the measure intuitively appears to make sense and delivers a seemingly easy to interpret result. However, a pure duration measure can also be highly arbitrary and favors quick returns rather than long-term wealth maximization[81], as it cuts off and ignores all cash flows after the payback point in time.[82] Further disadvantages[83] include for instance the neglect of the timing of cash flows that take place either before or after the payback time, problems when comparing investments with different sizes or risk profiles, and the disregard of the time value of money.

Several other static tools of investment appraisal exist, for example the cost comparison method[84] and the profit comparison method[85]. However, just like the accounting rate of return method and the payback period approach presented above, they all suffer from the major disadvantage of not taking into account the differing time value of money. The next sub-chapter addresses investment appraisal methods that overcome this particular drawback.

80 See for example Lumby (1988: p23), Röhrich (2007: p33), or Götze et al. (2007: p44) for more information on the respective decision rules.

81 See for instance McLaney (2006: p94) or Kruschwitz (2007: p40).

82 See for example Drury (2004: p510) or Blohm et al. (2006: p152).

83 See for instance Chadwick (1998: p157) for a discussion of further disadvantages of the payback period method.

84 See for example Röhrich (2007: p11ff), Götze et al. (2007: p32ff), or Schäfer (2005: p31ff) for further information on the cost comparison method.

85 See for instance Kruschwitz (2007: p33ff), Götze et al. (2007: p39ff), or Röhrich (2007: p24ff) for discussions of the profit comparison approach to investment appraisal.

2.3.3 Fundamental Dynamic Methods

A multitude of dynamic investment appraisal methods have been developed over the years. The two dynamic methods that receive by far the most attention in investment literature and that are also most frequently applied by companies[86], are the 'net present value' (NPV) method and the 'internal rate of return' (IRR) method. The basics of both methods are briefly introduced in the following sections[87].

Net Present Value Method

The net present value of an investment project equals the sum of the present values[88] of all net cash inflows minus the present value of the investment cash outflow.[89] "Alternatively expressed, the NPV is calculated by discounting a project's net cash flows at a specified rate" (Röhrich, 2007: p93). This rate, often called discount rate, can be either the cost of capital, a risk-adjusted rate, an arbitrary profitability target rate or any other rate that the evaluator deems suitable, as there is no universally defined and agreed discount rate to be used for calculating the net present value.[90] The decision rule underlying the net present value method states that the investment project with the highest NPV figure should be selected

86 See for example Watson/Head (2007: p199ff), McLaney (2006: p96f), or Drury (2004: p512) who quote several empirical studies that illustrate the importance of the NPV method and the IRR approach.

87 In line with the intention of this chapter, the following introductions are rather short, but additional references regarding the discussed methods are provided along with the respective descriptions.

88 See for instance Atrill/McLaney (2002: p197ff), Lumby (1988: p60), or Blohm et al. (2006: p50) for descriptions of the time value of money concept and how to proceed in order to discount cash flows from future values to present values.

89 See for example Drury (2004: p498), Lumby (1988: p63), or Chadwick (1998: p158).

90 See for instance Chadwick (1998: p158) for typical discount rates.

in a context with several competing opportunities; with regard to a single project setting, the project is accepted if its NPV is greater than zero.[91]

The NPV method exhibits several advantages. It includes all relevant cash flows and their respective timing, and it is in line with the traditional wealth maximizing objectives of most businesses.[92] In addition, it copes well with size disparities and cash flow timing pattern disparities when comparing competing investment alternatives.[93] Nevertheless, the net present value approach also possesses some disadvantages, most of them being related to inherent conceptual assumptions[94], for example addressing only a single target variable or assuming certainty[95]. In addition, the net present value method has some drawbacks when comparing mutually exclusive investments with different project durations.[96] Moreover, it is sometimes difficult to select a suitable discount rate, for example as the cost of capital is rather difficult to estimate.[97] Some other challenges that are frequently brought up in discussions of the NPV method – for example with regard to forecasting and data collection requirements – actually apply to all investment appraisal methods and are therefore not real disadvantages of the net present value approach, nor of any other particular appraisal method.

91 See for example Götze et al. (2007: p54) or Röhrich (2007: p64f) for details on the decision rules of NPV in different settings.

92 See for instance Atrill/McLaney (2002: p204) or Watson/Head (2007: p161).

93 See for example Dayananda et al. (2002: p103f) for a discussion of the suitability of the NPV method for comparing alternatives with different sizes or cash flow patterns.

94 See for instance Götze et al. (2007: p62ff) for a detailed discussion of the inherent assumptions of the net present value approach and their comparison with the real world situation.

95 See chapter 2.3.4 for variations of the NPV method that extend its applicability to situations of uncertainty, thus overcoming the mentioned disadvantage of the basic NPV method.

96 See for example Dayananda et al. (2002: p104ff) for a discussion of potential problems when comparing projects with unequal life spans.

97 See for instance Watson/Head (2007: p162).

Looking at both aspects of the NPV method, advantages and drawbacks, Watson/Head (2007: p161) draw the conclusion that "net present value is the *academically preferred* method of investment appraisal" and Röhrich (2007: p75) states that "net present value has no serious flaws". In addition, the NPV method also enjoys great popularity among the majority of companies, as the earlier mentioned empirical studies indicate.

Internal Rate of Return Method

The internal rate of return method is to a certain extent similar to the NPV method, but it approaches the appraisal task from a different starting point: "The internal rate of return is the discount rate which sets the net present value of an investment to zero" (Röhrich, 2007: p79). The calculation of the figure that produces an NPV of exactly zero[98] is often not straightforward[99], and usually requires the use of iterative procedures like diagrammatical approximation or arithmetic interpolation.[100] Based on the decision rule underlying the internal rate of return method, the investment with the highest calculated rate of return is chosen in a setting with several alternative projects; in the case of a single project, the investment is accepted if its IRR exceeds a pre-defined minimum rate of return.[101]

A key advantage of the IRR method is that its calculated result is intuitively easy to understand, as it is a percentage return, and most managers are familiar with return-type metrics from other occasions. In addition, the IRR method takes

98 See Atrill/McLaney (2002: p204f).

99 Under certain conditions, it is possible that the calculation yields two or more potential rates that each produce an NPV of zero, or that even no such solution exists; see for example Kruschwitz (2007: p109ff) or Dayananda et al. (2002: p99) for a discussion of this deficiency of the IRR method.

100 See for instance Röhrich (2007: p80f) or Blohm et al. (2006: p86ff) for examples of iterative procedures used to approximate the internal rate of return.

101 See for example Götze et al. (2007: p68), Atrill/McLaney (2002: p206), or Röhrich (2007: p79).

into account the amount and timing of all relevant cash flows[102] as well as their time value, and thus overcomes the major disadvantages of the earlier presented static appraisal methods. However, with regard to its inherent basic assumptions, the internal rate of return method suffers from the same deficiencies as the net present value approach. Furthermore, the IRR method has considerable disadvantages when comparing investments of different sizes, differing cash flow timing patterns, or unequal investment project life spans[103]. Due to this limited suitability for comparing mutually exclusive investments, the IRR method is often regarded as inferior to the NPV method.

However, despite the listed disadvantages and the theoretical inferiority to the NPV method in several comparative contexts, the IRR method is nevertheless still very popular among practitioners, and the earlier mentioned empirical studies indicate that, on average, companies use the internal rate of return method about as often as the net present value method. This is presumably mainly due to the seemingly intuitive and easy to understand representation of IRR as a return metric.

Various further dynamic methods of investment appraisal exist, including for example the discounted payback period method[104] – an enhancement of the presented payback period approach that additionally incorporates the discounting of cash flows to present values –, the profitability index approach[105], compound

102 See for instance Atrill/McLaney (2002: p206).

103 See for example Dayananda et al. (2002: p103f), Watson/Head (2007: p166f), Röhrich (2007: p86), or Drury (2004: p505ff) for a detailed discussion of the shortcomings of the internal rate of return method in these situations and the underlying reasons.

104 See for example Lumby (1988: p74ff), Götze et al. (2007: p75ff), or Schäfer (2005: p146ff) for further information on the discounted payback period method.

105 See for instance Proctor (2006: p189f), Lucey (2003: p423), or Drury (2008: p321) for additional information regarding the profitability index approach.

value models[106] and annuity models[107]. The common element of all these tools, including the ones presented earlier, is that they focus on one target variable and assume certainty in the standard version. In contrast, the following sub-chapter introduces more sophisticated approaches which address multiple attributes or support investment related decision making in the context of uncertainty.

2.3.4 Advanced Methods

In contrast to the previous two sub-chapters, the intention of this sub-chapter is not to give a basic understanding of specific appraisal methods, but rather to create awareness that there is a multitude of other appraisal techniques available for a large variety of potential purposes and contexts. The following sections focus in particular on examples of advanced methods from two areas: tools that support decision making in a context with multiple attributes, and methods that facilitate investment decision making under uncertainty. Approaches that go even beyond these two areas, for example tools for program decisions[108], are not addressed, as this would go far beyond the scope of this chapter's intention, and is also not necessary for future considerations in this thesis.

Methods for Multiple Attribute Decision Making

The appraisal of capital investments frequently demands that several goals and target measures are taken into account simultaneously, hence requiring methods

106 See for example Götze (2006: p110ff), Kruschwitz (2007: p59ff), or Blohm et al. (2006: p76ff) for discussions of compound value models.

107 See for instance Röhrich (2007: p76ff), Götze et al. (2007: p65ff), Schäfer (2005: p128ff), or Kruschwitz (2007: p76ff) for further information on annuity methods.

108 See for example Kruschwitz (2007: p241ff), Götze et al. (2007: p221ff), or Blohm et al. (2006: p271ff) for more information on methods addressing investment programs or simultaneous plans for program decisions (including for example investment, financing and/or production).

for multiple attribute decision making. A very well-known method for this purpose is the utility value analysis, also referred to as simple additive weighting. In this method[109], each relevant attribute is assigned a particular weight. Subsequently, each attribute receives a score that expresses the target fulfillment rate of this particular attribute. Finally, the scores of each attribute are multiplied with the respective weights and the sum of these products is calculated[110]: "the higher the weighted sum of the utility values, the better the alternative" (Geldermann/Rentz, 2007: p264ff). Accordingly, the alternative with the highest figure is chosen.

Other tools for multiple attribute decision making include for example the analytic hierarchy process[111], multiple attribute utility theory[112] (MAUT) methods and several so-called outranking models[113]. All these methods have the advantage of considering more than just one attribute, especially more than just financial figures, and can therefore often provide a better and more comprehensive picture of the decision situation. However, their major drawback is that they are rather complex and highly time-consuming to execute. Consequently, they are in general mainly applied in very complex decision situations that are of high importance.

---

109 See for instance Götze et al. (2007: p175ff) or Blohm et al. (2006: p155ff) for a detailed discussion of the utility value analysis and the detailed procedure of this method.

110 See for example Yoon/Hwang (1995: p32).

111 See for example Bhushan/Rai (2004), Saaty/Vargas (2001), or Götze et al. (2007: p179ff) for information on the analytic hierarchy process.

112 See for instance Dyer (2005), Hardaker et al. (2004: p219ff), or Kleindorfer et al. (1993: p137ff) for information on multiple attribute utilities and MAUT-based methods.

113 Outranking approaches comprise several special methods to addressing multiple attribute decision making; see for example Brans/Mareschal (2005), Geldermann/Rentz (2007: p265ff), or Götze et al. (2007: p203ff) for so-called PROMETHEE methods, Figueira et al. (2005) for so-called ELECTRE methods and Martel/Matarazzo (2005) for other outranking methods.

Methods for Decision Making under Uncertainty

During the appraisal of investments, the decision maker is frequently faced with several uncertain aspects[114]. These can be incorporated into the evaluative and judgmental process with the help of more advanced appraisal tools. The so-called 'correction methods'[115] constitute one type of such tools. These methods adapt and extend traditional appraisal techniques – often the net present value approach – in order to include some elements of uncertainty. One approach to correcting the NPV method is the risk adjusted discount rate method (RADR), which focuses on adjusting the discount rate in such a way that it "takes into account the time value of money as well as the risk associated with the project's expected cash flows" (Dayananda et al., 2002: p118), in order to yield a risk-adjusted net present value of the project.[116] The primary challenge of this approach is not the mathematical NPV calculation, but the estimation of the risk-adjusted discount rate, which incorporates several situation-specific risk factors and risk premiums. A similar approach of correcting and extending the traditional net present value method is pursued by the certainty equivalent (CE) method, which directly adjusts the cash flows that are used in the NPV calculation and uses modified expected cash flows instead.[117]

Further methods for addressing uncertainty – with regard to both ignorance and especially risk – in investment contexts exist, ranging from simple decision

---

114 See chapter 2.2.3 for a discussion of uncertainty.

115 See for instance Schäfer (2005: p223ff), Röhrich (2007: p111ff), or Blohm et al. (2006: p229ff) for a discussion of correction approaches.

116 See for example Dayananda et al. (2002: p115ff), van Horne/Wachowicz (2008: p401ff), Madura (2006: p429f), or Kinney/Raiborn (2009: p569) for additional information on the risk-adjusted discount rate method.

117 See for instance Groppelli/Nikbakht (2006: p175ff), Dayananda et al. (2002: p115ff), or Webster (2003: p678) for further information on the certainty equivalent method.

rules for ignorance contexts[118] to sophisticated tools for incorporating risk, for example sensitivity analysis[119], simulations and scenarios[120], and options pricing models like real options[121]. As today's business environment is characterized to a significant extent by uncertainty, the demand for – and importance of – these techniques has increased considerably over the last decades, despite the challenges related to the application of most of these tools, for example the high complexity and the time-consuming implementation.

This chapter described rationality and its underlying axiomatic requirements, for example the invariance principle, as the foundation and benchmark for evaluating capital investment decisions when adopting a normative perspective. Taking a descriptive perspective, the empirical research at a later stage of this thesis actually examines whether decision makers potentially violate certain of those basic rules of rationality during the appraisal of capital investments, for example due to the existence of cognitive biases. However, in order to prepare this empirical part, it is first necessary to address the theoretical fundamentals underlying cognitive psychology in general and cognitive biases in particular. This is done in the following chapter.

---

118 See for example Lucey (2002: p27ff), Schäfer (2005: p229ff), Wisniewski (2006: p184ff), or Barrow (2006: p90f) for a discussion of simple rules to adopt in the context of ignorance, including for instance dominance, maximin, maximax or the Hurwicz rule.

119 See for instance Dayananda et al. (2002: p134ff), Kinney/Raiborn (2009: p569ff), McLaney (2006: p151ff), or Blohm et al. (2006: p232ff) for further information on sensitivity analyses.

120 See for example Damodaran (2008: p145ff), Dayananda et al. (2002: p153ff), or Madura (2006: p30f) for additional information on various scenario and simulation approaches.

121 See for instance Guthrie (2009), Mun (2006), Götze et al. (2007: p296ff), Kruschwitz (2007: p424ff), or Schäfer (2005: p387ff) for discussions of option approaches in general and real options in particular.

3 Theoretical Foundations of Cognitive Biases

This chapter conveys a basic understanding of cognitive biases and their underlying theoretical foundations. The first part of this chapter describes the fundamentals of psychology in general and cognitive psychology in particular. The second part introduces the 'heuristics and biases' approach and discusses cognitive biases that result from three fundamental heuristics. Subsequently, a selection of further relevant biases is described. The fourth part finally critically discusses the most frequently raised critiques that the 'heuristics and biases' approach is confronted with.

The intention of this chapter – analog to the previous chapter – is to give an introduction to cognitive biases and their theoretical fundamentals. It explicitly does not intend to cover all potential aspects of cognitive psychology, heuristics, or biases, as this is far beyond the scope of this thesis and as there is a large number of suitable literature available[122]. Instead, the focus is explicitly on introducing the basic concepts that are relevant for later parts of this thesis.

3.1 Fundamentals of Cognitive Psychology

The foundations of cognitive biases are rooted in the more general domain of cognitive psychology. Therefore, this part introduces the fundamentals of this discipline. The first section addresses general psychology, focusing on its areas and sub-disciplines, in order to subsequently identify and classify cognitive psychology as one particular sub-discipline. Finally, the main areas of interest and the key concepts and approaches of cognitive psychology are introduced and described.

---

[122] See for example Gerrig/Zimbardo (2008) regarding psychology in general, Sternberg (2009) with regard to cognitive psychology, and Kahneman et al. (1982) or Gilovich et al. (2002a) for further information on the 'heuristics and biases' approach and several cognitive biases.

3.1.1 General Psychology and its Sub-Disciplines

"The word psychology is derived from two Greek roots: *psyche*, meaning 'mind', and *logos*, meaning 'study' or 'knowledge' " (Nevid, 2009: p4). Accordingly, psychology can be understood as the 'study of the mind', and is often referred to in general terms as "the science of behavior and mental processes" (Nevid, 2009: p14)[123]. However, this description is somewhat simplistic and partly limited, therefore Eysenck (2004: p3) suggests a more formal and concise definition: "Psychology is a science in which behavioural and other evidence is used to understand the internal processes leading people (and members of other species) to behave as they do". Given that the term 'behavior' is a key component of the above definitions, it is reasonable to clarify what it actually means in this context: "Behavior is the means by which organisms adjust to their environment" (Gerrig/Zimbardo, 2008: p4) and "refers to any overt (observable) response or activity by an organism" (Weiten, 2007: p8).

Psychology is a very large field that approaches its targets from several different perspectives. These are each based on a different set of assumptions and adopt a particular point of view. Gerrig/Zimbardo (2008: p11ff) distinguish seven psychological perspectives:

1. Psychodynamic perspective: claims that behavior is driven by powerful inner forces, for example inherited instincts and biological drives.
2. Behaviorist perspective: analyzes how environmental stimuli trigger and control particular types of behavior.
3. Humanistic perspective: assumes that people are innately good and capable of choice, and looks for patterns in peoples' life histories.

---

123 A similar definition is provided by Gerrig/Zimbardo (2008: p4) who define "psychology as the scientific study of the behavior of individuals and their mental processes".

4. Cognitive perspective: addresses human thought and all related processes as a decisive determinant of behavior.
5. Biological perspective: seeks behavioral causes in the functioning of genes, the nervous system, the brain, and the endocrine system.
6. Evolutionary perspective: focuses on the long-term processes of evolution and natural selection as explanatory base for behavior.
7. Sociocultural perspective: studies cross-cultural differences to find causes and consequences of behavior.

The detailed classifications of the psychological perspectives vary to a certain extent among some authors, but the core elements usually remain the same. For example, in his discussion of six major contemporary perspectives, Nevid (2009: p9) merges the biological and evolutionary perspectives to form a 'physiological perspective' that "examines relationships between biological processes and behavior".

As a consequence of the existence of a multitude of different perspectives, psychology is also characterized by a large variety of diverse fields of activity, often referred to as research areas or sub-disciplines. However, the detailed classification of these activities partly differs considerably between several authors. While for example Eysenck (2004: p4ff) describes six main sub-disciplines[124], Weiten (2007: p18f) lists nine major areas[125]. These areas illustrate the immense diversity of psychology, which is also reflected in the large variety of tasks and specialty areas of professional psychologists[126]. Furthermore, the

---

[124] Biological psychology, cognitive psychology, individual differences, developmental psychology, social psychology, and abnormal psychology.

[125] Developmental psychology, social psychology, experimental psychology, physiological psychology, cognitive psychology, personality, psychometrics, educational psychology, and health psychology.

[126] See for example Nevid (2009: p15ff) for a detailed overview and comparison of professional psychologists' specialty areas and major activities or duties; further information on this topic is for instance provided by Weiten (2007: p19ff) or Gerrig/Zimbardo (2008: p17f).

focus of psychology in general and the importance of each of its approaches and areas has changed considerably throughout history[127], largely driven by the contributions of individual psychologists and authors[128]. However, despite some substantial differences between the core beliefs and foci of some approaches of psychology, the fields of activity are by no means mutually exclusive; rather, they often overlap and even build on and incorporate each other's findings to a certain extent.

One element that is common in all four mentioned classifications of psychological perspectives and areas is the cognitive perspective, which is called cognitive psychology when referring to it as psychological sub-discipline. This sub-discipline is the focus of the next sections.

3.1.2 Introduction to Cognitive Psychology

Given that 'cognition' is a core term in cognitive psychology, this sub-chapter first briefly clarifies the meaning of 'cognition' before defining cognitive psychology itself and subsequently describing the basic assumptions about the mind underlying this particular psychological discipline.

"The word *cognitive* comes from the Latin word *cognare*, meaning 'to know' " (Balota/Marsh, 2004: p1). Accordingly, "cognition is a general term for all forms of knowing" (Gerrig/Zimbardo, 2008: p236).[129] The scientific discipline that addresses cognition and all related activities and processes is called cognitive psychology: in general, cognitive psychology is "the study of how the brain pro-

---

127 See for instance Weiten (2007: p3ff), Nevid (2009: p4ff), or Gerrig/Zimbardo (2008: p9ff) for detailed descriptions of the historical background and development of psychology and its different approaches and branches.

128 See for example Eysenck (2004: p11) or Weiten (2007: p10) for the results of research regarding the most eminent psychologists and the most influential contributors to psychology.

129 See for instance Andrade/May (2004: p1) for another example of a definition of cognition.

cesses information. In more everyday terms, it is about the mental processes involved in acquiring and making use of knowledge and experience gained from our senses" (Esgate et al., 2005: p2).[130] Sternberg (2009: p2) describes it as "the study of how people perceive, learn, remember, and think about information" and Eysenck (2006: p3) adds that it covers "the main internal psychological processes involved in making sense of the environment and deciding what actions might be appropriate". In summary, cognitive psychology is the science that analyzes how the mind and the psyche are organized, how they produce intelligent thinking and how the processes of thought that take place in the brain can be made visible and observable.[131] With regard to its historical development, similar to psychology in general, the foci and respective approaches of cognitive psychology have changed considerably over the decades and centuries[132].

Several basic assumptions about the mind underlie cognitive psychology. As a starting point, cognitive psychology is "based on the idea that we are like a computer when processing information and have an input, storage and retrieval function" (Brown, 2006: p6) and that "the mind is viewed as an information processing system through which people interact with the external world" (Andrade/May, 2004: p2). Early cognitive psychologists believed that this information processing is always bottom-up and serial: bottom-up processing means that the processing is triggered and directly affected only by external, environmental stimulus input[133], not by internal factors, and serial processing assumes that "only one process occurs at any moment in time [...] and means that

[130] See for example Brown (2006: p6) or Balota/Marsh (2004: p1) for additional definitions of cognitive psychology.

[131] See Anderson (2007: p1).

[132] See chapter 3.1.3 for an overview of the different approaches of cognitive psychology; for detailed information on the history and historical development of cognitive psychology and its psychological antecedents see for instance Sternberg (2009: p5ff), Andrade/May (2004: p11ff), Anderson (2007: p6ff), or Brown (2006: p9ff).

[133] See for example Andrade/May (2004: p2) or (Eysenck, 2006: p3) for further information on information processing assumptions and formal definitions of bottom-up processing.

the current process is completed before the next one begins" (Eysenck, 2006: p3). However, today it is known that this is a radical over-simplification[134]: cognition consists of both bottom-up and top-down processes.[135] In this particular context, "top-down processing refers to the influence of higher-level cognitive elements (goals, intentions, expectations, knowledge etc.) on lower-level processes" (Andrade/May, 2004: p2), which means that internal factors – for example an individual's expectations or past experience – actually do affect the processing of external stimuli.[136] Furthermore, processing is not only serial; instead, frequently parallel processing of information takes place: two or more cognitive processes occur in parallel at the same time[137].

Moreover, it is assumed that "the mind has resource and structural limitations, that is, it is a limited-capacity processor" (Andrade/May, 2004: p2). As a consequence, the mind cannot process an unlimited amount of information, neither simultaneously nor in a fixed period of time, as each processing activity takes time. As a consequence, the mind is open to mental shortcuts or rules of thumb – called heuristics[138] – in order to reduce the processing effort. In addition, many cognitive psychologists assume that cognitive processes operate in a modularized way. In this context, "modules are clusters of processes that function independently from other clusters of processes. Each module processes one parti-

---

134 See for instance Andrade/May (2004: p1).

135 See for example Bruner et al. (1951) for an illustrative demonstration of cognition being often a mixture of both top-down and bottom-up processing, based on color experiments.

136 See for instance Eysenck (2006: p4).

137 See for example Gerrig/Zimbardo (2008: p238) or Eysenck (2006: p4).

138 See chapter 3.2 for more information on heuristics and their effects on information processing outcomes.

cular type of information" (Andrade/May, 2004: p2).[139] This modularity becomes also evident in the classifications of topical subjects covered by cognitive psychology and the resulting approaches that form its sub-disciplines. These two aspects are addressed in the following sections.

3.1.3 Subjects and Approaches of Cognitive Psychology

Cognitive psychology encompasses a variety of subjects, or topical areas, that each cover particular modules or sets of functions of the brain. Although the detailed subject classifications partly differ between authors, they are usually similar with regard to the core components. According to Gerrig/Zimbardo (2008: p236) these include perception, attention, memory, language, human intelligence, and thinking and problem solving. Major differences between different authors' classifications concern the details of how the functions of the brain are 'clustered' into subjects, Anderson (2007) for example splits 'thinking and problem solving' into two parts – 'problem solving' and 'reasoning and decision making' –, and Andrade/May (2004) address comprehension as individual subject while others integrate that functionality of the brain into other subjects. In addition, several side topics exist, which are covered only by few authors – for example emotions[140] or artificial intelligence[141] – which could be summarized as "others" in a general classification of major subjects of cognitive psychology.

---

[139] This modularized layout also supports the assumption that particular functions are localized in specific areas of the brain, which forms inter alia the base for 'cognitive neuroscience', a sub-discipline that focuses on approaches that apply brain-imaging technologies; an overview of the major sub-disciplines of cognitive psychology is provided in chapter 3.1.3.

[140] See for example Eysenck (2006: p406ff) or Andrade/May (2004: p213ff) on emotions and cognition.

[141] See for instance Sternberg (2009: p528ff) for a cognition-based discussion of human and artificial intelligence or Bickhard/Terveen (1995) for artificial intelligence and cognitive science in general.

Cognitive psychologists today have an increasing multitude of tools and methods to analyze and examine the various information processing activities of the brain, which is to a certain extent also due to the technological advancements during the last decades. In line with these tools, five different approaches of cognitive psychology, also referred to as sub-disciplines by some authors, can be distinguished, which are briefly summarized in the following list: [142]

1. Experimental cognitive psychology: traditional approach of cognitive psychology that carries out experiments on healthy individuals and is mainly laboratory-based.
2. Cognitive neuropsychology: focuses on analyzing patterns of cognitive impairment that are shown by brain-damaged patients.
3. Computational cognitive science: highly interdisciplinary approach[143] that focuses on computational models and artificial intelligence.
4. Applied cognitive psychology: practice-driven approach that focuses on solving real-life problems and employs primarily real-world rather than laboratory experiments.
5. Cognitive neuroscience: applies various brain-imaging techniques and technologies to analyze the structure of the brain and its functions.

---

142 Based on a synthesis of the definitions and descriptions in Eysenck (2006: p4ff), Andrade/May (2004: p14ff), and Brown (2006: p6ff). Note that not all authors include all five sub-disciplines in their classifications, for example Eysenck (2006) and Brown (2006) skip applied cognitive psychology, while Andrade/May (2004) omit experimental cognitive psychology.

143 According to Friedenberg/Silverman (2006: p2) and Gerrig/Zimbardo (2008: p236), computational cognitive science is situated at the intersection of several different approaches, including philosophical, psychological, cognitive, neuroscience, network, evolutionary, linguistic, artificial intelligence, and robotics components.

Despite their different focus areas and applied methods, the above described sub-disciplines – which constantly evolve and change over time[144] – are not fully separated, but exhibit several overlaps and benefit from each other's findings.

Having defined cognition and cognitive psychology – which is one sub-discipline of general psychology – and described its subjects and approaches in general, the following sub-chapter focuses on so-called 'cognitive biases'. These are a result of simplified cognitive information processing activities, which are investigated in different ways by all of the above described sub-disciplines.

3.2 Heuristics and Biases

The following sections address and explore a core aspect of this thesis: cognitive biases. The first part introduces the 'heuristics and biases' approach and characterizes cognitive biases. The subsequent sections focus on three basic heuristics – availability, representativeness, and anchoring – and describe in detail the cognitive biases that directly result from the use of each heuristic.

3.2.1 Introduction to the 'Heuristics and Biases' Approach

The 'heuristics and biases' approach is based on research in the field of cognitive biases pioneered in the 1970s and 1980s[145] by Daniel Kahneman and Amos Tversky, who "developed theoretical approaches [...] to understand the limi-

[144] Both with regard to shifts in detailed content focus but also in linguistic terms: For example, the sub-discipline that is today called 'computational cognitive science' has earlier been referred to as 'cognitive science' by many authors.

[145] See Kahneman et al. (1982) for a compendium of early theoretical and empirical research.

tations of human judgment" (Eysenck, 2006: p333).[146] Cognitive biases result from unconscious mental activities of information processing that are inherent in every human being. They can be described as "mental errors caused by our simplified information processing strategies" (Heuer, 1999: p111), the so-called heuristics, and result in "predictable deviations from rationality" (Arnott, 2006: p59). These heuristics are 'mental shortcuts' or 'rules of thumb', that reduce complex tasks to simpler judgmental operations[147] and enable people, in the absence of "having complete, reliable, predictive information [...] to make inferences and predictions from what scanty and unreliable data are available" (Taylor, 1982: p191). Heuristics are usually applied unconsciously and function in an automated way, they "occur without the individual recognizing their presence or impact" (McCray et al., 2002: p49).

Heuristics are existent in every aspect of life. They can be as simple as classifying "a number as even or odd by paying attention only to the last digit" (Piatelli-Palmarini, 1994: p20) instead of looking at the full number, or they can unknowingly substitute highly complex mathematical calculations in everyday life, for example when catching a ball that flies through the air: instead of solving elaborated parabola equations and calculating trajectories for the ball, we unconsciously use a simple heuristic that enables us to catch the ball without any calculation.[148] Accordingly, very often in everyday life, "people's judgments rely

146 Detailed descriptions and extensive references regarding the historical development of the 'heuristics and biases' approach, as well as information on earlier decision making research that the approach builds upon, and current perspectives are for example provided by Goldstein/Hogarth (1997: p24ff), Gilovich/Griffin (2002), or Piatelli-Palmarini (1994: p171ff).

147 See Tversky/Kahneman (1974: p1124).

148 See for instance Gigerenzer (2008: p8ff), who illustrates the example of catching a ball in a baseball game and refers to the respective rule, which is unconsciously applied by players, as the 'gaze heuristic': "Fix your gaze on the ball, start running, and adjust your running speed so that the angle of gaze remains constant".

on heuristics rather than on formal methods of analysis" (Gerrig/Zimbardo, 2008: p262).

However, although heuristics are in general rather valid[149], and are thus usually very useful tools[150], they can, under certain conditions, lead to systematical distortions in the decision making process and accordingly produce systematically biased outcomes.[151] Tversky/Kahneman (1974: p1124) illustrate this at the example of a simple heuristic used in everyday life in order to determine how far away an object is: "the more sharply the object is seen, the closer it appears to be". This rule of thumb usually yields good results, however, it can be distorted by below-average visibility, for example a slight fog, or very good visibility – both influence how blurred or sharp an object is seen – which in consequence often causes an overestimation or underestimation of the actual distance. Analogously, similar distortions can happen to all information processing activities in decision making based on heuristics: accordingly, although these heuristics are usually right, they might, under certain circumstances, lead to biased judgments due to the effects of cognitive biases.

Pohl (2004: p2f) summarizes four defining features of illusions in general and cognitive illusions[152] in particular: they are *deviations* from a normative standard[153], which deviate "in a *systematic* fashion (i.e., in a predictable direction) rather than just randomly"; moreover, they "appear *involuntarily*, that is, without specific instructions or deliberate will", and are "*hard if not impossible to*

---

149 See for instance Gigerenzer et al. (1999) and Gigerenzer (2008) for discussions and examples of the suitability of heuristics in many contexts.

150 In fact, our everyday life would be impossible to handle without unconsciously applying any heuristics at all.

151 See for example Tversky/Kahneman (1974), Gilovich et al. (2002a), or Kahneman et al. (1982).

152 Some authors, for instance Pohl (2004), refer to 'cognitive biases' as 'cognitive illusions' or use the two terms as synonyms. For consistency, this thesis uses only the more common term 'cognitive biases' for the remaining parts.

153 In the case of cognitive biases, normative rationality is considered to be the normative standard.

avoid".[154] With regard to these features and their effects on people, cognitive biases are similar to optical illusions. The following example outlines this similarity:

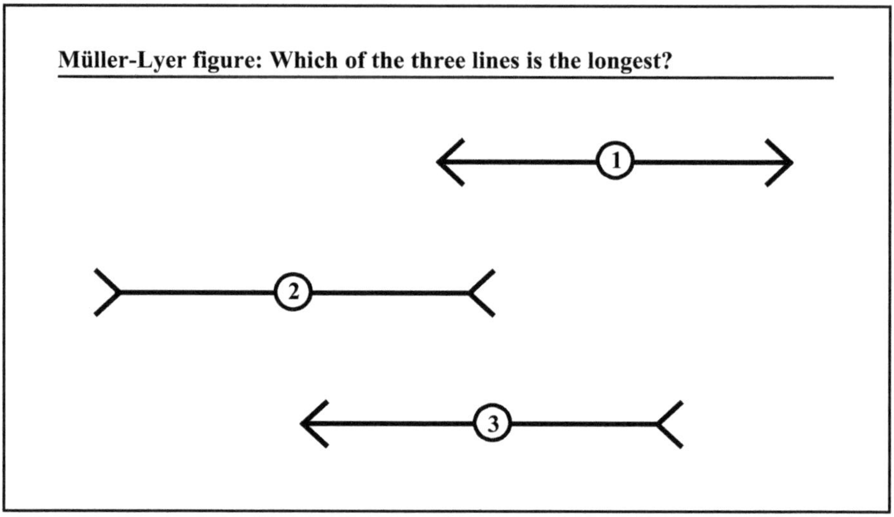

Illustration 5: Exemplary optical illusion[155]

When asked to select the longest line in the following illustration, the majority of people tend to choose number two, as it seems longer than the two others, due to

---

[154] Pohl (2004: p3) actually discusses a fifth feature – being "*distinct* from the normal course of information processing" and consequently 'sticking out' as 'something special' that 'piques curiosity' – to distinguish cognitive biases from ordinary errors or misunderstandings. However, the author believes that this requirement is already sufficiently provided for by the prerequisite of repeatedly producing *systematic* deviations, as random errors or faults, or misunderstandings, in general do not satisfy this criterion of a predictable deviation, but appear randomly.

[155] Adjusted variation of the Müller-Lyer illusion, originally based on Müller-Lyer (1889).

the arrows attached to each line, which distort the estimate of the lengths.[156] In fact, however, the three lines all have the same length.

With regard to the defining features listed above, this optical illustration satisfies all four of the above mentioned defining criteria of an illusion: the estimates of length deviate from reality (line two is perceived to be longer, although this is not the case), in a systematic way (it is predictable that it is line two that is perceived as the longest, and this is consistently the case), the illusion happens involuntarily (it just 'happens' that the second line is perceived as longer, without deliberate will or instruction) and it is hard to avoid (even though one knows that they all have the same length, one still continues to 'see' that number two seems longer): "the error remains compelling even when one is fully aware of its nature" (Heuer, 1999: p112). The same is true for cognitive biases[157].

Analyzing cognitive biases and their particularities, Piatelli-Palmarini (1994: p139f) goes one step further and summarizes eight common characteristics and traits of cognitive biases:

1. General: they are found in all humans, or at least in the majority of human beings[158].
2. Systematic: they occur in a systematical way and can be repeatedly reproduced with similar results.
3. Directional: their effects show a clear tendency in one particular, predictable direction, instead of being simply random fluctuations.

---

156 See for instance Nijhawan (1997) for a discussion of reasons underlying the optical illusion of the Müller-Lyer figure; interestingly, research, for instance by Segall et al. (1966), indicates that members of certain non-Western cultures seem less susceptible to this particular optical illusion.

157 However, despite the similarities in effect, cognitive biases are different from optical illusions with regard to the respective sources and underlying roots: cognitive biases are not due to perceptual, visual effects (which are the source of optical illusions), but due to information-processing-related mental activities and the use of heuristics.

158 Unless they are specifically trained to recognize and counteract a specific bias; further information on training and its suitability as countermeasure is provided in chapter 5.2.4.

4. Specific: they only appear under certain circumstances or conditions, not every time that a particular heuristic is applied.
5. Externally modulable: they can, to a certain extent, be adjusted and manipulated by experts in order to yield specific effects.
6. Subjectively incorrigible up to a certain point: being told about the bias does not immediately stop one from being subject to the bias.
7. Nontransferable: knowing the bias from a particular problem situation is not sufficient to become resistant against the same bias in different problem settings.
8. Independent of intelligence and education: neither intelligence, nor better education or being an expert in a particular area does stop one from being subject to the bias, if the difficulty of the decision problem is adjusted accordingly.

Based on these characteristics, Piatelli-Palmarini (1994: p140) concludes that "we are discovering something deep in human nature, and not just a trite statement of 'human stupidity' " and highlights the importance of addressing cognitive biases and their effects in different aspects of our life. However, the 'heuristics and biases' approach is also occasionally confronted with skepticism from some authors. Their major arguments and criticisms are discussed and analyzed later in detail in a separate sub-chapter[159].

3.2.2 Fundamental Heuristics and their Resulting Cognitive Biases

As discussed in the preceding sections, cognitive biases result from the unconscious usage of particular heuristics with regard to mental information processing activities. The following sections successively address three fundamental

[159] See chapter 3.4 for details.

heuristics that have been identified by Tversky/Kahneman (1974) – availability, representativeness, and anchoring – and discuss and illustrate in detail several cognitive biases that stem directly from the respective heuristic.

3.2.2.1 Availability Heuristic

The availability heuristic refers to the simple rule of using the "ease with which instances or occurrences can be brought to mind" (Tversky/Kahneman, 1974: p1127) as proxy for frequency or probability judgments. This use of accessibility of information in one's memory as proxy for such judgments is due to the fact that, "in general, instances of large classes are recalled better and faster than instances of less frequent classes; that likely occurrences are easier to imagine than unlikely ones; and that the associative connections between events are strengthened when the events frequently co-occur" (Tversky/Kahneman, 1982: p163). However, although these assumptions are generally valid in many cases, applying the availability heuristic can nevertheless lead to systematic errors, as "availability is affected by factors other than frequency and probability" (Tversky/Kahneman, 1974: p1127), for example the vividness or recency of information. A multitude of empirical experiments have demonstrated and illustrated these judgmental distortions.

When discussing the availability heuristic, it is important to highlight that people can in general assess availability quickly and accurately[160], in the absence of 'triggers' that initiate cognitive biases. This reinforces the notion that distortions regarding probability or frequency judgments are not random effects, caused by a general inability to assess availability, but that they are rather

[160] See for instance Tversky/Kahneman (1982: p165f) for empirical research on people's general ability to assess availability accurately.

systematic biases. The following sections address these cognitive biases[161] stemming from the availability heuristic one after another in detail.

Retrievability of Instances

The underlying rationale for the existence of this bias, that is also referred to as 'ease of recall' bias, is that "when the size of a class is judged by the availability of its instances, a class whose instances are easily retrieved will appear more numerous than a class of equal frequency whose instances are less retrievable" (Tversky/Kahneman, 1974: 1127). This means that many judgments based on availability are systematically distorted due to the vividness, recency, familiarity, or salience of information, but also due to the strength and relevance that one attributes to pieces of information based on one's values and beliefs[162]. Bazerman (2006: p18) illustrates this effect through a simple experiment asking participants to rank a set of given causes of death in the U.S. between 1990 and 2000. Options include, among others, 'poor diet and physical inactivity' and 'motor vehicle accidents'. While most participants estimate that the number of deaths due to motor vehicle accidents is much higher than those caused by poor diet and physical inactivity, the latter is in fact nearly 10 times higher than the former[163]. This demonstrates very well the 'ease of recall' bias, as instances of lethal motor vehicle accidents are much more available than deaths caused by poor diet or physical inactivity, because the former tend to be "exhaustively covered and sensationalized by the media" (Reber, 2004: p153). Similar distortions have been

[161] There is no common, universal terminology with regard to the names of cognitive biases; therefore, the names can vary between different authors. The terminology for the biases discussed in this section is primarily in line with the most frequently used names.

[162] See for example Tversky/Kahneman (1982), Reber (2004), or Bazerman (2006: p18f) for further information on the cognitive bias related to the retrievability of instances.

[163] See Mokdad et al. (2004: p1240) for empirical evidence of death causes.

illustrated in numerous studies, for example in experiments about the influence of fame on estimated frequencies of male or female names, demonstrating that familiarity influences the availability of instances and biases judgments.[164]

However, availability is not only influenced by the salience or vividness of individual events – as in the case of lethal accidents and other deaths –, or the familiarity with particular instances – as in the case of the names of famous persons. Tversky/Kahneman (1974: p1127) also explain that recency is an influencing factor, as "recent occurrences are likely to be relatively more available than earlier occurrences". In addition, "beliefs and values foster pre-conceptions that heighten the availability of certain evidence [by increasing the relevance and strength that one attributes to it], thus biasing the judgment process" (Taylor, 1982: p192). The result of all those effects is that availability-based judgments are systematically distorted due to the cognitive bias of retrievability of instances.

Effectiveness of a Search Set

This cognitive bias is based on the finding that the way how one's memory is structured and how information is stored in or retrieved from one's memory strongly influences the availability of information. This results in biased probability judgments, as probability – in contrast to the availability – is not affected by different ways of storing or retrieving information in the brain. Several researchers observed and analyzed this memory-structure-related bias via

---

[164] See for example McKelvie (1997) who replicated and extended the original experiments referred to by Tversky/Kahneman (1974). Participants' judgments are biased due to the familiarity with the names of famous persons (in contrast to non-famous persons) in such a way, that they estimated that a list with famous and non-famous names contained more famous names than non-famous names, although the opposite was actually the case – because famous names are easier recalled due to their familiarity, thus distorting the frequency judgment.

experimental research, for example with simple word frequency estimation tests[165] and word construction tasks[166]. These experiments demonstrated that judgments based on availability tend to be unconsciously distorted due to memory processes and structures.

Retrieval of information from the memory is for instance influenced by the effectiveness of a search set or search strategy[167]. This means that, depending on the way how one searches for information in one's memory, one finds particular pieces of information quicker or easier than others – they are thus more available –, which can in turn lead to a distorted judgment: "classes whose instances are readily recalled will be judged more numerous than classes of the same size whose instances are less available" (Tversky/Kahneman, 1982: p175). For instance, for most people searching for words that start with a particular letter is usually much quicker and more effective than looking for words that have a particular letter at another specific position of the word; as a consequence of this differing effectiveness of the two search strategies, examples of the former type of words are more available and are therefore perceived as being more numerous and more likely, although this is not necessarily the case.

In addition, the effectiveness of a search set bias "could also be produced by the selective retrieval of information from memory" (Ross/Sicoly, 1982: p180). For instance, if someone adopts primarily an egocentric perspective when searching for particular information in his or her memory, this can lead to a

165 See for instance Galbraith/Underwood (1973) or Tversky/Kahneman (1982: p166ff).

166 See for example Tversky/Kahneman (1982: p165).

167 See for instance Tversky/Kahneman (1974: p1127), Tversky/Kahneman (1982: p174ff), or Reber (2004: p150f).

selected retrieval of self-referential information[168] and a non-retrieval of relevant non-self-referential information.[169]

In summary, the above effects imply that "memory processes can make an availability-based judgment inaccurate" (Gerrig/Zimbardo, 2008: p263)[170] and therefore potentially induce wrong decisions.

Imaginability

In contrast to the above presented two biases, which are based on the ease of recall and retrieval of relevant instances, this cognitive bias is related to how easy or difficult it is to construct or imagine potential instances if no relevant instances are stored (and can thus not be recalled or retrieved): in this case, people often tend to evaluate "frequency or probability by the ease with which the relevant instances can be constructed" (Tversky/Kahneman, 1974: p1127) or generated from one's imagination. However, the actual frequency of instances is often not sufficiently and adequately reflected in the ease of constructing instances[171], which can lead to a systematic distortion of the decision making process and its result.

Tversky/Kahneman (1982: p169f) illustrate this bias for instance by means of an empirical experiment in which they tell their participants to consider a group of ten people that must form committees of x members, with x being a number that lies between 2 and 8. Subsequently, they ask them how many different committees of x members this group could potentially form. The results of this experiment yield a "decreasing monotonic function of committee size" (Tversky/

168 Although Ross/Sicoly (1982) focus primarily on cases of someone taking an egocentric perspective, selected retrieval can also occur if someone focuses on any particular perspective.

169 To a certain extent, this selected retrieval of information could be considered as a pre-stage of framing and the 'confirmation trap' bias, which are discussed in more detail in chapter 3.3.1.

170 These memory processes refer to both storage and/or retrieval of information.

171 See Tversky/Kahneman (1974: p1127).

Kahneman, 1974: p1128): the larger x is, the lower is the estimated number of possible committees. This is in sharp contrast to the correct values[172]. This distortion emerges because it is easier to imagine groups with two members than groups with more members[173], and accordingly large committees are less available than small committees, and vice versa.[174] As a consequence, "if frequency is assessed by imaginability, or by availability for construction, the small committees will appear more numerous than larger committees, in contrast to the correct bell shaped function" (Tversky/Kahneman, 1974: p1128). Other experiments[175] demonstrate similar judgmental distortions triggered by the use of the availability heuristic and the resulting cognitive bias.

Illusory Correlation

This cognitive bias, also known as 'presumed associations' bias, describes the tendency of people to overestimate the probability that two events co-occur[176] because they base their estimate on the number and availability of similar associations or examples that can easily be recalled or imagined.[177] The underlying

172 The correct calculation is done based on the binomial coefficient $\binom{10}{x}$ that reaches a maximum for x=5 members, is bell-shaped, and yields for instance the same result for both x=2 and x=8.

173 See Tversky/Kahneman, (1982: p169): "more such patterns are seen at first glance, they are more distinctive, and they are easier to visualize".

174 See Tversky/Kahneman (1982: p169).

175 See for instance Tversky/Kahneman (1982: p169) for a similar combinatorial experiment about different bus routes and bus stop patterns; Tversky/Kahneman (1974: p1128) briefly describe an example in which the ease of imagination can effect the perceived risk of a particular project.

176 Usually the probability is overestimated, but, depending on the particular circumstances, the probability can also be underestimated, if no co-occurrences come to mind or these are hard to imagine.

177 See for example Tversky/Kahneman (1974: p1128), Bazerman (2006: p20f), Fiedler (2004), or Tversky/Kahneman (1982: p175ff).

reason is that many people unconsciously violate basic rules of probability calculation by taking mental shortcuts. For example, when estimating the association or correlation between two instances, A and B, most people typically try to recall situations where A and B happened at the same time, or alternatively try to imagine situations in which A and B could co-occur. As a consequence, their judgment is based on the availability or plausibility (regarding imagined co-occurrences) and the number of those situations. However, a proper analysis would require examining all four possible combinations of occurrence (or non-occurrence) of A and B[178], and subsequently basing the judgment on their relative frequencies. However, the formally correct procedure is less intuitive, more complex and also time-consuming. As a consequence, people unconsciously rather take the presented 'shortcut' in the form of the availability heuristic, which can lead to systematic misjudgments of co-occurrence probabilities.

Bazerman (2006: p20f) exemplarily illustrates this by means of a task of estimating associations between marijuana use and delinquency[179]. In addition, the evidence from several empirical studies[180] supports and confirms the highly distortive effects of this cognitive bias.

Having described in the preceding sections the cognitive biases that result from the availability heuristic – which are in real life by no means as distinct as the separate discussions might seem to imply, but instead usually overlap and co-occur, thus potentially amplifying their distortive effects – the following sections address cognitive biases that result from the representativeness heuristic.

---

178 The four possible combinations of (non-) occurrences of A and B are: 'A and B', 'A and not B', 'B and not A' and 'not A and not B'.

179 In this example, "most people typically try to remember several delinquent marijuana users and either assume or not assume a correlation based on the availability of this mental data" (2006: p20) instead of going through the complete analysis that should contain all four combinations.

180 See for instance Chapman/Chapman (1969) or Ward/Jenkins (1965) for early research in this area, as well as Fiedler (2004) for several examples of more recent research.

3.2.2.2 Representativeness Heuristic

People using the representative heuristic unconsciously rely on similarity or stereotypes as the base for probabilistic judgments: "When you make judgments based on the representativeness heuristic, you assume that if something has the characteristics considered typical of members of a category, it is, in fact, a member of that category" (Gerrig/Zimbardo, 2008: p264), or, as Tversky and Kahneman (1974: p1124) describe it, "probabilities are evaluated by the degree to which A is representative of B, that is, by the degree to which A resembles B".

In general, the representativeness heuristic is a useful strategy that can be applied in a large variety of situations where no relevant additional information is available[181]. However, people also tend to rely on representativeness-based strategies if the available information – which they base their judgment on – is insufficient or irrelevant, and even if additional, better information exists that would enable a more accurate judgment[182]. Instead, these other pieces of relevant information are then ignored. As a consequence, "this approach to the judgment of probability leads to serious errors, because similarity, or representativeness, is not influenced by several factors that should affect judgment of probability" (Tversky/Kahneman, 1974: p1124), for example base-rates or sample sizes. Despite this clear disadvantage, the representativeness heuristic is nevertheless very frequently used.[183] This fosters the emergence of several cognitive biases that systematically distort decision making. The following sections briefly address and

---

181 See for instance Nisbett/Ross (1980: p7) who describe that, in the absence of additional information, botanists often use the representativeness heuristic to assign a newly discovered plant to a known species or family, based on its particular (representative) features.

182 See for example Bazerman (2006: p9) or Gerrig/Zimbardo (2008: p264).

183 Teigen (2004: p166) attributes this to the fact that the representativeness heuristic is easy, requires only a minimum of cognitive resources, and can be used in a large variety of situations.

illustrate the most important cognitive biases that result from the representativeness heuristic.[184]

Insensitivity to Base Rates

This cognitive bias, also referred to as 'insensitivity to prior probabilities', describes the tendency to neglect or ignore base rate information if descriptive data is available.[185] In one of the earlier research experiments[186] demonstrating this effect, participants receive a short description of a (fictional) person, Steve, prepared by Steve's neighbor. They are asked to estimate the probability that Steve is engaged in particular occupations and to rank them and pick the most likely profession: Steve is described as "very shy and withdrawn, invariably helpful, but with little interest in people, or in the world of reality. A meek and tidy soul, he has a need for order and structure, and a passion for detail" (Tversky/Kahneman, 1974: p1124). The choices available for Steve's occupation include farmer, salesman, airline pilot, librarian and physician. The results[187] illustrate that participants assess the probabilities purely based on the similarity of the description to their stereotypes of the professions. However, considerations of base rate frequency – there are more salesmen than librarians in the world – are

184 In addition to the biases that are discussed in the following sections, Tversky/Kahneman (1974: p1126) originally also described two other biases, which are related to predictions: 'insensitivity to predictability' (insensitivity with regard to the suitability of information for predictive uses and with regard to predictability in general) and 'illusion of validity' (distorted confidence in predictions based on the degree of representativeness of available input information). However, as these seem of lower relevance in literature, and due to considerations of scope, the discussion in the following sections focuses only on the five most frequently discussed and most well-known biases that stem from the representativeness heuristic.

185 See for instance Tversky/Kahneman (1974: p1124) or Bazerman (2006: p21f).

186 See Kahneman/Tversky (1973) for details on this empirical study.

187 The profession that receives the highest probability estimate and that is also most frequently selected is 'librarian'.

neglected. This distorts the judgment, because base rates do affect the actual probability, but they do not affect the perceived similarity – and thus the representativeness – of Steve in relation to the given professions.[188] Analogous results are obtained from similar experiments: people utilize base rates properly if no other evidence is given, but ignore base rates if additional descriptive information is provided, even if this information is worthless[189]. As a consequence, this cognitive bias of insensitivity to base rates can lead to systematically distorted judgments and decisions.

Insensitivity to Sample Size

This cognitive bias describes the tendency to ignore the size of a sample when unconsciously basing one's judgment on the representativeness heuristic, because "sample size is rarely a part of our intuition" (Bazerman, 2006: p23). As a consequence, people tend to assess the probability of obtaining a specific sample result from a particular population purely by the similarity – and thus the representativeness – of this sample result to the general population, without considering the sample size.[190] However, while the similarity between a sample and the corresponding population is not dependent on the size of the sample, the actual probability does depend on the sample size.

This effect of neglecting the sample size is demonstrated in several studies[191], for instance in a frequently cited and replicated empirical experiment[192]: being

188 See Tversky/Kahneman (1974: p1124).

189 See for instance Kahneman/Tversky (1973).

190 See Tversky/Kahneman (1974: p1125).

191 See for instance Bar-Hillel (1982: p79ff) for discussions of several experiments about sample size and the representativeness heuristic.

192 See for example Bazerman (2006: p23f), Bar-Hillel (1982: p81f), or Tversky/Kahneman (1974: p1125).

presented a situation with two hospitals in a town, participants are asked whether the number of days, on which more than 60% of the newborns are boys, is bigger in the larger or in the smaller hospital, or roughly equal in both, over a year. In addition, participants are told that one hospital has on average 45 newborns a day while the other has 15, and that on average about 50% of newborns are boys, but the specific percentage fluctuates each day. The majority of participants judge that the probability is the same in both hospitals, because both samples seem "equally representative of the general population" (Tversky/Kahneman, 1974: p1125). However, the probability is actually much higher in the smaller hospital than in the larger hospital, because smaller samples tend to fluctuate more than larger ones. Nevertheless, "people ignore the issue of sample size – which is critical to an accurate assessment of the problem" (Bazerman, 2006: p23), and therefore fall victim to this cognitive bias.

Misconceptions of Chance

This cognitive bias is caused by the tendency of people to "expect that a sequence of events generated by a random process will represent the essential characteristics of that process even when the sequence is short" (Tversky/Kahneman, 1974: p1125). This means that people expect that a random sequence is representative of the 'typical' sequence they imagine and that it also 'looks' and 'appears' like a random sequence.[193] As a consequence, a sequence that seems more representative is assigned a higher probability than a sequence that seems less representative, even if both sequences have exactly the same probability.

193 See for instance Bazerman (2006: p23ff), Teigen (2004: p167ff), or Tversky/Kahneman (1974: p1125f).

This 'misconceptions of chance' bias[194] is often illustrated using simple empirical experiments[195] about probability judgments of coin-flips:[196] "people regard the sequence H-T-T-T-T-H to be more likely than the sequence H-H-H-T-T-T, which does not appear random [due to the seemingly unusual clusters of heads and tails], and also more likely than the sequence H-H-H-H-T-H, which does not represent the fairness of the coin [due to the seeming imbalance of heads and tails]" (Tversky/Kahneman, 1974: p1125). However, all three sequences actually have the same probability. In a replication study, Smith (1998) explicitly includes an additional option that states that all sequences are equally likely[197]; nevertheless, the majority still wrongly selects the option that looks most representative instead. This indicates the strong persistency and tenacity of this particular cognitive bias.

Regression to the Mean

This cognitive bias describes that people tend to neglect the natural tendency of repeated activities to regress towards the mean.[198] This tendency – which is for example common for random variables that follow a Normal distribution – means

---

194 Two special cases of the 'misconceptions of chance' bias are sometimes discussed as individual biases on their own: the 'gambler's fallacy' (for example people wrongly believe that after a long run of red on the roulette wheel, the chance for black is higher in the next trial) and the 'hot hand phenomenon' (the opposite of the gambler's fallacy: people believe that a sports player with several successful trials in a row, for example in basketball, has a higher than usual chance for another successful throw in the next trial due to his 'hot hand', which is actually not the case, as empirical research, for instance by Gilovich et al. (2002b), demonstrates).

195 See for example Tversky/Kahneman (1974: p1125) or Teigen (2004: p167f).

196 In the following description, it is assumed that the coin is fair, that is both heads ('H') and tails ('T') have the same chance of 50%.

197 In the very first experiments, this option of "all are equally likely" has not been explicitly provided, but participants were mostly asked to rank the sequences according to likelihood.

198 See for example Tversky/Kahneman (1974: p1126) or Bazerman (2006: p25ff).

that it is likely that an extremely good outcome, for example a specific test result, is succeeded by an outcome that is worse[199] than the previous one, for example the result of a subsequent test. The same applies in the opposite direction: an extremely bad outcome is usually succeeded by a relatively better outcome, because of the regression to the mean. However, "people do not develop correct intuitions about the phenomenon" (Tversky/Kahneman, 1974: p1126). Instead they "tend to naively develop predictions based on the assumption of perfect correlation with past data" (Bazerman, 2006: p27), or construct non-existent causalities[200], and neglect the probabilistic concept of distributions and their regression to the mean with repeated trials.[201] As a consequence, considerable distortions and misjudgments can result due to this cognitive bias.

Conjunction Fallacy

The cognitive bias referred to as 'conjunction fallacy' describes that people tend to violate basic statistical rules when judging conjunctions – that is when assessing probabilities for conjunctive events – due to the representativeness heuristic[202]: "a conjunction will be judged more probable than a single component descriptor when the conjunction appears more representative than the component descriptor"

---

199 Worse means in this case that the outcome is in relative terms not as extremely good as the previous outcome, although it might still be good in absolute terms.

200 For example, Kahneman/Tversky (1973) describe that flight trainers experienced that praise for an exceptionally good landing was usually succeeded by a worse landing, and harsh criticism after a very poor landing was usually succeeded by a better landing; from this experience, the instructors drew the conclusion – based on their perceived causality – that praise is detrimental and punishment is beneficial. However, they did not take into account the regression towards the mean and that it is usual that an excellent landing is succeeded by a less excellent landing.

201 Bazerman (2006: p27) notes that in very extreme cases people realize the exceptional character and take into account the regression towards the mean, for example if a soccer player scores four goals in a single match, most people do not expect this to happen again the next time. However, people "generally do not recognize the regression effect in less extreme cases".

202 See for instance Tversky/Kahneman (1983) or Bazerman (2006: p27ff).

(Bazerman, 2006: p28). However, it is a statistical fact that a conjunction cannot be more likely than any of its components, but at most equally likely.

In a well-known experiment, Tversky/Kahneman (1983) illustrated this effect: they showed participants the description of a (fictional) person, Linda, and asked them to rank several statements about Linda according to probability. The result revealed that most people ranked the statement that 'Linda is a bank teller and is active in the feminist movement' as more likely than 'Linda is a bank teller', which is a clear violation of the statistical conjunction rule, as the former statement is a sub-set of the later statement and can thus not be more likely. Tversky/ Kahneman (1983) attribute this to the representativeness heuristic[203]. In a similar, less abstract experiment, Tversky/Kahneman (1983: p302) demonstrate the same effect: with regard to the Wimbledon finals in 1981, people ranked the statement that Björn Bork, one of the finalists, 'will lose the first set but win the match' as more likely than 'Borg will lose the first set', because the first statement seemed more representative of the tennis player Björn Bork.[204] However, this is again a clear violation of the conjunction rule, because the second statement actually also includes the second one. As a consequence, the application of the representativeness heuristic and the neglect of the proper statistical calculation lead to a cognitive bias that potentially entails systematically distorted decisions.

The preceding sections illustrated in detail several cognitive biases related to the representativeness heuristic, and highlighted their potential detrimental effects on

[203] The 'Linda'-experiment is probably the most frequently and most controversially discussed experiment conducted by Tversky and Kahneman. Several authors have analyzed, replicated, adapted and changed this experiment in order to prove or disprove potential alternative explanations and competing theories. See for instance Fisk (2004: p23ff) for a detailed discussion of potential explanations. However, none of the alternative explanations has sufficiently satisfied all controversial positions.

[204] Being an excellent tennis player, but often rather weak in the first set, requiring some time to get into the match.

decision making. Similarly distortive consequences can also result from the third and final fundamental heuristic, which is covered in the subsequent part: anchoring and adjustment.

3.2.2.3 Anchoring and Adjustment Heuristic

The anchoring and adjustment heuristic refers to the simplifying strategy to "make estimates by starting from an initial value that is adjusted to yield the final answer" (Tversky/Kahneman, 1974: p1128). However, this procedure creates systematic errors, because people frequently "fail to make sufficient adjustments" (Das/Teng, 1999: p760) to their initial anchors[205].[206] Consequently, with regard to exactly the same question, "different starting points yield different estimates, which are biased toward the initial values" (Tversky/Kahneman, 1974: p1128), because "judgment is 'anchored' too firmly to an original guess" (Gerrig/ Zimbardo, 2008: p265). As a consequence, the application of the anchoring and adjustment heuristic leads to a cognitive bias that entails systematically distorted decision making.[207]

The generally used procedure for empirical verifications of the anchoring effect is a two-step process[208]: subjects are first asked to compare the target value

205 See for instance Slovic/Lichtenstein (1971) for further research on insufficient anchor adjustments.

206 The two dominating cognition-based causes potentially underlying this insufficient adjustment are described in more detail at the end of this chapter.

207 In contrast to the previous sections, the discussion of the anchoring heuristic is not split into different cognitive biases that result from its use, because the result of the anchoring effect itself is regarded as the (only) cognitive bias. Tversky/Kahneman (1974) originally described two additional cognitive biases: one is concerned with distortions of evaluating conjunctive events, and the other one with biased calibrations of estimating confidence intervals. However, these are regarded as being only marginally attributable to the anchoring heuristic (Tversky/Kahneman stated this themselves). Actually, the first corresponds to the 'conjunction fallacy' discussed in chapter 3.2.2.2 and the second to the 'overconfidence bias' addressed in chapter 3.3.4.

208 See for instance Tversky/Kahneman (1974: p1128ff) or Chapman/Johnson (2002: p121).

to the anchor, and state if it is higher or lower than the anchor, and then to provide their own estimate. In general, anchors can be either explicitly provided by the experimenter or the decision description, or they can be self-generated by the participants. In the latter case, "people adjust from values they generate themselves as starting points known to be incorrect but close to the target value" (Epley/Gilovich: 2006: p312).[209] In the case of externally provided anchors, several approaches are used to point out the completely uninformative and irrelevant nature of the anchor value[210]: for instance spinning a wheel of fortune in front of the participants[211] – and using the result as anchor value for the comparison – or constructing an anchor value from the participant's social security number or telephone number[212]. However, both types of anchor produce the distortive anchoring effect.

Chapman/Johnson (2002: p123f) discuss and outline two necessary conditions for the anchoring bias to occur: firstly, subjects must take note of and attend to the anchor in some form[213] – if the anchor value is not seen or does not come to mind at all, anchoring cannot occur –, and secondly, the anchor must be on the

209 Epley/Gilovich (2006: p312) provide an example for the self-generation of anchors from one of their experiments that asked participants to estimate the year when George Washington was elected president of the United States: although most don't know the exact year, they "can quickly generate an estimate by adjusting from the date of the Declaration of Independence in 1776 – a date known to be close to the correct answer".

210 Chapman/Johnson (2002: p122) explicitly point out that, for empirical experiments on anchoring, it is important that the anchor is obviously uninformative, because otherwise "subjects might attend to anchors and incorporate them into their judgments because they reason that the experimenter would not have mentioned the anchor were it not informative or relevant".

211 See for example Tversky/Kahneman (1974: p1128).

212 See for instance Russo/Shoemaker (1989: p90).

213 Wilson et al. (1996) state that it is not necessary that an explicit comparative step takes place (which is the case in most experiments), but that it is sufficient if the participant is adequately exposed to the anchor, for instance visually or acoustically, and properly attends to it.

same numerical scale as the target response[214], for example both values are expressed as percentages or as dollars, and not of different types, for example dollar values for the target and percentages for the anchor.

Extensive research has demonstrated the persistency and robustness of anchoring effects: they occur in a huge variety of judgments in many different domains[215], including professional contexts[216], also work for extreme and even implausible anchors[217], are not reduced if payments are rewarded for accuracy[218] and even occur if participants are explicitly made aware of the anchor's effects[219]. However, anchoring effects can result from different psychological mechanisms.[220] There exist several possible cognition-related causes[221] for the observed anchoring effects, of which two seem to prevail and thus dominate the discussion: On the one hand, insufficient adjustment due to an too early termination of the adjustment process[222]: "people adjust insufficiently from an initial anchor value because they stop adjusting once their adjustments fall within an implicit range of plausible values" (Epley/Gilovich, 2006: p316). On the other hand, insufficient

214 Strack/Mussweiler (1997) note that the anchoring effect is even stronger if both anchor and target response are in addition expressed in the same underlying dimension, for example the height or width (both are measures in meters, but are different dimensions of an object).

215 See for instance Mussweiler et al. (2004: p185f) for an extensive list of research examples.

216 See for example Joyce/Biddle (1981) for empirical support of the anchoring effect being present among practicing auditors of the Big Four accounting firms.

217 See for instance Strack/Mussweiler (1997) or Chapman/Johnson (1994).

218 See for example Tversky/Kahneman (1974: p1130) or Chapman/Johnson (2002: p125).

219 See for instance Chapman/Johnson (2002: p125) or Wilson et al. (1996).

220 See Epley/Gilovich (2006: p316).

221 See for example Chapman/Johnson (2002: p126ff) for a discussion of different potential cognitive causes for anchoring effects.

222 See for instance Epley/Gilovich (2006) or Epley/Gilovich (2001) for discussions on insufficient adjustment due to the termination of adjustment once a plausible value is reached as potential explanation for the anchoring effect, especially with regard to self-generated anchor values.

adjustment due to enhanced accessibility of anchor-consistent information[223], in such a way that "the existence of an anchor leads people to access information that is consistent with that anchor [...] and not access information that is inconsistent with the anchor" (Bazerman, 2006: p29), which results in an adjustment that is less strong than it should be. However, despite slightly different explanatory approaches to locate the exact underlying cognitive reason, all authors agree on the existence of the anchoring effect and that this cognitive bias can lead to severe distortions of judgmental outcomes.

The previous parts have introduced the general approach and discussed a multitude of cognitive biases. Nevertheless, there are many more on top of those. These are addressed in the following sub-chapter. However, as it is neither possible, nor the purpose of this thesis, to cover all of them, the subsequent sections highlight only a selection of the most prominent and relevant biases, some of which will also be part of the empirical section of this thesis later on.

3.3 Selection of Further Biases and Effects

Building on the principles discussed in the previous sections, this sub-chapter addresses four groups of further cognitive biases that were selected based on their popularity, empirically tested validity, and their relevance for the subsequent empirical part: framing effects, irrational relativity, action and inaction preferences, and overconfidence effects. In addition to these distortions and the ones addressed in the previous sub-chapter, many additional biases exist,

223 See for example Mussweiler et al. (2004) or Strack/Mussweiler (1997) for discussions of the enhanced accessibility of anchoring-consistent information as potential explanation for the anchoring effect.

including for example zero effects[224] and the halo effect[225], but it would be far beyond the scope and the intention of this thesis to address them as well.

3.3.1 Framing Effects

"Framing refers to alternative wordings of the same objective information that significantly alter the model decision" (Bazerman, 2006: p43). This means that different representations of the same problem can lead to differing preferences and choices, thus producing preference reversals[226]. However, according to the normative rules of rationality, particularly the invariance principle[227], "different representations of the same choice problem should yield the same preference" (Tversky/Kahneman, 2000: p213). This is in sharp contrast to observed decision making behavior, indicating that "the presentation of the options [seems to] make a difference" (Kühberger, 1997: p129), resulting in preference reversals. As a consequence, framing effects constitute violations of rationality and its normative invariance requirements.

Tversky/Kahneman (1981: p453) first demonstrated this effect in the well-known 'Asian disease' experiment. The participants are presented a situation in which a country "is preparing for the outbreak of an unusual Asian disease, which is expected to kill 600 people". A choice is to be made between an option with a certain outcome and a risky option.[228] Half of the participants receive the options described in terms of gains – that is, people saved – and half of them in an equivalent description in terms of losses – that is, people killed. The results show

[224] See for example Ariely (2008: p49ff) or Shampanier et al. (2007) for additional information regarding zero effects.

[225] See for instance Rosenzweig (2007) for a detailed discussion of the halo effect.

[226] See for example Slovic (2000) or Stalmeier et al. (1997) for more information on preference reversals in general and different types of preference reversals.

[227] See chapter 2.2.2 for a discussion of rationality in general and the invariance principle in particular.

[228] The risky option has exactly the same expected value for the outcome as the certainty option.

that the majority of participants presented with the 'positive framing'[229] selected the first, risk-averse option, while the majority of participants presented with a 'negative framing'[230] overwhelmingly favored the second, risk-seeking option. Content-wise, they answered exactly the same problem – '200 people are saved' is exactly equivalent to '400 people die' in the situation at hand –, but the effects of framing, in this case a slightly different description, provoked a drastic reversal of preferences.[231] One potential explanation[232] for this particular example is that participants in the two cases unconsciously use different reference points and compare gains or losses relative to their reference point, with losses weighing stronger than the equivalent gains. This behavior has been formally described in the so-called Prospect Theory[233].

However, framing can be more than just exchanging some words, as the above example and the term 'alternative wordings' in the first definition above might imply. The term 'frame' refers to a particular description of a situation[234], usually with alternative choices, and this description can differ in several aspects: Accordingly, Soman (2004: p382ff) distinguishes three different types of framing: outcome framing, structure framing, and task framing. The 'Asian disease' experiment is a typical example of outcome framing: the outcome of a decision is described in differing ways. In this case, the outcome is framed as gain

---

229 "200 people will be saved for sure" vs. "1/3 probability that 600 will be saved, and 2/3 probability that no people will be saved".

230 "400 people will die for sure" vs. "1/3 probability that nobody will die, and 2/3 probability that 600 people will be die".

231 See for example Shafir/Tversky (1995: p83f), Bazerman (2006: p41ff), or Soman (2004: p383f) for further discussions of the 'Asian disease' experiment.

232 See for instance Soman (2004: p383f).

233 See for instance Kahneman/Tversky (1979), Tversky/Kahneman (1992), or Jungermann et al. (2005: p220ff) for details on the Prospect Theory.

234 See Gerrig/Zimbardo (2008: p266).

or loss. Other ways of outcome framing[235] include aggregate vs. disaggregate quantities[236] or different scaling[237] of the outcomes. Preference reversals due to framing of outcomes are usually explained by means of the Prospect Theory. While outcome framing alters the verbal or numerical description of a decision situation, structure framing changes the structural format of the decision. Typical approaches[238] include the integration or segregation of information[239], reframing as aggregated or sequential decisions[240], or adjusting the scope and breadth of the respective frame[241]. Preference reversals due to structure framing are for instance attributed to the 'bracketing effect'[242], the 'pseudocertainty effect'[243] and 'mental

---

235 See Soman (2004: p382ff).

236 Framing of an outcome with two components in such a way that it is either described and subsequently evaluated as one joint, integrated outcome or as two separate, disaggregated outcomes. For example, "people are happier winning two lotteries that pay $50 and $30 separately, than winning a single lottery that pays $80" (Soman, 2004: p385).

237 Framing of an outcome using different scales for exactly the same value. For example, expressing the outcome in differently scaled (usually fictitious) foreign currencies (and explicitly providing the exchange rate, so that it is clear that the value in the original currency is the same) gives rise to the so-called 'money illusion'. For further information regarding this cognitive bias see for instance Fisher (1928) or Shafir/Tversky (2000).

238 See for instance Tversky/Kahneman (1981) or Soman (2004: p390ff).

239 See for instance Tversky/Kahneman (1981: p454f) for a framing example where a problem is presented either as one decision, or it is split into two paired decisions (with equal additive outcome) that have to be taken at the same time and in consideration of each other.

240 The decision situation is described either as one decision, or as two sequential decisions (with equal additive outcome). See for instance Tversky/Kahneman (1981: p455f) for an example.

241 See for instance Soman (2004) for an example of framing the structure of a decision problem (cancel the last day of a four-day skiing trip due to bad weather?) by providing either a narrow frame (having purchased in advance four daily tickets which each cost $40; thus the focus is on the individual ticket bought for the forth day, and the perceived 'loss' is directly calculable) or a broader frame (having paid in advance $160 for a four-day ticket; thus the focus is on the total four-day period, and the 'loss' could be partly reduced by potential gains in the first three days).

242 See for instance Read et al. (1999).

243 See for example Tversky/Kahneman (1981) or Bazerman (2006: p46ff).

accounting'[244]. Finally, task framing refers to different ways of specifying how the task is to be conducted. The most frequently used method is "to frame the task as a decision to choose one option from a given set, or a decision to reject options from the set" (Soman, 2004: p393). Depending on the task presented, participants can display substantial preference reversals[245], for example in such a way that exactly the same option is selected – thus regarded as better – in one version and rejected – hence regarded as worse – in the other version. A potential explanation is that people focus more on information which is consistent with the task, and that this information is more available and also attributed more value than disconfirming information.[246]

Framing effects are in general very persistent, as "people tend to adopt the frame presented in a problem and evaluate the outcomes in terms of that frame" (Shafir/Tversky, 1995: p84), because they unconsciously avoid the cognitive effort of reframing. Furthermore, framing effects also seem to affect experts, as Shafir/Tversky (1995: p84) note after an experiment involving radiation therapy as treatment for lung cancer: "Surprisingly, physicians were just as susceptible to the effect of framing as were graduate students or clinic patients".

A cognitive bias that is very closely related to framing is the 'confirmation trap' bias, which describes the tendency to prefer and consider primarily confirming information and at the same time neglect counter-evidence or disregard the search for disconfirming information.[247] To a certain extent, this means that one unconsciously imposes a particular frame on oneself and consequently

---

244 See for instance Bazerman (2006: p52ff), Pompian (2006: p171ff), or Thaler (1994: p25ff) for more information on mental accounting.

245 See for example Shafir (1993) or Shafir/Tversky (1995: p92ff) for examples and additional information on task structuring.

246 See the next but one paragraph for information regarding a similar bias, the so-called 'confirmation trap' bias.

247 See for example Pompian (2006: p187ff), Manktelow (1999: p66ff), or Bazerman (2006: p35f) for further information on the 'confirmation trap' bias.

focuses more on particular aspects of a decision. This can happen in all three above described types of framing, but it is particularly obvious in the case of task framing.

In summary, the above sections have illustrated that framing effects can be highly influential; they lead to substantial preference reversals, thus violating the normative rules of rationality, particularly the invariance principle. The following sections cover another group of cognitive biases that likewise break with normative rationality.

3.3.2 Irrational Relativity

Irrational relativity addresses two phenomena linked to an irrational treatment of relativity, exhibited by the reversal of relative preferences among two options in a choice set. With regard to such relative preferences, the 'independence of irrelevant alternatives' principle of normative rational decision theory demands that the "preference between options does not depend on the presence or absence of other options" (Tversky/Simonson, 2000: p518). However, two effects systematically violate this fundamental principle of rationality: the 'compromise effect' and the asymmetric dominance effect[248]. Both biases significantly influence and shift the relative preferences between two existing options by adding a third option to the choice set.[249]

In the case of the 'compromise effect', the preferences between two existing options are shifted by adding a third option in such a way that it makes one of the other two options a 'middle' option; this 'compromise' option is "evaluated more favorably when it is seen as intermediate in the set of options under con-

[248] The asymmetric dominance effect is also referred to as 'attraction effect' or 'decoy effect' in literature, and the three names are used synonymously. For consistency reasons, the term asymmetric dominance is used throughout the whole thesis, except for direct quotations.

[249] See for example Simonson (1989), Jungermann et al. (2005: p309ff), or Huber et al. (1982).

sideration" (Kelman et al., 2004: p963) than it was in the previous two-options setting. One reason for this is a tendency toward extremeness aversion: "options with extreme values within an offered set will be relatively less attractive than options with intermediate values" (Tversky/Simonson, 2000: p524). Accordingly, decision makers tend to gravitate towards the non-extreme option, and preference reversals can occur.

With regard to the asymmetric dominance effect, the preferences between two existing options are shifted by adding a third option in such a way that it is asymmetrically dominated. This means that the third option "is dominated by one item in the set but not by another" (Huber et al., 1982: p90). As a consequence, the option that dominates the newly-added third option is evaluated more desirable than before, in comparison to the second initially existent option.[250]

The following illustration presents a simple overview of the decision situations for both asymmetric dominance and the 'compromise effect'. In the depicted example, A and B are the two available, original options in the initial set-up in a two-dimensional decision situation with no dominant option.

250 See for instance Huber et al. (1982), Colman et al. (2007), or Ariely (2008: p8ff) for further information on asymmetric dominance.

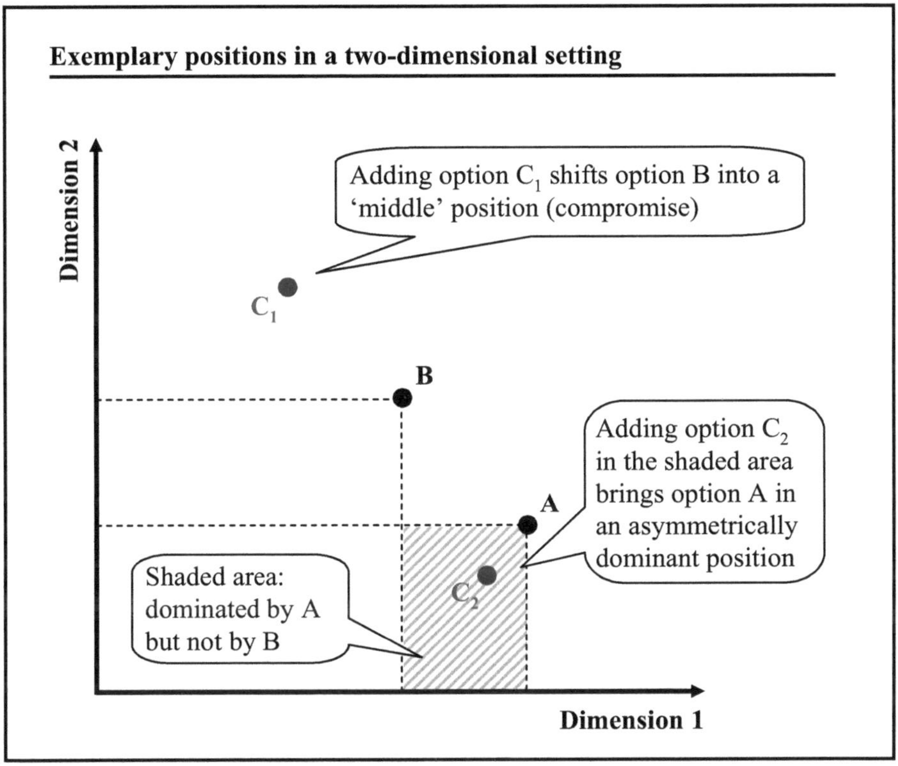

Illustration 6: Asymmetric dominance and the 'compromise effect'[251]

Assuming, for simplicity, that preferences are initially spread equally between A and B[252], the following happens if a third option is added to the choice set: On the one hand, if option C_1 is added, this creates a situation where B is in a 'middle' position, and according to the 'compromise effect' option B would be more

[251] Illustration based on descriptions and discussions in Simonson (1989), Jungermann et al. (2005: p309ff), and Huber et al. (1982).

[252] Preferences can actually be distributed in any way between A and B, but for illustrative purposes the simple assumption of roughly equally distributed preferences is taken.

preferable than A, which is now an extreme option. On the other hand, if instead option C_2 is added to the choice set, option A would be more preferable than option B according to the asymmetric dominance effect, because option A dominates option C_2 while option B does not dominate option C_2. This is a clear violation of the above mentioned 'independence of irrelevant alternatives' principle, because, depending on the position of the third option, option C, either option A is preferred over option B, or option B is preferred over option A – although both options A and B remain exactly the same, and the ranking of and relative preference between those two options should normatively not be affected at all by any other option, independent of its existence or position. Nevertheless, a large number of empirical evidence from different domains support the existence of irrational relativity effects and also demonstrate that they are very robust and persistent.[253]

Several potential reasonings have been suggested for explaining this irrational treatment of relativity[254]. Huber et al. (1982) propose that the asymmetrically dominated option changes perceived weights of the dimensions in such a way that the dominating option benefits because its 'stronger' dimension receives more weight and its 'weaker' attribute weighs less. A similar explanation is based on the Prospect Theory and suggests that the existence of more options in a particular segment of the decision space unconsciously creates a reference point against which all options are judged.[255] Another potential explanation, also initially proposed by Huber et al. (1982), states that the reason could be found in the evaluation process: in the case of a pairwise comparison, option A wins over

253 See for example Colman et al. (2007), Park/Kim (2005), or Hedgcock/Rao (2009) for recent empirical evidence as well as for a large number of references to earlier research.

254 Discussions in literature focus significantly more on potential explanations for the asymmetric dominance effect and hardly address the 'compromise effect' (the most frequently stated potential explanation for this is extremeness aversion, which is already mentioned above).

255 See for instance Pettibone/Wedell (2000).

option C_2 while option B only ties with option C_2, thus favoring option A over option B. Similarly, another reasoning suggests that a third option, in combination with particular evaluation processes, enables an easier justification of the decision, both internally and externally.[256] Alternatively, Luce et al. (1999) focus on trade-off-aversion and suggest that the introduction of an asymmetrically dominated option reduces the trade-off difficulty, as well as the unconscious inherent cost of thinking[257]. However, despite substantial evidence for all the above explanations, it is still not entirely clear today which of them prevails under which condition. Nevertheless, all of them demonstrate the robustness and importance of this cognitive bias.

Summing up, as a consequence of the irrational treatment of relativity illustrated in this sub-chapter, an important principle of normative rationality is systematically violated. However, while these violations are related to cognitive biases that are concerned with selection decisions among different available options, the following section focuses on cognitive biases that affect whether a decision is taken at all.

3.3.3 Action and Inaction Preferences

In the majority of the illustrated cases, decision making is concerned with which alternative to take from a particular choice set. However, even the decision whether to take action or not to act at all already gives rise to several distortions. Important and wide-spread cognitive biases with regard to such action or inaction preferences are the 'status quo' bias, elicited by 'loss aversion' and the 'endowment effect', and the 'omission bias'. These four biases are to a certain extent interrelated and partly reinforce each other.

---

[256] See for example Simonson (1989).

[257] See for instance Shugan (1980).

The 'status quo' bias describes people's "preference for the current state" (Kahneman et al., 2000: p160) or as few changes as possible. This means that, "an individual is relatively more reluctant to move away from some state identified as the status quo than from any alternative state not identified as the status quo" (Pompian, 2006: p249). As a consequence, people tend to be biased towards not acting and maintaining the status quo[258], if a status quo exists and if it is possible to retain this state[259]. Several empirical experiments, both in the laboratory as well as in the field, have demonstrated this tendency.[260] The underlying reasons for this preference of the 'status quo' are presumed to be to a small extent anchoring effects[261] and especially the implications of 'loss aversion', in combination with the effects underlying the Prospect Theory.[262] However, Samuelson/Zeckhauser (1988) argue that the considerations of other factors – for instance unconscious transaction costs, cognitive costs of thinking, or psychological commitment to prior choices – can also trigger the 'status quo' bias without the explicit influence of 'loss aversion'.

'Loss aversion' refers to the tendency of people to strongly prefer avoiding losses compared to acquiring equivalent gains[263], because "changes that make things worse (losses) loom larger than improvements or gains" (Kahneman et al., 2000: p165). This tendency is illustrated by and incorporated into the value

---

258 See for example Samuelson/Zeckhauser (1988), Pompian (2006: p248ff), or Kahneman et al. (2000: p163ff).

259 See for instance Beach (1990: p54ff) who distinguishes between 'optional change' (one can make a change, thus the status quo can be retained) and 'non-optional change' (one must make a change, thus the status quo cannot be retained).

260 See for example Kahneman et al. (2000) and Samuelson/Zeckhauser (1988).

261 See for instance Pompian (2006: p249).

262 See for example Jungermann et al. (2005: p318) and Kahneman et al. (2000: p165).

263 See for instance Tversky/Kahneman (1991), Pompian (2006: p208ff), or Kahneman et al. (2000: p165ff).

function of the Prospect Theory, which is steeper for losses than for gains.[264] One implication of this is the above mentioned 'status quo' bias: due to 'loss aversion', the disadvantages of departing from the status quo loom larger than the respective advantages, and consequently, "loss aversion induces a bias that favors the retention of the status quo over other options" (Tversky/Kahneman, 1991: p1042).

Another bias that potentially results directly from 'loss aversion' is the 'endowment effect', which is also very closely linked to the 'status quo' bias. The 'endowment effect' describes the tendency to value something higher if one possesses it than if one does not possess it[265]. More formally expressed, it refers to the observed discrepancy between "the minimum amount that people are willing to accept (WTA) to give up a good they own and the maximal amount they would be willing to pay (WTP) to acquire it" (Tversky/Kahneman, 1991: p1054). According to standard economic theory and normative rationality, willingness to pay and willingness to accept should be equal. However, the evidence from a large number of experimental studies[266] demonstrates that the 'endowment effect' systematically violates this principle, because people tend to "demand much more to give up an object than they would be willing to pay to acquire it" (Soman, 2004: p387).

In simple versions of such experiments[267], half of the participants receive a particular object – for example a lottery ticket, a chocolate bar, or a pen, depending on the experiment – and the other half receive the equivalent monetary value. Subsequently, participants are allowed to swap the object and the money, either with the experimenter or with each other, again depending on the particular

---

264 See for example Kahneman/Tversky (1979), Tversky/Kahneman (1991: p1039ff), or Shafir/Tversky (1995: p78ff).

265 See for instance Thaler (1980), Kahneman et al. (2000: p160ff), Knetsch (2000), or Ariely (2008: p127ff).

266 See for example Kahneman et al. (1994), Samuelson/Zeckhauser (1988), Knetsch/Sinden (1984), or Kahneman et al. (2000: p160ff) for a selection of empirical experiments on the 'endowment effect' and for references to further studies.

267 See for example Knetsch/Sinden (1984) or Kahneman et al. (2000).

experiment. However, the number of trades is usually considerably lower than expected, and the vast majority of participants prefer to keep what they receive: for instance "the pens were worth more money to those subjects who started with pens than to those show started with money" (Kahneman et al., 2000: p162). This behavior is usually regarded as a consequence of the effects of 'loss aversion' and the 'status quo' bias. The 'endowment effect' also persists in considerably more advanced experiments[268], which devised complex simulations of interactive markets.

Another bias closely related to the issue of action and inaction preferences is the so-called 'omission bias', which describes the tendency to judge harm caused by an action as worse than the equal harm caused by omission, that is caused by a lack of action.[269] The results of several experiments[270] demonstrate this effect: participants "display an irrational preference for harms of omission [...] over harms of commission [...], even when the harms of inaction are much larger than the harms of action" (Bazerman, 2006: p55). In a well-known series of experiments about vaccinations against a particular disease, Ritov/Baron (1990) report that many participants display a preference to not "vaccinate children against a disease that was expected to kill ten out of 10.000 children when the vaccine itself would kill five out of 10.000 through side effects" (Bazerman, 2006: p55). The prevailing explanation for this behavior is the effect of the above mentioned 'status quo' bias, which favors a lack of action. In addition, another possibly influential factor with regard to the 'omission bias' is "anticipated regret,

---

268 See for instance Kahneman et al. (1994) for a series of such experiments.

269 See for example Ritov/Baron (1990) or Jungermann p320ff.

270 See for instance Spranca et al. (1991) or Ritov/Baron (1990) for early experiments with regard to the 'omission bias'.

with the level of anticipated regret being greater when an unwanted outcome has been caused by an individual's own actions" (Eysenck/Keane, 2005: p498).[271]

All the above mentioned cognitive biases can exert a significant influence on decision making by affecting the judgment whether to take action or not to act at all. The following sections finally address a very different aspect: the belief that one has concerning one's ability to take correct decisions.

3.3.4 Overconfidence Effects

Overconfidence effects influence the level of confidence that one attributes to the accuracy and precision of one's judgments.[272] Accordingly, the 'overconfidence bias' describes the tendency that "people are often more confident in their judgments than is warranted by the facts" (Griffin/Tversky, 2002: p230) and consequently "overestimate the precision of their knowledge" (Glaser et al., 2004: p536). Overconfidence is typically classified into two types[273]: the miscalibration of the average level of accuracy[274] – corresponding to a shift in the estimated level of accuracy compared to the actual level – and the distortion of the ranges of confidence intervals – the confidence interval is too narrow and the estimated

---

271 However, see for example Gilovich/Medvec (1995) for findings that suggest that although in the short-run actions generate more regret, in the long-run the regret due to omission is larger.

272 Given that overconfidence is a very large field, characterized by many ambiguities and unclarities on the theoretical rationales, the focus of the following sections is limited to the major aspects of overconfidence, in line with the intention of this chapter, which is to give a brief introduction to the topic, but not to conduct a deep-dive analysis of this particular topic.

273 See for instance Hoffrage (2004: p235ff).

274 See for example Lichtenstein et al. (1982) and Metcalfe (1998): people seem to be able to properly recognize and rank the difficulties of questions, but they miscalibrate their estimated average accuracy level in such a way that it shifts upwards from the actual level. For instance, if they are correct in 60% of the cases their estimate is 80% and if they are correct in 70% of the cases their estimate is 90%.

outer boundary limits are too close to the estimated mean. Although the estimated accuracy level in the first type of overconfidence is usually shifted 'upwards', under particular conditions the opposite can be the case, which means that in general, "decision makers tend to be overconfident for difficult problems and underconfident for easy problems" (Bukszar, 2003: p33).

An empirical demonstration of the second type of overconfidence is for example provided by Alpert/Raiffa (1982: p301ff), who asked participants to provide 98% confidence intervals for several estimation tasks[275]. The results showed that 42.6% (out of 1.000 instances)[276] actually fell outside the estimated 98% confidence interval limits, presumably because participants exhibited a significant 'overconfidence bias' and therefore set the boundaries much too narrow. With regard to both types of overconfidence, an innumerous number of empirical research has been conducted over the years[277], demonstrating that the 'overconfidence bias' exists in a multitude of domains.

However, despite the large body of evidence for the existence of the 'overconfidence bias', the underlying reasons are not entirely clear so far. A frequently stated potential explanation is the effect of the earlier mentioned 'confirmation bias': when asked to estimate the accuracy of an estimate, the decision maker searches primarily for reasons that confirm his or her option and neglects the search for disconfirming evidence; consequently more confirmatory evidence is available and the judgment seems more accurate than it actually is.[278] However,

---

275 The actual task prompted participants to provide several fractiles, including among others .01 and .99 fractiles, from which the 98% confidence interval can be deduced.

276 According to probability theory, about 2% of all instances should fall outside a 98% confidence interval. In addition, given the large size of 1.000 instances (of which 426 are outside the range), it can be assumed that this is not just a purely random, statistical fluctuation.

277 See for example Lichtenstein et al. (1982) for extensive empirical evidence for the existence of overconfidence effects and Hoffrage (2004) for a large number of references to more recent studies in this field.

278 See for instance Griffin/Brenner (2004: p185ff).

there is a large variety of potential explanations and different competing models[279], but none of them sufficiently explains all findings related to overconfidence. Furthermore, some recent studies[280] extend the scope of analysis and thereby raise new issues. Therefore, additional studies are required in order to clearly identify the underlying rationale(s) of overconfidence. Nevertheless, although the exact sources of the 'overconfidence bias' might not be fully known yet, "it is prevalent, often massive, and difficult to eliminate" (Griffin/Tversky, 2002: p248), and therefore a very important aspect with regard to decision making.

Several other biases are closely linked to the 'overconfidence bias', for example the 'hindsight bias' and the 'planning fallacy'. While the planning fallacy[281] is concerned with future events and describes the general tendency to underestimate completion times of tasks[282] – the decision maker exhibits a particular form of overconfidence, with regard to one's abilities[283] –, the 'hindsight bias' causes systematic distortions with regard to judgments concerning past

---

279 See for instance Hoffrage (2004) or Griffin/Brenner (2004) for a detailed discussion and comparison of several potential explanations and models with regard to overconfidence, including simple concepts like the 'confirmation bias' as well as sophisticated approaches like ecological and error models.

280 For instance, Bukszar (2003) suggests that the magnitude of overconfidence can differ between the judgment phase (which is usually the object of overconfidence experiments) and the actual subsequent action based on this judgment: decision makers actually seem to 'think twice' before acting on a previous judgment, thus reducing the detrimental effects of the 'overconfidence bias'.

281 See for example Buehler et al. (2002), Griffin/Buehler (1999), or Buehler et al. (1994) for additional information and examples of the 'planning fallacy'.

282 See for instance Eysenck (2004: p22) who defines the 'planning fallacy' as "the tendency to underestimate how long a work task will take to complete in spite of evidence from similar tasks completed in the past".

283 A comparable form of such overconfidence is for example the 'illusion of control': "People falsely believe that they can control uncontrollable events […] and they overestimate the extent to which their actions can guarantee a certain outcome" (Bazerman, 2006: p70).

events. In general, the 'hindsight bias'[284], also known as the 'I-knew-it-all-along' effect, describes "the tendency to mold one's interpretation of the past to fit how events actually turned out" (Weiten, 2007: p28). As a consequence, one sees past events as more predictable than they actually were before they took place, which is a special form of overconfidence: "in hindsight, people consistently exaggerate what could have been anticipated in foresight" (Fischhoff, 1982a: p341).

For instance, Weiten (2007: p528) describes an experiment[285] in which groups of students received the results of (fictitious) experiments: "each group of students could 'explain' why the studies turned out the way they did, even though different groups were given opposite results to explain". Furthermore, similar to the distortions with regard to one's own earlier judgments, "when assessing others' knowledge, people are unable to ignore knowledge that they have that others do not have" (Bazerman, 2006: p38) or did not have.[286] The most frequently suggested reason for the 'hindsight bias' is a combination of anchoring[287] – the actual outcome or knowledge serves as anchor, but the adjustment is insufficient, leading to an overestimation of predictability of the outcome or other people's knowledge – and the availability heuristic[288]: actual knowledge is more available than previous knowledge, because it is more recent, more salient and potentially interferes with or even replaces previous knowledge in memory.

---

284 See for example Fischhoff (1975) or Hawkins/Hastie (1990) for detailed information on the 'hindsight bias'.

285 See Slovic/Fischhoff (1977) for additional information on this particular experiment.

286 See for instance Camerer et al. (1989) for further information on this effect, which they labeled 'curse of knowledge'.

287 See Bazerman (2006: p38).

288 See for example Agans/Shaffer (1994), Fischhoff (1982a) or Slovic/Fischhoff (1977) for detailed discussions of the role of the availability heuristic with regard to the 'hindsight bias'.

In summary, the previous sections described several overconfidence effects that occur in various situations. This complements and completes the overall picture drawn by the earlier described biases in this chapter and shows that cognitive biases can substantially distort decision making in a large variety of ways. However, this point of view is not shared by all authors and accordingly occasionally confronted with skepticism. Therefore, the next sub-chapter addresses and critically discusses in detail the major criticisms raised against it.

3.4 Critical Discussion of the 'Heuristics and Biases' Approach

Over the years, the 'heuristics and biases' approach has repeatedly triggered debates and critiques, with Gerd Gigerenzer being one of the most prominent and most fierce critics[289]. In order to better understand the 'heuristics and biases' approach and its potential limitations, it is important to address the major issues[290] raised against it and the underlying reasons, and to discuss their validity. Overall, the major critiques can be classified to fall into three general areas[291]: critiques regarding the approach's general orientation and focus, its scientific adequacy, and its content and research set-up.

3.4.1 Critiques Regarding the General Orientation and Focus

Arguments in this area mainly criticize the general focus and impression that the 'heuristics and biases' approach seems to suggest. Key criticisms are the 'one-sided view' – meaning that the approach focuses too much on the flawed cases of

---

289 See for instance Gigerenzer (1991) or Gigerenzer (1996).

290 The following discussion focuses on the major and most frequently raised critiques, as it is impossible to locate and analyze each potentially critical comment. However, all critiques encountered so far are, at least to a large extent, very similar to the major ones discussed.

291 This classification is not based on a particular classification in literature, but on the author's analysis and synthesis of the most frequently raised critiques.

decision making and ignores those cases where heuristics result in correct decisions[292] – and the 'we cannot be that dumb' critique, meaning that the approach "offers an overly pessimistic assessment of the average person's ability to make sound and effective judgments" (Gilovich/Griffin, 2002: p8).

These criticisms are to a certain extent justified, the 'heuristics and biases' approach indeed focuses primarily – but not solely – on the faulty cases, and aims to find out why they occur and under which conditions. However, it does this by building on the traditional normative model of rational decision theory as benchmarks and comparing it to the observations made, adopting a descriptive decision theory perspective. It were these real-life observations of deviations that actually triggered the whole research on 'heuristics and biases', assuming that a deviation between normative and descriptive outcomes indicates something worthwhile of being analyzed. Furthermore, it is not unusual, neither in the real world nor in science, to focus on 'faulty' cases – that is, on deviations from the normatively claimed outcome – even if they only represent a minority (which is also not unusual for deviations). For example, most improvement efforts in business do this, for instance six sigma or total quality management. Consequently, although the 'heuristics and biases' approach does indeed focus primarily on 'faulty' cases – because these deviations are actually the relevant objects of examination –, this does not constitute a real shortcoming.

However, the opponents of the 'heuristics and biases' approach do make a fair point if their arguments are to be interpreted in such a way that they criticize that "studies in this tradition have paid scant attention to assessing the overall ecological validity of heuristic processes [...]; the focus has been on identifying the cues that people use, not on evaluating the overall value of those cues" (Gilovich/Griffin, 2002: p8). This could be seen as a small shortcoming. In addition, although supporters of the 'heuristics and biases' approach rightfully

---

292 See Pohl (2004: p11).

point out that "a meaningful overall characterization of the quality of human judgment is neither possible nor sought after" (Gilovich/Griffin, 2002: p9), this only partly relativizes the above mentioned small weakness, which needs to be addressed in the future and provides an opportunity for further improving the approach.

Moreover, although the 'heuristics and biases' approach might at first glance indeed seem to describe an overly pessimistic picture of human abilities with regard to decision making, this is actually not the case. Instead, its supporters clearly state – and have always pointed out – that cognitive biases only occur under particular conditions – not always and everywhere –, that the application of heuristics only sometimes leads to errors[293] – but by no means always –, and that cognitive biases are thus not the rule, but the exception[294]. If this is considered, in addition to the earlier mentioned points, the above critique can in summary be rebutted.

3.4.2 Critiques Regarding the Scientific Adequacy

Critical comments in this area mainly address the concept of the 'heuristics and biases' approach and its scientific adequacy. On the one hand, critics complain about the lack of explanatory power and theoretical progress of the approach. They argue that the heuristics are not proper explanations, but merely paraphrase the observations[295], and criticize insufficient theoretical progresses[296] as well as a "lack of rigorous investigation and detailed modeling" (Pohl, 2004: p12). On the

---

[293] See for example Tversky/Kahneman's (1974: p1130) very first article, which already clearly stated that heuristics only "occasionally lead to errors in prediction or estimation".

[294] For instance, Piatelli-Palmarini (1994: p193) responds to this critique and clarifies that "no one ever claimed that every projection from past experience, and every memorization of typical situations, leads to fallacies and cognitive illusions. The thesis is that they *sometimes* do, and that among the cases in which they do so there are many that prompt us to correct ourselves".

[295] See for instance Pohl (2004: p11).

[296] See for example Gigerenzer (1991: p101).

other hand, opponents of the 'heuristics and biases' approach criticize its 'conceptual vagueness', meaning for example that "representativeness is a very broad concept, applicable to a number of situations. This generality makes it both imprecise and difficult to falsify" (Teigen, 2004: p177). Adding both points, critics argue in effect that the approach might not sufficiently fulfill the scientific requirements expected and demanded from a generally acceptable theory.

Before discussing the individual points, it is important to highlight that 'heuristics and biases' started as a descriptive approach to decision making, not as a normative approach. As a consequence, the focus was primarily on describing and understanding the observed phenomena. However, in the meantime, the theoretical backing and the normative perspective have received considerably more attention than earlier, but it is undisputable that the descriptive contributions still dominate.

Moreover, critics are right that explanatory power is still low for particular phenomena, but supporters of the approach are also correct if they argue that explanatory power is much better for many other instances. Nevertheless, critics undoubtedly have a point if their critique is interpreted in such a way, that the 'heuristics and biases' field is still in an early phase of its existence and that there are still innumerous questions to be answered; however, that is by no means questioned by the supporters of the 'heuristics and biases' approach; rather, they fully agree and admit themselves that still many answers are not known yet.

Concerning the theoretical progress argument, it is also definitely true that many of the underlying basic principles, for example the fundamental heuristics, are today still the same as in the early days of the approach. However, depending on the perspective, this can be seen either negative ('no progress') or positive ('robust concept'). Furthermore, the detailed cognitive biases concepts and approaches, as well as the related research practices, have been considerably refined since, both from an empirical and especially from a theoretical perspective.

With regard to the conceptual vagueness critique, one has to admit that for instance representativeness is indeed a very broad concept and on its own not sufficient as an explanatory theoretical construct. "However, representativeness was originally proposed as a more descriptive term, capable of elucidating some general characteristics of human reasoning under uncertainty" (Teigen, 2004: p177), not as a universally applicable explicatory model for all related effects. Furthermore, the development of the 'heuristics and biases' approach did not stop at the level of the fundamental heuristics, but progressed and advanced considerably and distinguishes by now between many different cognitive biases, that relate in some way to the respective heuristic, but have each their own underlying theoretical model. Each cognitive bias is considerably less vague than the original heuristic, is clearly defined and described, can be tested, and has its own specific theoretical cognition-based explanation. As a consequence, the respective heuristics have in the meantime become rather a kind of overarching concept that connects several elements, but they are not the theoretical model themselves anymore. For instance, while anchoring biases were earlier usually attributed 'just' to the anchoring heuristic – accompanied by a short statement that the adjustment is insufficient, but without any relevant in-depth theoretical explanation –, the discussion today focuses on understanding and elucidating the underlying cognition-related causes of this insufficient adjustment[297] and on establishing the respective theoretical models. This constitutes a significant progress for the overall approach.

Summing up, some of the critiques raised in this area are definitely justified with regard to the rather slow theoretical development of the 'heuristics and biases' approach in the first years and decades. However, since then considerable progress has been made, particularly in the last ten to fifteen years, and the theoretical base and understanding of many cognitive biases has been refined and advanced. Nevertheless, both supporters and critics of the 'heuristics and biases' approach agree that there is still considerable space for further progress.

---

[297] See chapter 3.2.2.3 for additional information on these causes.

3.4.3 Critiques Regarding the Content and Research Set-Up

The majority of critiques are related to this area, and are primarily concerned with the content and research set-up of the experiments that lead to the findings of the 'heuristics and biases' approach. The key criticism here is the allegation of 'artificiality', which describes the claim that the observed biases are only due to specific laboratory circumstances and to purposely setting-up traps for participants, and that consequently "the biases revealed in this research are merely the product of fiendish (or clueless) experimenters who ask misleading questions" (Gilovich/Griffin, 2002: p11). For instance, critics argue that the use of non-probabilistic formats would make the biases disappear.[298]

There is undoubtedly some merit to this claim of artificiality, at least with regard to particular individual experiments. Also, it is true that the initial experiments were primarily set in the laboratory and some of them seemed rather artificially 'staged' or 'set-up'. However, in the meantime many experiments have been replicated in the field, with problem formulations being adjusted accordingly in a less 'artificial' way, and the effects of many cognitive biases have been observed in real life. Actually, it was the observation of those distortions in real life that in the first place initially motivated the related research. Furthermore, "just as it is clear that some individual experiments are open to critique, it is equally clear that the main biases uncovered in this research tradition [...] are not. These have been demonstrated in countless contexts and with varied paradigms and dependent measures, and with domain experts as well as student volunteers" (Gilovich/Griffin, 2002: p11f). In addition, the fact that the 'heuristics and biases' approach has exerted such an influence on a wide range of applied domains, including business contexts[299], constitutes a strong indication that the 'artificiality' critique might be exaggerated, as this influence would not exist in such an extent

---

298 See for example Gigerenzer (1994).

299 See chapters 4.1.1 and 4.1.2 for examples related to various business contexts.

if the approach dealt only with purely artificial problems.[300] Moreover, even critics do admit "that the accusation of artificiality applied only to a few illusions, while others are 'true illusions' without doubt" (Pohl, 2004: p11).

A popular general claim is that the bias disappears if particular (content-related) features of the experimental situation are changed or removed. The validity of this rather general claim can be illustrated by drawing on the earlier described analogy to optical illusions[301], in particular the Müller-Lyer illusion[302]: this claim is equivalent to stating that an optical fallacy, in this case the Müller-Lyer illusion, disappears if certain parts are changed or removed, for instance if all arrows are erased. This will, of course, make the optical illusion disappear, as it is only reduced to three lines. However, that does not mean or prove that it has not been an optical illusion in the original situation (with the arrows). Similarly, demonstrating that a specific cognitive bias does not exist anymore in a particularly altered situation does not prove that the bias is also non-existent in every other situation (including the original situation). Accordingly, this claim seems too general to support any of the two sides. However, the next paragraph analyzes and discusses a very particular version of this general claim.

Probably the most frequently stated claim of many critics is that the evidence presented in the 'heuristics and biases' approach would disappear if frequencies where used instead of probabilities[303], for example because evolutionary survival required humans to cope with frequencies, not with probabilities.[304] However, a large number of different studies demonstrated that in some cases this indeed slightly improved judgments – although "judgments based on frequencies were only marginally more accurate than those based on probabilities" (Eysenck, 2006: p331) –, in other cases, presenting frequencies instead of probabilities made

300 See for instance Gilovich/Griffin (2002: p11).

301 See for example Piatelli-Palmarini (1994: p192) for a similar reasoning.

302 See chapter 3.2.1.

303 See for example Gigerenzer (1994).

304 See for instance Pinker (1997).

judgments even worse, and very often it did not influence the quality of judgment at all.[305] Moreover, the bias did not disappear, as claimed. Furthermore, in a lot of studies conducted in the 'heuristics and biases' tradition, the participants did not receive any probabilistic information at all, but cognitive biases emerged nonetheless.[306] Taken together, both points provide a strong indication that this particular critique is unjustified[307].

In summary, the above discussions of all three areas of criticism indicate that although some of the critical arguments are valid to a certain extent, many of the key criticisms regarding the core of the 'heuristics and biases' approach and especially its content and findings are not reasonably sustainable.

This chapter laid the theoretical foundations necessary to understand cognitive biases, the way they function and the characteristics they possess. Each cognitive bias constitutes a violation of the normative rules of rationality, which have been introduced in the second chapter, with a particular focus on capital investments and their appraisal. Being equipped with the necessary theoretical background from both previous chapters, the following one brings them together.

---

305 See for instance Gilovich/Griffin (2002: p14) for several references to frequency-probability comparison studies with all three types of result: improve, deteriorate, and indifferent.

306 See Gilovich/Griffin (2002: p15).

307 It might apply to a very limited set of particular biases, but in order to properly assess this, further analyses would be required.

4 Cognitive Biases in the Capital Investment Context

This chapter merges the two preceding chapters' fundamentals in order to examine the relevance of cognitive biases in the context of capital investments. The first part discusses preparatory theoretical considerations by describing, on a basic level, the effects of cognitive biases in several general business contexts. The second part addresses two illustrative case examples and their potential impact in a capital investment environment. Afterwards, the third part describes eight empirical experiments conducted for this thesis and analyzes their results. The last part of this chapter finally discusses potential conclusions and analyzes limitations with regard to the presented theoretical and empirical findings.

4.1 Preparatory Theoretical Considerations

Although the majority of research conducted in the 'heuristics and biases' tradition focuses on non-business situations, it is highly likely that the effects of cognitive biases are also relevant in economic contexts in general, and in a capital investment environment in particular. The following sub-chapter approaches this issue from a theoretical perspective, with the intention to provide a high-level picture, which will be complemented by more detailed considerations in later sub-chapters. The first section of this sub-chapter illustrates the effects of cognitive biases in a general business context, including for instance marketing and human resource management. Subsequently, an excursus on behavioral finance addresses theoretical implications and empirical evidence with regard to cognitive biases in a financial investment context. The concluding section finally translates and transfers the above arguments into the capital investment context.

4.1.1 Cognitive Biases in the General Business Context

There is a large variety of general business-related incidents where the effects of heuristics and cognitive biases are obvious – and some cases in which these are even fostered on purpose. For example, marketing commercials rely strongly on the effects of the availability heuristic[308] and intentionally try to exploit, among other cognitive biases, the 'ease of recall' bias[309] through advertising. The availability of a particular product or brand in the mind of a consumer is increased by means of frequency – the advertising message is regularly repeated – or vividness – for instance via attention-grapping or surprising commercial spots – in order to influence the purchasing decision. As a consequence, the consumer tends to exhibit a stronger preference for the particular product because the advertising message, including the presented 'advantages', is more available. Likewise, the effects of the representativeness heuristic are triggered by manipulating the size of a product's packaging[310]: a larger packaging is representative of more content and therefore implies a better deal for the purchaser; however, if the packaging is not completely filled, but partly empty, a consumer judging by the representativeness heuristic might wrongly believe that a larger packaging size also means a larger quantity of a product. In a similar fashion, many of today's marketing efforts incorporate a large variety of cognitive biases.[311]

Another example of a business-related context in which heuristics and biases can influence decision making is human resource management. For example, when being faced with hiring or promotion decisions, a personnel manager can be subject to the representativeness bias[312]: for instance, if certain traits or characteristics of an applicant are representative of a particular stereotype or of an existing group of employees, the judgment regarding this particular applicant

308 There is of course much more to marketing than this, but the availability heuristic is an important foundation for the functioning of advertising.

309 See the 'retrievability of instances' section in chapter 3.2.2.1.

310 See for example Calver (2004) for detailed discussions of considerations related to packaging.

311 See for instance Ariely (2008: p2ff) for an exemplary description of the use of asymmetric dominance in pricing decisions.

312 See for example Dipboye/Macan (1988).

might be unconsciously influenced by this stereotype or the performance of the particular group of employees that the applicant is believed to be representative of. As a consequence, hiring decisions might be biased towards favoring a particular type of employee, which would lead to an overly homogeneous workforce. In extreme cases, hiring decisions based on representativeness can even favor discrimination.[313] Another important activity of human resource management, performance appraisals, can potentially be distorted by the 'halo effect'[314], for instance if a very good performance rating in a particular category spills over to other performance rating areas and biases the overall picture. Furthermore, anchoring effects can also bias performance evaluations, because "past performance can also be an anchor that influences judgments about current performance" (Tenbrunsel et al., 1996: p327). Likewise, cognitive biases can impact several other activities of human resource management.[315]

A third example of the relevance of cognitive biases in a general business context are negotiations. A typical distortive effect that can influence negotiations is anchoring.[316] The first offer made in negotiations often establishes a strong anchor and can thus influence the outcome: "especially when the other party is uncertain about the correct, fair, or appropriate outcome, they are likely to gravitate towards any number that helps them focus and resolve their uncertainty" (Malhotra/Bazerman, 2007: p27f). Accordingly, setting the right (counter) anchor at the right level at the appropriate point in time is an important challenge in any kind of negotiations, in order to ensure that one can exploit the biasing effects and is not oneself being distorted by the other party's anchors. Another influential

313 See for instance Cann et al. (1981) or Graves/Powell (2006) for examples of discrimination.

314 See for example Rosenzweig (2007) for a detailed discussion of the halo effect.

315 See for instance Tenbrunsel et al. (1996: p326f) for further references and several other examples of how cognitive biases influence human resource management.

316 See for example Lax/Sebenius (2004) or Malhotra/Bazerman (2007: p27ff) for discussions of anchoring effects in negotiations.

cognitive bias in negotiations is framing.[317] Depending on the particular frame provided, for instance by adapting formulations and adjusting reference points, the same suggestion or offer could for example be either perceived as a gain or a loss, or as a stronger or weaker effect. Such distortions of negotiation decisions caused by cognitive biases can apply to all types of negotiations, ranging from bargaining the price during a car purchase or an individual's payment negotiations to negotiating the terms of merger and acquisition activities.[318]

Having illustrated that cognitive biases can be very relevant in a general business context – although of course not always and everywhere, but only in specific situations –, the next step is to focus on their potential effects with regard to investments.

4.1.2 Cognitive Biases in the Financial Investments Context: Behavioral Finance

The application of cognitive biases to the domain of financial investments, generally referred to as 'behavioral finance', has already received substantial coverage, both from a theoretical as well as from an empirical perspective. The following sections briefly describe some of the major findings of behavioral finance. However, given that financial investments are not in the focus of this thesis, the intention of this short excursus is only to provide a very high-level understanding of the fundamentals and demonstrate some empirical findings of

317 See for instance Malhotra/Bazerman (2007: p120ff).

318 See for example Lovallo et al. (2007) for a discussion of cognitive biases in the context of mergers and acquisitions.

behavioral finance[319], in order to enable the subsequent part to draw certain parallels between financial and capital investments with regard to cognitive biases.

Pompian (2006: p4) defines behavioral finance as "the application of psychology to finance". Accordingly, "behavioral finance studies how people actually behave in a financial setting [...] [and] how psychology affects financial decisions, corporations, and the financial markets" (Nofsinger: 2008: p4f).[320] Despite being a relatively young discipline[321], it has already received a large amount of attention and its findings strongly influence today's capital markets and the respective players. In general, two different streams of behavioral finance can be distinguished[322]: a micro perspective and a macro perspective. While macro behavioral finance "detects and describes *anomalies* in the efficient market hypothesis that behavioral models may explain" (Pompian, 2006: p9), micro behavioral finance "examines *behaviors or biases of individual investors* that distinguish them from the rational actors envisioned in classical economic theory" (Pompian, 2006: p9) and discusses how and why the investment decisions of individual investors are distorted by particular biases.

One distortion of financial investment behavior is the 'overconfidence bias'[323], which describes in this case the "tendency to believe that one can pick mutual

---

319 See for example Nofsinger (2008), Montier (2007), Shefrin (2002), or Pompian (2006) for detailed discussions of behavioral finance in general and particular cognitive biases with regard to financial investments.

320 Although behavioral finance is very closely linked to heuristics and cognitive biases, it is today not limited to these mental distortions, but also addresses distortions caused for instance by emotions and mood, which are not due to the use of simplifying information processing heuristics.

321 See for instance Shefrin (2002: p7ff) or Pompian (2006: p4ff & p19ff) for further information on the history of behavioral finance as well as its development and main contributors in the past decades.

322 See Pompian (2006: p8ff).

323 See chapter 3.3.4 for a more detailed discussion of the theoretical rationales underlying the 'overconfidence bias'.

funds or stocks that will perform better than the market" (Bazerman, 2006: p107). One consequence of this wide-spread distortion is an increased trading volume: as one believes that one is particularly good in picking winners, one trades more actively. However, several studies indicate that investors with a high level of trading activity perform significantly worse than the market[324]. Other potential direct consequences of the 'overconfidence bias' include an underestimation of downside risks and an insufficient diversification of the portfolio.[325] Very closely linked to overconfidence is the so-called 'self-attribution' bias, which "leads people to believe that successes are attributed to skill while failure is caused by bad luck" (Nofsinger, 2008: p11). Taken together, both biases can create a continuous vicious cycle that reinforces and amplifies each of the two distortions.

Another source for cognitive biases that distorts financial investments is the representativeness heuristic. In line with this heuristic, investors often tend to pick stocks or mutual investment funds that have performed above-average in a previous period[326], because "investors consider this past return to be representative of what they can expect in the future" (Baker/Nofsinger, 2002: p100). However, by doing this, they fall prey to several resulting cognitive biases[327], for instance 'misconceptions of chance'. In this case, investors neglect sample sizes and ignore statistical considerations of chance: "viewed in the context of the thousands of investment managers, a given manager's three-year track record is just as likely an indication that the manager has benefited from luck as it is an indication of skill" (Pompian, 2006: p73). Furthermore, investors frequently neglect 'regression to the mean': stocks that perform particularly well during a given period of time

324 See for example Barber/Odean (2000) for an empirical analysis of trading volume and performance compared to the market.

325 See for instance Pompian (2006: p60f).

326 See for instance Bazerman (2006: p103ff).

327 See chapter 3.2.2.2 for a discussion of biases that stem from inappropriately applying the representativeness heuristic.

tend to perform worse in following periods, and vice versa. For instance, de Bondt/Thaler (1985) conducted an empirical study and compared the performance of previous periods' winners and losers in the following periods, and found that the previous winners perform significantly worse than the previous losers. As a consequence, people who unconsciously base their financial investment decisions on the representativeness heuristic are subject to several cognitive biases and therefore on average yield lower returns than would be possible other-wise.

Decision makers in a financial investment context are also susceptible to biases that result from the availability heuristic. If a particular security is readily available in an investor's mind, he or she is more likely to invest in this particular security than in another option that is less available or less familiar. An increased availability can be caused by several reasons, for instance because one knows the company or its products from their usage or advertisements, because a friend spoke about a particular investment, because the respective company has a regional or local business presence[328], or even because one works for this particular company[329]. These aspects favor for instance the 'ease of recall' bias and thus distort the investment decision. However, given that none of those factors that influence availability is directly linked to the quality of the respective security – nor to its future performance –, relying on availability, or familiarity, can lead to substantially lower returns. Nevertheless, several studies indicate that investors do actually overweigh stocks of companies that they are familiar with[330], thus indicating that they fall prey to availability induced cognitive biases.

---

328 See for instance Huberman (2001); with regard to overweighing national or domestic stocks compared to international stocks, this phenomenon is often referred to as 'home bias'.

329 See for example Benartzi (2001) for an empirical analysis of pension plans demonstrating a strong tendency of people to invest in the company that they work for, although this does actually increase risks for the individual investor.

330 See for instance Nofsinger (2008: p66ff) or Baker/Nofsinger (2002: p101f).

The exemplarily described cases demonstrate the large influence that cognitive biases can have with regard to financial investment decisions. The question whether these biases can also be relevant in capital investment contexts is addressed in more detail in the following section.

4.1.3 Cognitive Biases in the Capital Investments Context

Despite several similarities between financial and capital investments and the intrinsically obvious hypothesis that cognitive biases might therefore also exist in the latter domain, this area has not attracted noteworthy research yet. The following sections address an important reason why this domain has not been adequately addressed to date by highlighting several differences between financial and capital investments related to the analysis of potential effects of cognitive biases. Subsequently, those phases in the capital investment process with the potentially highest relevance for cognitive biases are identified from a conceptual perspective and several examples of cognitive biases in the capital investment context are briefly named. However, the intention of this part is to provide primarily an overview from a conceptual perspective; more detailed considerations regarding cognitive biases for capital investments follow in the subsequent sub-chapters.

An enormous advantage that behavioral finance research strongly benefitted from – and definitely fostered the interest in this discipline and its success – is the large amount of relatively easily available, high quality data for analysis: innumerous financial transactions take place every day, usually with a high level of standardization and transparency, and with transaction data being collected and stored centrally. Accordingly, researchers get access to very large data sets[331]. In

[331] For instance, Barber/Odean (2000) analyzed the stock exchange transaction data from 78.000 accounts for a 5-year period, and Benartzi (2001) analyzed the 401(k) pension plan data of more than 2.5 million participants.

addition, it is relatively simple to evaluate and compare most financial investment decisions, for instance based on absolute returns or relative returns compared to the market. Consequently, it is rather easy to test hypotheses with regard to cognitive biases and their influences on financial investments and to reveal appealing demonstrations. Furthermore, the results and findings are usually easy to illustrate, and there is a large number of potentially concerned and thus interested parties – ranging from private investors to corporate and institutional investors. As a consequence, behavioral finance quickly received a high level of attention – both from the scientific as well as from the non-scientific sector –, attracted many researchers, and collected significant funds for further research.

With regard to capital investments, many of the above factors that favor the analysis of cognitive biases and their effects are not present or applicable. The number of capital investments is considerably lower, they are mostly highly individualized to the specific needs and targets – hence not standardized –, and data is not collected and stored in a centralized fashion[332]. Moreover, due to their high degree of individualization, there is no simple, universal means of evaluating and comparing the performance or success across different capital investments. Consequently, the disposability of transaction information about capital investments is extremely low and available data is highly unstandardized, which makes large analyses – as they are done in behavioral finance – hardly possible or even impossible.[333] This is a very strong impediment to empirically testing potential hypotheses about cognitive biases and their effects, and probably constitutes one important reason why this domain has not received noteworthy attention to date.

---

[332] Although some companies collect and store data about their own capital investments in some way, which is often already hard to do in a standardized and transparent way due to the diversity of investments, there is no central entity that collects comparable data across companies.

[333] In addition, many capital investment decisions are of high importance for the respective company, and therefore the company might not be willing to share and provide this data for analyses by external researchers.

Furthermore, the nature of capital investments differs to a certain extent from that of financial investments. For instance, capital investments often involve large amounts of money that are bound for a considerable amount of time, they are normally not easily reversible, and there is usually no proper market for trading capital investments. Nevertheless, despite those – partly substantial – differences between financial and capital investments, the essence and rationale of both types of investments is quite similar: they consist of a series of cash outflows and cash inflows – for instance in the form of dividends or interest for financial investments and revenues for capital investments – over a particular period of time, with the aim to achieve a profit.[334] Moreover, the basic principles and foundations relating to decision making are also very similar. For example, although the specific investment appraisal tools for capital and financial investments have to take into account the special characteristics and traits of the respective investment type, their core ideas and fundamentals possess several common features, for instance the time value of money concept and the resulting discounted cash flow logic. Therefore, despite the existence of several differences, there are also many similarities between capital and financial investments, especially with regard to decision making approaches and fundamentals. Accordingly, as the distortive effects of cognitive biases are related to information processing activities during decision making, these similarities foster the previously stated hypothesis that cognitive biases are also existent and relevant in a capital investment related decision making environment.

However, cognitive biases might not be equally relevant in all stages or phases of the typical investment life cycle. With regard to the capital investment process discussed earlier[335], and given the particular characteristics of cognitive biases, the core activities conducted in the planning phase – primarily activities

---

[334] See chapter 2.1.1 for a discussion of definitions of investments in general.

[335] See chapter 2.1.3 for a discussion of the different phases and core activities of the capital investment process.

concerned with decision making or the respective preparation – seem especially susceptible to such biases. To a certain extent, some of the activities conducted in the disinvestment phase[336] might also give rise to certain cognitive biases. In contrast, the implementation and realization phases seem less prone to the mental information processing related distortions discussed so far, because they include mainly executing and operational activities that build on the decisions taken in earlier phases. The following illustration summarizes, on a very general level, the expected degree of vulnerability of each phase in the capital investment process and names, for the three most relevant phases, exemplary cognitive biases that potentially affect the activities conducted in the respective stage:

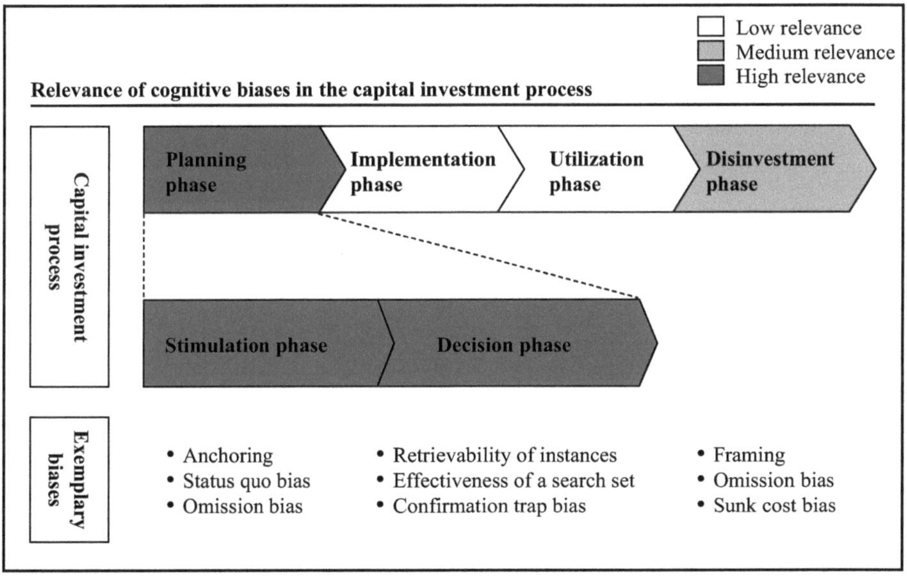

Illustration 7: Relevance of cognitive biases in the capital investment process[337]

336 For example the analysis of disinvestment options and the respective decision; other activities like the operational execution of the deconstruction are less susceptible to cognitive biases.

337 Illustration is based on discussions in earlier parts relating to the capital investment process and the characteristics and effects of the respective cognitive biases.

Cognitive biases that can affect the stimulation phase include, for instance, anchoring effects, the 'status quo' bias, or the 'omission bias'. All three distortions can potentially influence whether the investment process is actually initiated or stopped. For example, the 'status quo' bias causes a tendency to be biased towards not acting and maintaining the status quo, which could potentially impede that the capital investment process is started.[338] Likewise, if someone is for instance anchored too firmly to a specific strategy or business target, the need for a particular capital investment to adjust or change this strategy or target might not be properly realized or attributed sufficient weight, and the process is not triggered at all.

In the decision phase, several cognitive biases can for example influence which alternatives are identified in the first place, for instance the 'retrievability of instances' and 'effectiveness of a search set' biases might favor the identification of alternatives that are more available in one's mind due to salience, recency, vividness or specific search strategies, but disadvantage less available options that are actually also important. Likewise, the evaluation of identified alternatives is potentially affected by the 'confirmation trap' bias if one searches primarily for information confirming that a particular capital investment alternative is attractive, and at the same time neglects the search for disconfirming evidence. With regard to the disinvestment phase, framing effects could potentially influence the outcome, depending on the particular frame used. For instance, the same disinvestment decision could be framed either as a loss – for example with regard to revenues or jobs – or as a gain – for example with regard to increased liquidity or less working capital being tied up. The outcome could also be influenced if the responsible person falls prey to the 'sunk cost' bias and falsely incorporates irrelevant considerations into the decision process. In

[338] A similar effect can be provoked by the 'omission bias', for instance if potential harm caused by actively initiating the capital investment process is wrongly judged to be higher than by not triggering this process.

addition, the effects of the 'omission bias' can mean that a necessary disinvestment is not executed yet, because the harm caused by taking an action – executing the disinvestment and scrapping the plant – is perceived as larger than the harm caused by inaction – not conducting the disinvestment –, although the opposite might actually be the case.

In summary, all the exemplarily mentioned instances above indicate that cognitive biases seem to be relevant in a capital investment environment and potentially influence core activities of the respective decision making process. In order to substantiate these preliminary considerations, the following sections introduce two illustrative case examples that cover capital investment decisions.

4.2 Illustrative Case Examples

Having approached the existence and relevance of cognitive biases in the capital investment context from a theoretical perspective and having adumbrated some short examples in the previous sections, the following sub-chapter describes a more detailed picture of cognitive biases and their effects in typical capital investment situations by providing two fictitious case examples. Each case consists of two components: a short description of a typical, simplified capital investment decision making situation and a subsequent discussion that addresses how cognitive biases could potentially influence and affect the outcome in the described situation.

4.2.1 Identification and Evaluation of Risks for a Capital Investment Project

The illustrative case example in this section briefly describes that and how cognitive biases can potentially influence the identification and evaluation of risks related to a capital investment project. The intention of this case is to exemplarily point out potentially interesting aspects and issues with regard to cognitive biases and capital investments, but not to present a detailed model of the particular situation or discuss each aspect in depth.

Description of the Situation

Lucy Inc. is a multinational conglomerate with several business units. One of them produces components and spare parts for the automotive industry, focusing on safety technologies. A few days ago, the South American country manager of the business unit learned that the Brazilian government is about to announce a three year program that aims at drastically reducing lethal traffic accidents and therefore offers high financial rewards for Brazilian car drivers who equip their car with a particular additional safety feature that can easily be installed in any existing car. However, the financial bonus is only eligible for locally produced safety equipment, not for imported products. The business unit management considers upgrading the technology in the Brazilian plant in such a way that the respective site could produce that particular safety product. In order to determine if this capital investment is worthwhile, the managers assemble a project team to analyze the business opportunity. Mike, a senior marketing analyst, is assigned to the project team, in addition to his regular operational duties.

One day before the weekly project meeting with the senior managers of the business unit, the project team leader, Tom, hears that they also want to discuss potential risks involved in this project – although this topic was initially scheduled for a later meeting. In order to be able to provide some insights in the upcoming meeting, Tom asks Mike to address this issue and generate a short-list containing the five most important and most relevant risks, which will require further analysis and increased attention later in the decision process. Given the time constraints, Mike suggests to address this task in the following way: in a first step, he will create a preliminary list with ten to fifteen risks that come to his mind. In the second step, he will very briefly evaluate these risks and select the five most important ones from the preliminary list to go onto the short-list. Tom agrees with the proposed approach, as this procedure seems reasonable to him.

Discussion of Potential Implications induced by Cognitive Biases

In the situation described above, the effects of cognitive biases potentially influence the final outcome by triggering distortions in both phases: in the identification phase, several biases – for instance those resulting from the availability heuristic – influence which potential risks or roadblocks are put on the preliminary list, and in the evaluation phase a number of biases – for example those resulting from the representativeness heuristic – influence the relevance or importance attributed to each item, and hence potentially affect which specific risks are selected for the final short-list.

In the identification phase, cognitive biases can distort the outcome – in this case the preliminary list – primarily in two ways[339], if compared to an ideal, unbiased outcome: risks that are on the list should not be on it, and risks that should be on the list are actually not there. Given that Mike has a strong marketing background, it is likely that the availability of marketing-related risks – for example with regard to pricing, distribution channels, promotional budget overruns, etc. – is relatively high, because he can recall such risks rather easily. This increased availability can for instance be due to the fact that he frequently comes across such risks in his daily business or that he remembers them in a vivid or salient way – giving rise to the 'ease of recall' bias –, or because his unconscious search strategies focus too much on the marketing area – resulting in the 'effectiveness of a search set' bias. As a consequence, the preliminary list potentially contains a disproportionately high number of marketing-related risks. For similar reasons, technology-related risks, among others, might be under-

339 Comparable to committing 'type I' (alpha) errors and 'type II' (beta) errors in statistics; see for instance Black (2008: p300f) for futher information.

represented because of their relatively low availability in Mike's mind. Hence, the list potentially does not contain sufficient risks from that area and could be rather unbalanced.

In addition to clusters of risk that exhibit a higher or lower availability, individual risks can also be more or less available. For instance, Mike might remember very vividly the recent example of a problem caused by another safety product of the business unit that did not correspond to the cultural usage habits and therefore had disastrously low sales figures. Accordingly, Mike might put the issue of cultural product acceptance risks on the preliminary list due to their high availability, caused by the 'ease of recall' bias, although culture-related issues are actually not so important here as the product is largely pre-specified by the Brazilian government. Contrarily, if Mike does not recall any instance of a problem caused by exchange rate fluctuations, this potential risk might not come to his mind and therefore might not appear on the preliminary list at all, although it might be relevant.

With regard to the evaluation phase, similar distortions and errors are potentially caused by cognitive biases: particular risks are supervalued and ranked higher than they should actually be, or specific ones are undervalued and ranked lower than they ought to be, hence resulting in a distorted final short-list. For example, with regard to operational technology risks, Mike knows that until now only one other plant has been upgraded with a similar technology, a few weeks ago, and that so far no major operational problems have been reported with regard to technology issues. Accordingly, Mike might judge that operational risks related to the particular technology are very low, seemingly even lower than with the old technology that causes about 3 to 4 shut-downs per year. However, the obtained sample size of one plant for only a few weeks is probably too small to give an appropriate picture of the magnitude of potential risks, and Mike therefore would have fallen prey to the 'insensitivity to sample size' bias and the 'insensitivity to base rates' bias, as he neglects the long-term average of the old technology and decides that this base rate is not applicable to the new technology, based on very weak evidence. Furthermore, Mike's judgment of risks related to intellectual property rights infringements or technology theft might be distorted by the use of the representativeness heuristic: he knows that the above mentioned problems are big issues in many emerging countries, for example in China, a country that is frequently grouped together with Brazil as one of the four 'BRIC' countries[340]. Given that both China and Brazil are representative of emerging countries, this stereotype judgment might lead Mike to conclude that intellectual property rights infringements and technology theft are also a very important problem for this particular project in Brazil, although this is not necessarily the case. Similarly, Mike's evaluation of the importance of political risks might be distorted by cognitive biases caused by the representativeness heuristic: if Mike knows about the political instability in some South American countries and judges Brazil to be representative of South America, he might falsely conclude that this particular risk is highly important and thus rank it considerably higher than it should actually be.

As a consequence of the above mentioned examples, the final short-list might not properly mirror the actual importance of the risks related to this particular project: some risks are ranked high on the list although they are of relatively low relevance, other ones are ranked considerably lower than their actual importance would demand, and some risks are completely missing. Moreover, the list might differ depending on the person who actually conducts the task. For instance, if an engineer had compiled the list instead of Mike, the final short-list might have been very different, though potentially also biased, for example due to the different background and hence unequal individual availabilities of particular risk types.

340 BRIC is an acronym for a group of four important emerging economies: Brazil, Russia, India, and China.

The above case illustrates that the effects of cognitive biases can exert considerable influence on decisions related to capital investments. However, although the example is of course hypothetical and intentionally exaggerates slightly for illustrative purposes, it is by no means unrealistic.

4.2.2 Preparation and Analysis of a Business Case for a Capital Investment Opportunity

This section introduces a second simplified case, which addresses how cognitive biases can potentially influence the preparation and analysis of a business case for a capital investment opportunity. Analog to the previous example, this short case does not intend to develop an in-depth model of the particular situation, but rather exemplarily point out potentially interesting aspects to build upon them later on.

Description of the Situation

ITA is a European-based entertainment company with significant international operations. ITA is active in different segments of the entertainment sector. One of their divisions develops, produces and markets board games for children and adults. At the weekly steering meeting, the division's management discusses, among other topics, a recent niche trend to equip traditional board games with miniature microchips and interactive high-tech gadgets. Supporters state that this increases for instance the interactivity of the respective game, expands available options for board game designers and makes the game more attractive for those customer groups that switched from traditional board games to video games. Opponents argue that this drives up the development and production costs, increases the likelihood of defects and probably overstrains traditional customer groups that are less technology experienced.

Given the controversial discussion, the management is hesitant to invest funds into that area, but at the same time acknowledges that this niche might be very lucrative. Therefore, the managers decide that the controlling department will develop a rough preliminary business case, which will then be discussed in the next regular steering meeting, in order to decide whether to look in more depth at this opportunity or to abandon it before assigning considerable monetary and human resources to it.

After the meeting, the head of controlling entrusts Sally, a well-respected analyst working in the controlling department, with this task. Sally holds an MBA from a prestigious business school and joined ITA seven years ago. After six years in ITA's toys division, she decided to switch to the board games business unit. Before going on a long-planned five-day fishing trip with his family, the head of controlling provides Sally with a detailed briefing for her task, recapitulates the major arguments raised in the meeting and states his position regarding this issue. He asks Sally to prepare and analyze the preliminary business case within the next days, so that he can present it in the next steering meeting.

Discussion of Potential Implications induced by Cognitive Biases

In the situation above, a multitude of cognitive biases could potentially influence the business case preparation. The following section exemplarily describes three distortive effects – the 'confirmation trap' bias, anchoring, and a group of biases relate to associations and interrelations – in more detail and illustrates the potential effects of each of them on the final outcome of the task.

One distortion that is usually relevant for tasks similar to Sally's assignment is the 'confirmation trap' bias[341]. As described earlier, this bias refers to the tendency to prefer and consider primarily confirming information and at the same time neglect counter-evidential information or the search for disconfirming evidence. However, this bias normally only manifests itself as soon as Sally has a first opinion or hypothesis. Given Sally's high level of prior knowledge and industry

341 See chapter 3.3.1 for general information on the 'confirmation trap' bias.

experience, it is very likely that she has – at least unconsciously – formed a first opinion very early. In addition, as the head of controlling named the positions discussed in the meeting and also explicitly stated his opinion, Sally has potentially integrated some arguments into her own opinion. As a consequence, Sally might conduct the collection of information in a biased way. For instance, she could seek information that potentially evaluates and confirms the expected attractiveness of the niche, analyze primarily competitors that already target this niche, try some of the existing board games of other market players, or assess synergies with other segments, for example economies of scale. Although all these activities seem logical and objective at first sight, they are actually biased towards yielding confirmatory evidence rather than providing disconfirming information. For example, Sally might assess synergies based on the existence or non-existence of potential economies of scale, but underestimate the existence or magnitude of counteracting diseconomies of scale.[342]

Similarly, due to the 'confirmation trap' bias, confirmative information might be attributed a higher value than disconfirming information. For example, if Sally finds out that four companies already entered this particular niche during the last nine months – three are still in the market and one withdrew after a short period of time – the one company that left the market might be considered as an 'outlier', and thus disregarded, as the three seemingly positive examples dominate the one negative example, although this conclusion might not incorporate the whole picture. As a consequence, this effect and the other distortions caused by the 'confirmation trap' bias might distort Sally's preliminary business case.

Another potentially distortive factor influencing the preparation of the business case is the effect of the anchoring heuristic. In the described case example, anchoring can occur in several ways. For example, if Sally wants to

[342] See for instance Hansen et al. (2009: p101ff) for a detailed discussion of complexity costs and diseconomies of scale with regard to capital investments.

estimate the number of board games that could potentially be sold every year in this niche, as input factor for the business case calculations, she might start with a very rough estimate, for instance based on a similar niche, and then adjust and refine this first estimate. However, due to the effects of the anchoring heuristic, the adjustment is potentially not sufficient, and consequently Sally's estimate might be too high or too low, depending on her starting point. Furthermore, assuming that Sally needs several input assumptions for preparing and analyzing the business case, the biased estimates might amplify each other, leading to a result that could be even more biased than each individual assumption.[343]

In addition, anchoring could also apply to the final overall outcome. Given that Sally's superior, the head of controlling, explicitly stated his opinion, it is possible and likely that this unconsciously serves as anchor for Sally. For instance, as soon as Sally finishes the calculation part and obtains a first result, she might unconsciously compare this result to the 'expected' or anchored outcome. If the calculated outcome corresponds to the 'expected' outcome, this might favor that the assumptions are accepted too quickly and not sufficiently critically reviewed a second time, as the result already seems to 'fit'. Contrarily, if the initially calculated outcome does not correspond to the anchored value, Sally might conduct a critical review of all assumptions, and as a result potentially slightly adjust some of them. However, this second review likely leads to an outcome that is closer to the anchored value than the original one. As a consequence, the result of the business case preparation and analysis might be different, depending on the initial anchor's position, which constitutes a distortion of the outcome due to the effects of cognitive biases induced by the anchoring heuristic.

[343] It is also possible that the individual deviations due to insufficient adjustments of input values cancel each other out. However, in the majority of cases the individual deviations will probably neither all tend in the same direction (and create totally extreme results) nor will they fully cancel each other out, but an intermediate effect will occur.

Finally, a group of cognitive biases related to associations and interrelations might also influence the outcome of Sally's business case task. For instance, due to the 'imaginability' bias, sequences of events or combinations of events which are easier to imagine are more available, and are thus judged as more likely than sequences or combinations that are less easily imaginable. With regard to Sally's task, this means that enriching the business case with a seemingly logical story or chain of events might make the business case more appealing and increases the perceived likelihood of the presented scenario, and therefore potentially influences whether it is accepted or rejected. Similarly, two other biases discussed earlier – the 'presumed associations' bias and the 'conjunction fallacy' bias – might distort probabilistic judgments of certain scenarios or assumptions that Sally incorporates into the business case. To provide a very simple example, if Sally makes three independent assumptions that are necessary for a certain scenario to unfold, and she is very confident that each of them is likely, she might unconsciously conclude that the overall consideration is also very likely, although that is not necessarily true: for instance, three independent assumptions that each have a seemingly high probability of 80% yield only about 51% probability of occurring all three. Consequently, if Sally falls prey to any of these cognitive biases, this will result in potentially substantial distortions of probabilistic judgments with regard to the preliminary business case that Sally is preparing.

In summary, the exemplary cases described above – although they are fictitious – highlight that the effects of cognitive biases can very well influence decision making in a capital investment context. However, as already stated before, this is not applicable to every single decision, but it can happen in certain situations.[344] Moreover, there are several factors that favor the emergence of cognitive biases,

---

[344] To date, it is not entirely clear which particular features of a situation lead to cognitive biases. Additional, dedicated research is required to clarify this issue, as pointed out in chapter 6.2.

for instance time pressure or workload issues like being responsible for a project in addition to one's daily operational responsibilities. None of these two factors is extremely unusual in today's business environment, which increases the likely-hood of the potential existence and relevance of cognitive biases in real life capital investment contexts.

4.3 Empirical Experiments

This sub-chapter extends the theoretical considerations discussed in the previous chapters by describing empirical experiments that examine the existence and relevance of cognitive biases in simplified capital investment contexts. The first part provides a short overview and introduces the overall approach underlying the series of empirical experiments. The subsequent sections describe in detail the design, execution and analyses of each experiment, which cover three different cognitive biases: anchoring, framing, and asymmetric dominance.

4.3.1 Overview and General Approach

This section describes and explains the general approach that has been chosen in order to empirically test whether cognitive biases are relevant in a capital investment context. The intention of this section is to introduce the selected approach and the applied procedures in general and address those aspects and methodological issues in more detail that are equally applicable to all empirical experiments; aspects that differ between some experiments, for example the parti-cular choice of statistical test for the respective experiment, are not discussed in this section, but in the part that addresses the individual experiment. With regard to certain statistical considerations and analyses, the following sections assume knowledge of basic statistics terminology[345] and fundamental theory of statistics, which is

[345] See for instance Gravetter/Wallnau (2009) or Black (2008) for definitions and explanations of basic terminology (population, sample, independent variable, etc.) and related concepts.

therefore not explicitly described. Statistical considerations that go beyond the fundamental level are addressed in the respective sections.

Based on the traditional modus operandi of scientific research and empirical testing of hypotheses[346], and considering necessary adaptations to reflect the particular requirements and characteristics of the intended empirical research, an overall approach is developed that includes eight distinct steps:

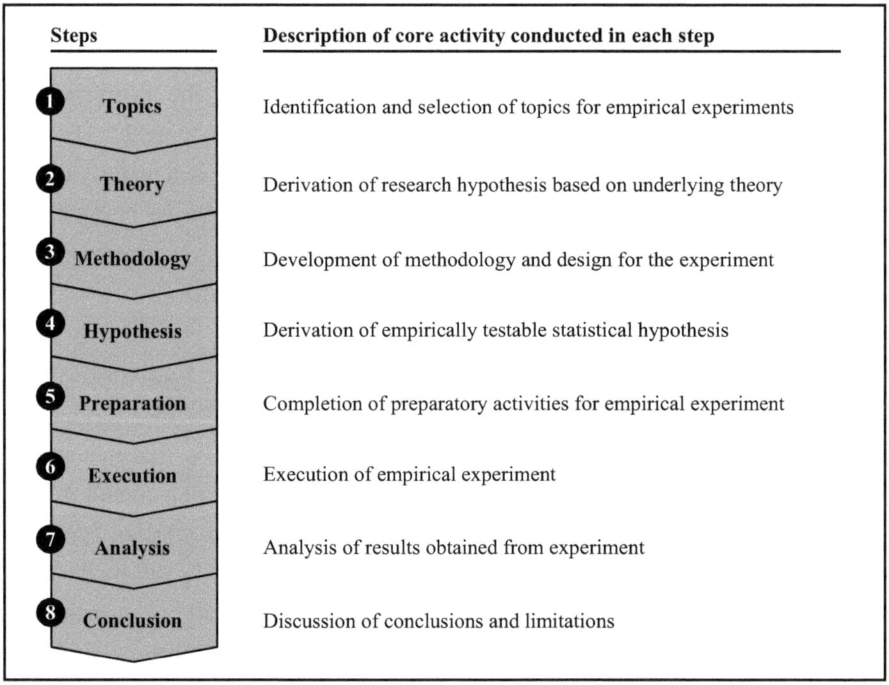

Illustration 8: Overview of the general approach for empirical experiments[347]

---

346 See for example Gerrig/Zimbardo (2008: p26ff) for a general discussion of the 'process of research' or Black (2008: p290ff) for a detailed 'introduction to hypothesis testing'.

347 Based on discussions and considerations in Black (2008: p290ff), Gerrig/Zimbardo (2008: p26ff), and Gravetter/Wallnau (2009: p8ff).

Step 1: Identification and Selection of Topics

The first step addresses the identification and selection of suitable topics, in this case particular cognitive biases, for the subsequent empirical experiments. This selection constitutes the foundation for the remaining parts of the process. In the earlier chapters, several potentially interesting cognitive biases have already been introduced. In order to ensure that a sufficiently diverse variety of effects are covered in the empirical experiments, three different cognitive biases have been chosen: anchoring, framing, and asymmetric dominance. This selection includes on purpose very different types of biases, in order to illustrate the wide range of potential effects that cognitive biases can have on capital investments: one bias (anchoring) that results from one of the three basic heuristics, a widely spread and very influential general cognitive bias (framing), and a less well-known but nevertheless very impactful bias (asymmetric dominance). In addition to the general target of selecting a large spectrum of different types of cognitive biases, several other considerations influenced the particular selection.

With regard to choosing one of the fundamental heuristics, anchoring was also taken because the two other heuristics, availability and representativeness, have already been addressed in detail in the illustrative case example chapter. Furthermore, according to the earlier described empirical evidence from other domains, the anchoring bias is highly influential and robust, and therefore believed to be also of high relevance in the capital investment context.

For similar reasons, framing was selected to be part of the experiment. Moreover, the fact that framing can lead to preference reversals, thus openly violating normative rational decision theory, is another potentially very important and interesting aspect for real-life capital investment decision making.

In contrast to framing and anchoring, asymmetric dominance is a less basic and rather special topic that nevertheless possesses, in general, highly distortive powers, as the earlier discussions[348] have demonstrated. Its irrational effects with

[348] See chapter 3.3.2 for detailed information on asymmetric dominance.

regard to relativity in choice situations might especially be relevant for capital investment decisions regarding the determination of relative profitability, for instance when selecting between several mutually exclusive investments. Furthermore, its influence has already been demonstrated in some general business areas, particularly in marking. However, published studies in marketing so far concentrated on consumer choices[349], not on the choices of professionals in a business-to-business context. Moreover, asymmetric dominance seems to not have attracted any research in behavioral finance yet. However, it is unclear whether these aspects are indications that asymmetric dominance might not be relevant in a non-consumer business context, or whether these areas have just not been addressed yet. Accordingly, choosing this particular cognitive bias for the upcoming empirical experiments might actually help to shed light on this issue, which also constituted one reason for its selection.

In summary, compared to empirically testing only one bias or several very similar effects, selecting three totally different types of cognitive biases is expected to give a much better picture of their relevance in the capital investment context.

Step 2: Derivation of Research Hypothesis based on Underlying Theory

In this second step, the underlying theory of each of the three biases is described by briefly recapitulating major aspects from the respective theoretical sub-chapter and, where appropriate, enriching them with additional details and theoretical sophistications to establish a better connection to capital investments and empirical testability. Based on these theoretical considerations, a research hypo-

349 See for instance the discussions and references in chapter 3.3.2.

thesis[350] is derived for each of the three experimental foci, which states in general terms what the expected outcome would be according to the theory. This general statement is in a later step transformed into a more formal, empirically testable statistical hypothesis.

Given that this second step is highly individual for each of the three selected cognitive biases, the details are discussed in the respective section that describes the individual experiment.

Step 3: Development of Methodology and Design for the Experiment

This step addresses the methodology and design of the empirical experiments. While the overall aspects are common for all three experimental areas, and are thus discussed in this section, the detailed design and set-up of each experiment varies and is accordingly described in the corresponding section.

The very first methodological step is actually already the decision to opt for an experimental research method and conduct real 'experiments'. However, in contrast to the general meaning of the word experiment used in everyday language, which people usually refer to for all kinds of studies, the scientific 'experiment' "must include manipulation of an independent variable and rigorous control of other, extraneous variables" (Gravetter/Wallnau, 2009: 15). If this is not the case, the approach is classified as a nonexperimental method[351]. Further information with regard to how the two essential features of an experimental method, manipulation and control, are handled for the respective cognitive biases experiments is provided later.

---

[350] According to Black (2008: p294), a 'research hypothesis', also frequently called 'scientific hypothesis', is "a statement of what the researcher believes will be the outcome of an experiment or a study", expressed in general terms, and not referring to the particular experimental design yet.

[351] See for instance Gravetter/Wallnau (2009: p15ff) for further information on nonexperimental methods, for example the 'nonequivalent groups' approach or 'pre-post studies' methods.

Due to the fact that no prior research on the effects of cognitive biases on capital investment decisions is available so far, and given that the design of an adequate field study would strongly benefit from being based on experiences and findings from prior experiments, the intended series of experiments are conducted in a laboratory setting, but with the intention of nevertheless being as close to reality as possible.[352] Analogous to the majority of empirical studies conducted about the effects of cognitive biases in general, students are selected to serve as participants.[353]

In line with the above stated intention of being as close as possible to reality, the experiments are set up in the form of hypothetical scenarios, which are essentially simplified versions of a role play that takes place with pen and paper. The participant assumes the role of the CFO of a multinational corporation who has to help and advise the managers of several business units with regard to a number of capital investment decisions. Every decision situation is individually described and explained in detail, and the respective decision task is presented. Once the decision is taken, the participant moves on to the next situation. This hypothetical scenario design has the advantage of being very flexible and thus allows extensive manipulations of the independent variable while at the same time keeping many external variables constant. However, the major disadvantage of hypothetical scenarios is that participants might be tempted to answer what they believe the researcher wants them to answer.[354] In order to reduce this potential distortion, the participants are not told the true purpose of the tasks or that they

---

352 Other reasons for opting for a laboratory based design instead of a real life field study include resource constraints, both monetary and time-related, and the earlier mentioned fact that companies are highly hesitant to reveal data on their capital investment activities, especially due to their strategic importance and because no empirical evidence exists so far for these effects.

353 Additional information on the participating students and their demographic characteristics is provided in the respective 'execution and analysis' section.

354 See for instance Baron (2007: p40) or Gerrig/Zimbardo (2008: p30f).

are participating in a real research experiment; instead, the students were presented with the tasks during their regular course.[355] In addition, the scenario situations and decision choices are also designed in such a way that the participant can not simply deduct which answer might be the expected answer. Comparing advantages and disadvantages, for instance Baron (2007: p40) concludes that "hypothetical decisions may be just as useful as real ones for finding out how people think about certain types of problems".

Based on the above considerations and the described set-up of the experiments, a between-subjects design is adopted instead of a within-subject design.[356] This means that the participants of each experiment are randomly and unknowingly divided in two groups – both groups answer, under the same conditions, the same questions, with one exception: the independent variable, in this case one piece of information provided in the description of the situation, differs slightly between the two groups –, and the results of the groups are compared to see if the difference in the independent variable influences the dependent variable, that is the decision option chosen by the participant.

The above described random assignment of participants to one of two groups[357] is an important measure used to rule out the influence of environmental and participant variables, that is to "eliminate confounding variables that relate to

---

355 The students are told by their course supervisor that the university's business faculty is currently developing a business game for its students and that it needs the student's help for testing some of the questions. The students are also told that this task is not linked to their course performance rating and that it is anonymous and not marked. This background information provides a very reasonable and credible justification for the existence of the task and at the same time unconsciously appeals to the student's helpfulness. This resulted in a high willingness-to-help, that is even reinforced by the course supervisor clearly pointing out to the students that their help is very valuable and highly appreciated.

356 See for example Baron (2007: p47f) or Gerrig/Zimbardo (2008: p32f) for a short discussion of between-subjects vs. within-subject designs.

357 In practice, two different paper versions of the same situation – both absolutely identical apart from the change in the independent variable – were created and randomly mixed and distributed.

individual differences among potential research participants" (Gerrig/Zimbardo, 2008: p32). In combination with a sufficiently large sample, random assignment "makes it quite likely that the two groups will be similar in important ways at the start of an experiment" (Gerrig/Zimbardo, 2008: p32) and that differences in the dependent variable are not due to differences in participant characteristics.[358] While random assignment helps to eliminate the influence of participant variables, an important method to eliminate the influence of environmental variables is holding them constant.[359] With regard to this research on cognitive biases, this means for example that all participants face the same experimental situations in the same environment under the same conditions, they are all provided with the same background information and the same instructions, they are all given the same time to answer the respective set of questions, they are all supervised during the task to prevent talking to each other, collusion, or the use of additional tools, etc. Accordingly, it is very likely that the influence of environmental variables is low and does not distort the outcome. Taken together and referring back to the earlier stated requirements of an experiment in the scientific sense, the two areas of action described above – manipulation of the independent variable and control of environmental and participant variables – essentially fulfill the defining necessities of a scientific experimental method.

Step 4: Derivation of Empirically Testable Statistical Hypothesis

In the fourth step, the empirically testable statistical hypothesis is derived for each experiment, based on the research hypothesis established in the second step

358 See Gravetter/Wallnau (2009: p14) who also mention an additional method of eliminating differences in participant variables: matching (assess each participant's characteristics and then assign groups in such a way that the distribution of the characteristics of the groups is the same). However, this procedure is not suitable and practicable for the intended purpose and set-up.

359 See for example Gravetter/Wallnau (2009: p14).

and the methodological considerations and design of the particular experiment in step three. The statistical hypothesis is the formal expression of the hypothesis test and contains both the null hypothesis and the alternative hypothesis.[360] However, given that this step is highly individual for each of the selected empirical experiments, the respective statistical hypotheses are derived and stated in the corresponding individual sections.

Step 5: Completion of Preparatory Activities for Empirical Experiment

This fifth step addresses certain preparatory activities that refine the set-up of the empirical experiments. These activities include two types of tests, which are only conducted when necessary for the particular experiment: scaling tests, in order to roughly calibrate the characteristics of some investment objects or choices in such a way that they have a similar 'attractiveness' in an unbiased environment, and pre-tests, in order to ensure that participants correctly understand the description of the situation and the task, verifying for instance if explanations of technical terms are adequately understood, if the instruction is clear, if the completion time limits are appropriate, etc. Both activities are optional, but reduce the likelihood that the experiment is not evaluable due to formal mistakes, ambiguities, or misunderstandings.

This step is also very specific for each individual experiment, and is only necessary and relevant for some of the selected experiments. Accordingly, it is addressed in detail when discussing the respective experiment.

Step 6: Execution of Empirical Experiment

In the sixth step, the empirical experiments are finally executed. In total, eight different experiments related to capital investment decisions were conducted,

[360] See for instance Black (2008: p294ff).

covering two different situations for anchoring – with two variations each –, two distinct settings for framing, and two situations for asymmetric dominance. However, every participant only received a subset of all possible situations, with the exact composition and number of situations varying slightly between the course group sessions, for instance due to different time constraints set by the respective course supervisor. However, within each course session all participants received the same experimental situations, and the two different versions of each experiment – which only differ with regard to the value of the independent variable – were randomly assigned to about half of the participants in each session.

Step 7: Analysis of Obtained Results

In the seventh step, the results of each experiment are analyzed in detail, including both descriptive and inferential analysis methods. Finally, either the null hypothesis or the alternative hypothesis from the original statistical hypothesis is rejected. This step is again highly individual for each experiment and is therefore covered in the respective section.

With regard to overall participant demographics, a total number of 376 participants in 10 different course sessions across 4 German universities[361] took part in the overall experimental series conducted in summer and autumn 2009[362]. The majority of participating students in the main study were undergraduate students

---

[361] Chemnitz University of Technology, University of Bayreuth, ESB Reutlingen Business School, and University of Applied Sciences Hof.

[362] These total figures include both the main study (303 participants in 8 sessions) and the short MBA replication study (73 participants in 2 sessions). The following parts only refer to the main study, which is the primary focus. The MBA replication study is introduced and addressed in more detail in chapter 4.4.4.

in their third year, mainly studying business sciences[363]. About 51% of participants were female, and 49% male. The vast majority of participants were between 21 and 25 years old.[364]

Step 8: Discussion of Conclusions and Limitations

In this final step, potential conclusions are drawn from the results of the analyses of each experiment. Subsequently, these are discussed together with the potential limitations. However, although there is undoubtedly also a corresponding individual component for each experiment, this critical discussion of conclusions and limitations primarily takes place in an additional sub-chapter[365], which also explicitly addresses potential arguments of skeptics.

In total, the above sections outlined the selected approach and the respective overarching methodological considerations. Having clarified this, the following sections address in detail each of the selected experimental clusters.

4.3.2 Empirical Experiments: Anchoring

This sub-chapter addresses and explains in detail four empirical experiments related to anchoring. The first part very briefly recapitulates and summarizes the major underlying theoretical considerations. Subsequently, the second part

363 Some participants also majored in business-related studies, for example 'industrial engineering', and attended the respective course as part of their regular curriculum.

364 Participants were not directly quoted for their age, but at the end of the experiments they were asked to select the appropriate age group (each group consisting of 5-year intervals). Accordingly, an exact average of the participant's age cannot be calculated, but as a similar number of participants stated they were older than 25 or younger than 21, it might be assumed that the average is roughly in the middle of the major interval, hence around 23 to 24 years.

365 See chapter 4.4.

focuses on the individual methodological considerations and preparations of each experiment. In the third part, the results are finally analyzed and discussed.

4.3.2.1 Underlying Theory

According to the anchoring heuristic[366], people make estimation judgments by starting at an initial value – the anchor – and adjusting this value step-by-step towards the final value. However, the adjustments are often insufficient. Consequently, different starting points yield different estimates, and the estimate is systematically biased in the direction of the anchored value. Potential reasons for this cognitive bias and the resulting violation of normative rationality are enhanced accessibility of anchor-consistent information and a stop of the adjustment process as soon as a plausible value is reached.

In general, the anchored value that represents the starting point can be either externally provided or self-generated.[367] In the case of an empirical experiment, using an externally provided anchor is considerably easier to implement – the experimenter can for example integrate the anchor directly into the description, or create a comparable stimulus, for instance by spinning a wheel of fortune –, and also much better traceable than relying on anchors that are self-generated by the participants. In addition, three different types of anchor values can be used: realistic, extreme, and implausible anchors. While realistic anchors are moderately close to the actual value, extreme anchors are not seen as realistic values but are still theoretically possible – for instance, when estimating market share, an anchor value of 80% is usually not realistic, but it is theoretically possible –, and implausible values are so far off that they are simply not possible, for example a

---

366 See chapter 3.2.2.3 for a detailed discussion of anchoring in general and the major aspects summarized in this paragraph.

367 See for example Epley/Gilovich (2006: p312), Russo/Shoemaker (1989: p90), or Tversky/Kahneman (1974: p1128).

market share above 100%. However, research has demonstrated that the distortive effects are triggered even if implausible values are used as an anchor.[368]

With regard to the potential applicability of anchoring effects to the capital investment context, the demonstrated persistency and robustness of these effects in a large variety of different domains[369] indicate a high likelihood of being relevant for capital investment decisions as well. In addition, the earlier described case example[370] briefly illustrated that anchoring could potentially be relevant for this domain, both with regard to final outcome values and estimates of input values, for example assumptions for a business case calculation.

Based on the above considerations, the respective research hypothesis is that anchoring effects do exist in capital investment contexts[371], that externally provided anchors then significantly influence and distort evaluations and judgments in the capital investment process and that these distortions affect capital investment decisions in a systematic way, meaning that the estimation or judgment is reproducibly[372] biased in such a way that being exposed to a higher anchor leads, on average, to a higher estimate compared to being exposed to a lower anchor. The following section builds on this research hypothesis and describes methodological considerations and preparatory activities related to the design of a series of experiments to test the derived research hypothesis.

---

368 See for instance Chapman/Johnson (1994) or Strack/Mussweiler (1997).

369 See for example Mussweiler et al. (2004: p185f) for an extensive list of research examples.

370 See chapter 4.2.2.

371 However, this is of course not the case for every single decision under all potential circumstances, but relates only to some occasions and depends on the particular situation.

372 In relation to this research hypothesis (and the other ones in this thesis), the claim of being 'reproducible' is to be understood as 'emerging in more than one situation', and must in this case not to be confused with the notion of being 'replicable' (emerging repeatedly in the same situation), which is implicitly addressed at a later stage by means of a small replication study.

4.3.2.2 Methodology and Preparation of Empirical Experiments

All anchoring experiments follow the overall specifications discussed in the general section: in a pen-and-paper based hypothetical scenario, consisting of several episodes, the participant assumes the role of the CFO of a multinational company who helps the business unit managers in taking a number of capital investment related decisions. In a standardized environment, every participant randomly receives one of two experimental versions, which are identical apart from a change in the independent variable, in this case the anchor value.

Methodology and Design of the Experimental Situation

Anchoring is in general primarily relevant for judgments related to estimation tasks. This limits the number of potential set-ups for anchoring experiments in a capital investment context, because for instance pure selection tasks[373] are not relevant. Nevertheless, the capital investment environment actually also provides a large number of estimation tasks, for example estimating the value of input variables – future sales figures, market shares, interest rates, completion times, etc. – for appraisal procedures. The developed experiments include estimation tasks for two of the above mentioned input variables, integrated into the setting of a post-acquisition situation.

In particular, the background situation presented to the participant for the anchoring experiment is the following[374]: the company, whose CFO the participant takes, just acquired another company, which recently started an important capital investment project: building a production and distribution facility for a new product. The CFO is asked to quickly assess this project, in particular

[373] For instance the final selection decision which machine to purchase or where to build a plant.

[374] The following information provides only a rough, strongly abbreviated recapitulation of the situation that the participant is presented with; the complete version is provided in the appendix.

focusing on the probability that the capital investment is completed on time, and on the future market share[375] of the respective product for which the capital investment has been made. Accordingly, two different estimation judgments have to be made with regard to this capital investment, each constituting one experiment. For each judgment, the CFO-participant is provided with qualitative information that is characterized by varying degrees of uncertainty and represents a mixture of positive, neutral and negative indications or evidence. For instance, with regard to the completion of the project, the information includes, among other pieces of information, that the CFO recalls that the other company has in the past usually finished its investment projects on time, that he reckons that the take-over might have implied some delays, that it seems as if, compared to the original plan, additional staff has been allocated to the project as countermeasure, etc.

In line with the traditional methodology in empirical anchoring experiments[376], a two-step procedure is used: the participant is first asked to compare the value of the target variable – for instance the likelihood of finishing a project on time – to an anchor value, and state if it is higher or lower than the anchor value. Subsequently, the participant provides his or her own estimate of the target value. For this series of experiments, based on the outlined scenario and intention, it was decided to use an externally provided anchor, which is integrated into the task description, and to use a realistic anchor instead of an extreme or implausible anchor.[377] As discussed earlier, when using externally provided anchors, it is extremely important to highlight and undoubtedly clarify the uninformative nature of the anchor.[378] This is established in two different ways: in experiments 1 and 2, the task description explains that the particular value for comparison was

---

375 Actually, participants are asked to estimate the expected market share after 1 year in the market.

376 See for instance Tversky/Kahneman (1974 p1128ff) or Chapman/Johnson (2002: p121).

377 See chapters 3.2.2.3 and 4.3.2.1 for further information on anchor types (externally provided vs. self-generated and realistic vs. extreme vs. plausible).

378 See for example Chapman/Johnson (2002: p122).

randomly generated (by a random generator) in the process of printing the document, and explicitly states that this number has no meaning or informational value for the particular task, but is completely uninformative. In experiments 3 and 4, the anchor value to be compared with in the first step is introduced as a seemingly spontaneous guess made by a new assistant, but the description additionally stated that the CFO did observe, a minute before, that this assistant simply rolled two ten-sided dices[379] which resulted in exactly this number, and it states explicitly that accordingly the 'guess' is completely uninformative and irrelevant, and that the CFO-participant has to form his or her own opinion. Despite being to a certain extent a bit artificial – the latter probably less so than the former – both versions clarify and highlight undoubtedly that the given value should be regarded as completely uninformative and irrelevant.

Preparatory Activities: Scaling Test and Pre-Test

With regard to the exact positions of the anchors, the classical approach is to set anchors "at one standard [deviation] above and below the mean estimates of a calibration group that answered [only the] absolute questions" (Mussweiler et al., 2004: p184). In line with this standard procedure, a preparatory scaling test has been carried out for each of the two experimental parts – likelihood of completion on time and expected market share – in which the respective participants only had to answer the absolute estimation task, and the anchor was removed[380]. However, although this calibration exercise helps to balance the experiment and set anchors within a realistic range, this step is by no means obligatory, as anchoring also occurs with less realistic anchors. In addition, usually only a relatively small

[379] With values from 0-9 each, thus allowing any possible value between 00% and 99%.

[380] Except for the removal of the first task – the comparison with the anchor value – the description used in the scaling test was identical to the original experiment.

sample size is necessary for the scaling test, because a rough estimate of mean and standard deviation is sufficient.

In total, each of the two scaling experiments was presented to 20 scaling test participants. In the first scaling experiment (likelihood of completion on time), the sample mean was 60% and the sample standard deviation was 24%. Accordingly, anchors were determined to be at 84% and 36% for the final experiments.[381] In the second scaling experiment (market share after one year), the sample mean was 15% and the sample standard deviation was 7%. Accordingly, anchors were determined to be at 22% and 8% for the final experiments.[382]

Subsequent to the scaling tests, pre-tests have been carried out, in order to test if participants correctly understand the description of the situation and the task, to verify if explanations of technical terms are adequately understood, to check if the instruction is clear, etc. Accordingly, pre-tests were conducted in one-on-one situations with students, to better observe the immediate reactions of the participant and also give him or her the possibility to ask for clarifications, if needed, and provide direct feedback afterwards. Although this step is also not imperatively required, it helps to ensure a high quality of the test and the obtained results and reduces the likelihood that the experiment is not evaluable due to formal mistakes or ambiguities.

The conducted pre-tests indicated no unclarities or ambiguities, the descriptions and tasks were properly understood and the scenario and set-up seemed plausible[383]. If explicitly asked about the randomly generated or dice-rolled (anchor) value in the description, the participants stated that they were aware of its uninformative nature, that they accordingly disregarded it for the second part

---

381 High anchor: 60% + 24% = 84%; Low anchor: 60% - 24% = 36%.

382 High anchor: 15% + 7% = 22%; Low anchor: 15% - 7% = 8%.

383 In the light of the standard 'background story' detailed earlier (testing questions for a business game for students currently being developed by the university).

and that they were not influenced by the anchor value.[384] In summary, the pre-tests revealed that no changes of the designed experiments were necessary.[385] Consequently it was decided that the version used for the pre-tests is also used identically for the real experiments.

Having clarified all methodological considerations and described all preparatory activities, the following part addresses the execution and analysis of the experiments.

4.3.2.3 Analysis and Conclusions

In this sub-chapter, the four empirical experiments that are conducted with regard to the effect of anchoring in a capital investment environment are dis-cussed and analyzed in more detail. At the beginning, the selected statistical test method is introduced, subsequently each of the four experiments is addressed one after the other, and finally the preliminary conclusions are discussed. Within each of the four experiment sections, first the particular situation and set-up are very briefly described, subsequently the specific statistical hypothesis is stated, followed by descriptive and inferential analyses.

With regard to the anchor incorporation, in the first two experiments, the earlier discussed 'likelihood of completion on time' (experiment 1) and 'expected market share in one year' (experiment 2) scenarios are equipped with the 'random-generator' version of presenting the anchor. In experiments 3 and 4, the 'roll-the-dice' version of presenting the anchor is applied for the respective two scenarios.

---

384 This belief of not being influenced by the anchor is common in anchoring experiments. However, contrarily to participants' believes, they usually are influenced by the anchor, even if they deny it. See for instance Chapman/Johnson (2002: p125) or Wilson et al. (1996).

385 Apart from very few minor changes to adjust for accidental mistakes in spelling and grammar, for instance comma setting.

Statistical Test Method

Based on the earlier stated research hypothesis[386], and considering the general design and set-up of the anchoring experiments, a statistical method is needed that can test whether the mean of the group exposed to the higher anchor is statistically significantly different from – and in the second step higher than – the mean of the group exposed to the lower anchor. Accordingly, the statistical method needs to test the difference in means of two independent – that is non-grouped or not paired – samples. In addition, the population variances are not known, and as it is also not certain that the population variances of the two groups are equal.[387] Both pieces of information are important to select the appropriate statistical procedure.

With regard to unknown, possibly unequal variances, the statistics literature is split in two groups. Many authors claim that the requirements of equal variances and normality of the distribution can be dropped if both samples are sufficiently large[388], and that consequently a regular t-test[389] or a regular z-test[390] based on the standard normal distribution can be applied. Other authors[391] argue that a special version of the t-test with a more complex degrees-of-freedom component has to be used as approximation. In order to increase the quality of the hypothesis testing procedure and avoid potential criticisms regarding the formal inadequacy of the statistical test method used, the decision is to apply the more sophisticated

---

386 See chapter 4.3.2.1.

387 Although it is likely that they are similar due to the random allocation of participants to the groups.

388 However, authors differ with regard to which sample size per group is necessary in this case to be considered as large enough: Diekhoff (1992: p140) states 25, Schwarze (2006: p223) and Bamberg/Baur (1991: p193) say 30, and Vogel (1999: p237) suggests 40. In addition to the requirement of a large sample, Diekhoff (1992: p140) demands that the two sample sizes should be roughly equally large.

389 See for instance Vogel (1999: p237), Diekhoff (1992: p140), or Schwarze (2006: p223).

390 See for example McClave/Benson (1991: p394) or Bamberg/Baur (1991: p193).

391 See for instance Montgomery/Runger (2007: p358), Bosch (1993: p418), or Black (2008: p358).

statistical test and not opt for the simplifying method, although the sample size would be sufficiently large to get a rough approximation with the easier method. Accordingly, a t-test with the following test statistic and degrees-of-freedom formula is selected to test the null hypothesis H_0: $\mu_1 = \mu_2$ [392] and the alternative hypothesis[393] H_1: $\mu_1 \neq \mu_2$ for a two-tailed test:[394]

$$t = \frac{(\bar{x}_1 - \bar{x}_2) - (\mu_1 - \mu_2)}{\sqrt{\frac{s_1^2}{n_1} + \frac{s_2^2}{n_2}}} \quad \text{with} \quad df = \frac{(\frac{s_1^2}{n_1} + \frac{s_2^2}{n_2})^2}{\frac{(\frac{s_1^2}{n_1})^2}{n_1 - 1} + \frac{(\frac{s_2^2}{n_2})^2}{n_2 - 1}}$$

Furthermore, in order to reduce the likelihood of wrongly rejecting a true null hypothesis, the alpha value applied for the tests is decided to be at the $\alpha = 0.01$ level, which is a rather demanding level for a first-of-its-kind series of experiments in a new domain, but helps to reduce the potential vulnerability of the findings with regard to formal critiques.

Anchoring Experiment 1

The first experiment refers to the previously outlined 'likelihood of completion on time' scenario in combination with the 'random-generator' version of presenting the anchor. In line with the earlier described results of the scaling test, participants in group 1 were exposed to a high anchor (84%) and participants in group 2 were presented the low anchor (36%). The full description of the experiment is provided in the appendix.

---

392 Which is equivalent to H_0: $\mu_1 - \mu_2 = 0$.

393 For the one-tailed test, the alternative hypothesis to be tested is H_1: $\mu_1 > \mu_2$, assuming that group 1 is presented with the high anchor and group 2 with the low anchor. The test itself is identical.

394 See for example Montgomery/Runger (2007: p358), Black (2008: p358), or Bosch (1993: p418).

In total, 148 participants took part in this experiment, thereof 73 randomly allocated to group 1 and 75 to group 2. For group 1, the sample mean is 0.739, which corresponds to an average 'likelihood of completion on time' estimate of 73.9%, and the sample variance is 0.016. In contrast, the sample mean for group 2 is 0.501 – signifying an average 'likelihood of completion on time' estimate of 50.1% – and the sample variance is 0.039. The following diagram illustrates and contrasts the histograms of the two groups' judgments:

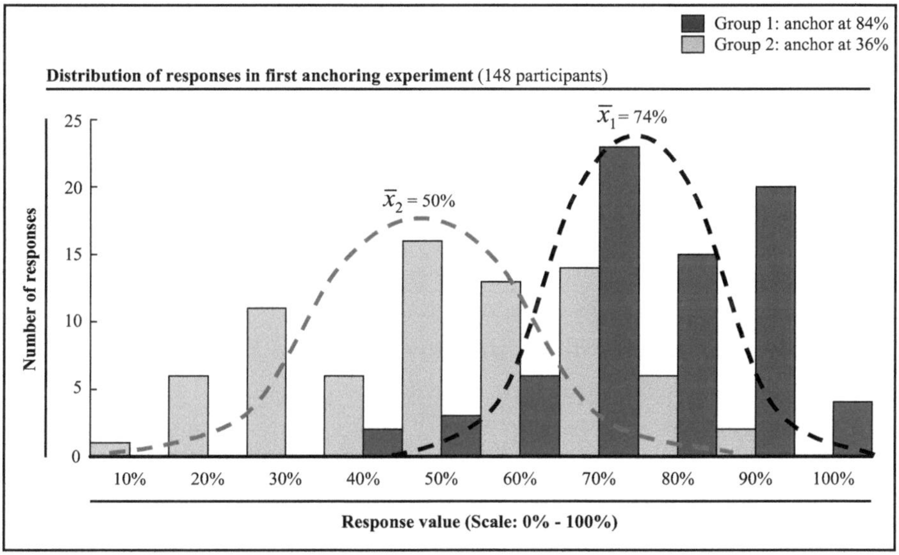

Illustration 9: Comparison of histograms for the first anchoring experiment[395]

In the above histograms, the number of participants whose estimate lies in a particular 10%-interval is depicted. For instance, the column at 30% includes the number of responses that are above 20% and equal or less than 30%. At first

[395] The bell shapes in this diagram (and in the respective charts of the three other anchoring experiments) are schematically illustrated.

sight, both groups' histograms each roughly reflect the bell-shape typical of a Normal distribution. The comparison of the two sample histograms and the two sample means seems to depict a substantial difference between the two groups, which would indicate the existence of a distortive cognitive bias. However, an inferential analysis is required to properly determine whether this indication of differing means is actually statistically valid.

The sample sizes of both groups are sufficiently large to apply the earlier selected inferential statistical test method. As outlined before, the statistical hypothesis for this experiment consists of the null hypothesis H_0: $\mu_1 = \mu_2$ and the alternative hypothesis H_1: $\mu_1 \neq \mu_2$ for the two-tailed test[396]. The respective two-sample t-test for unequal variances yields for $\alpha = 0.01$ and the number of degrees-of-freedom being df = 127 a critical value of $t_{0.005,127} = \pm 2.615$. The observed t-statistic value is t = 8.757, which is larger than 2.615, and accordingly the null hypothesis is rejected in favor of the alternative hypothesis. Actually, the p-value for this test is $p < 10^{-13}$.[397] This results means that there is a statistically significant difference between the means of the two groups.

For the one-tailed test with the alternative hypothesis H_1: $\mu_1 > \mu_2$, the critical value of $t_{0.01,127} = 2.356$ is likewise exceeded by the observed t-statistic value, with the respective p-value being $p < 10^{-14}$. Consequently, the null hypothesis is also rejected in the one-tailed case, in favor of the alternative hypothesis. This implies that the mean of group 1 is statistically significantly higher than the mean of group 2. Given that the only difference between the two groups in the

396 The two-tailed test is used to analyze whether there is a difference in means, that is whether there are distortive effects. In the second step, the one-tailed test is used to examine the direction of these distortive effects, that is whether a higher anchor does indeed produce higher means than the lower anchor.

397 According to the calculation based on Microsoft Excel, which is used because the respective value is far beyond the scope of standard critical value tables for the t-statistic. Similarly, Excel is applied for calculating the p-values in all following hypothesis tests.

experiment is the position of the anchors, it can hence be concluded that the anchors' positions caused that distortive deviation.

Anchoring Experiment 2

The second anchoring experiment addresses the 'market share after one year' estimation scenario that was described earlier and also presents the anchor in the 'random-generator' version. In line with the traditional procedure in anchoring experiments, the assignment of high and low anchors was swapped: participants in group 1 this time received the low anchor (8%) and participants in group 2 attended to the high anchor (22%). The full description of the experiment is provided in the appendix.

The same 148 participants as in the first experiment also took part in the second experiment[398]. The sample mean of group 1 is 0.116 – signifying an average 'market share after one year' estimate of 11.6% – and the sample variance is 0.003. For group 2, the sample mean is 0.204 and the sample variance is 0.007. The following diagram depicts and compares these results. The two histograms display the number of participants whose estimate is in a particular 5%-interval. The 5% steps are selected because they enable better insights, given that the estimations are much closer to each other, because a market share estimate is demanded and because – in absolute terms – both anchors are considerably closer to each other compared to the previous experiment. Accordingly, the histograms also only span the continuum from 0% to 50%:

[398] The post-merger scenario of having to review a large investment project of the target company spans and connects both situations. However, both estimation judgments are independent and should not influence each others' answers, as two totally different aspects of the project need to be estimated. However, even if the first answer did influence the second answer, this spill-over effect would work contrary to the anchoring effect, because high and low anchors are exchanged in the second question, and would thus diminish the anchoring effect (and reduce the likelihood of observing a statistically significant result in the second experiment).

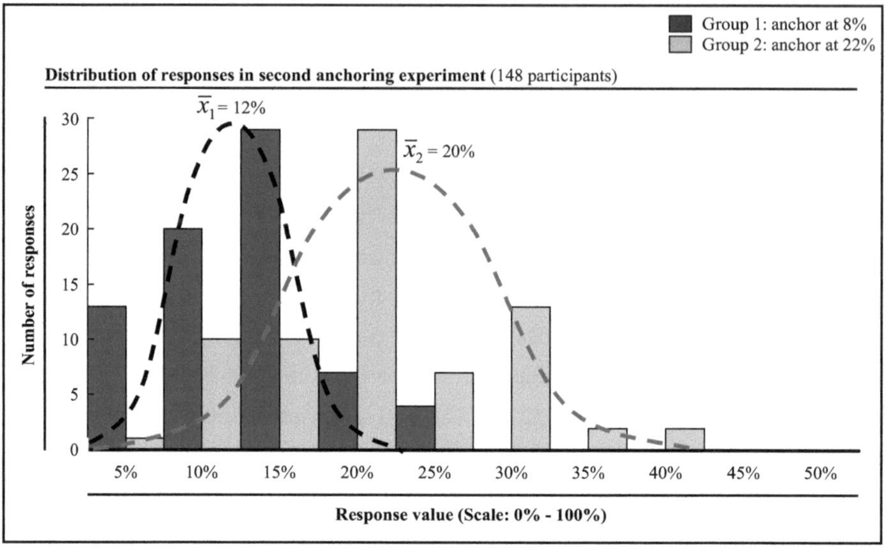

Illustration 10: Comparison of histograms for the second anchoring experiment

The bell-shape in the above diagram is slightly less salient than in the first experiment, which is presumably due to the smaller step size selected. Nevertheless, in line with the expected pattern, the estimates of the first group – which was exposed to the lower anchor – seem to be lower than those of group 2, which again indicates a significant difference between the two groups' means and thus points towards the existence of a distortive cognitive bias.

Conducting the two-tailed two-sample t-test for unequal variances with the null hypothesis H_0: $\mu_1 = \mu_2$ and the alternative hypothesis H_1: $\mu_1 \neq \mu_2$ results in a critical value of $t_{0.005,122} = \pm 2.617$ if the significance level is set at $\alpha = 0.01$. As the obtained t-statistic value of $t = -7.632$ is smaller than -2.617, the null hypothesis is rejected in favor of the alternative hypothesis. Calculating the respective p-value, which is $p < 10^{-11}$ confirms this, which signifies that the means of the two groups are statistically significantly different.

The obtained t-statistic value of the one-tailed test with the alternative hypothesis H_1: $\mu_1 < \mu_2$[399] is also far below the critical value of $t_{0.01,122} = -2.357$. The corresponding p-value is again $p < 10^{-11}$, resulting in the null hypothesis being rejected in favor of the alternative hypothesis. As the two samples only differ with regard to the position of the respective anchor, this statistically significant result implies that the anchoring bias provoked that distortion.

Anchoring Experiment 3

The third experiment in this empirical experimental series on anchoring is basically a modified variant of the first experiment, in which the anchor is not presented as the result of a 'random generator', but instead integrated via the earlier described 'roll-the-dice' version[400]. While the 'random generator' version is extremely artificial, the 'roll-the-dice' version is somewhat less artificial and is incorporated in such a way that its uninformative nature is already very clear from the situation itself; in addition, this uninformative nature and the resulting irrelevance is also explicitly highlighted. Apart from the different version of presenting the anchor, the experiment is identical to the first anchoring experiment. The full description of the experiment is provided in the appendix.

55 of the 115 participants were randomly allocated to group 1, the remaining 60 to the second group. The following illustration summarizes the descriptive statistics and contrasts the resulting histograms:

---

399 Given that group 1 was exposed to the lower anchor and group 2 to the higher anchor, the alternative hypothesis for the one-tailed case must this time be the other way round, in contrast to the first experiment (which was characterized by the opposite anchor arrangement).

400 See chapter 4.3.2.2 for detailed information on the actual integration via the assistant's result of rolling the dice.

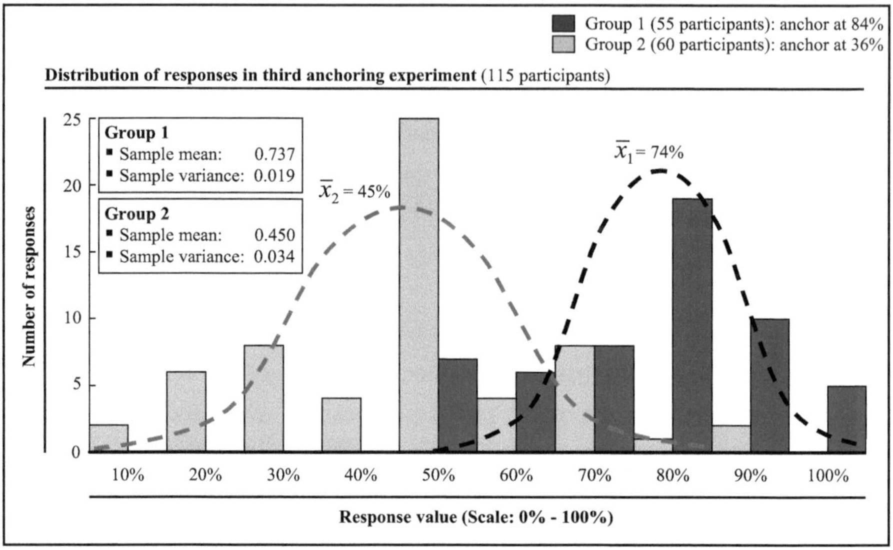

Illustration 11: Comparison of histograms for the third anchoring experiment

The descriptive information and the depicted histograms in the above diagram are very similar to those from the first anchoring experiment. This indicates that the different way of integrating the anchor did not substantially influence the estimation judgments. Repeating the inferential statistics conducted in the first experiment yields analog results: the deviation is statistically significant in the two-tailed[401] and the one-tailed[402] hypothesis tests, and the null hypothesis is rejected twice in favor of the alternative hypothesis, which is a very strong indication for the existence and the impact of an anchoring-induced cognitive bias.

---

[401] The observed t-statistic value ($t = 9.447$) is larger than the critical value ($t_{0.005,109} = \pm 2.622$), with $p < 10^{-15}$. The lower degrees-of-freedom number, compared to experiment 1, is due to the lower sample size of the third experiment.

[402] The critical value ($t_{0.01,109} = 2.361$) is exceeded by the observed t-statistic value, with $p < 10^{-15}$.

Anchoring Experiment 4

The final anchoring experiment is a modification of the second one, addressing the 'market share after one year' estimation scenario, with the anchor being incorporated in the 'roll-the-dice' version, analog to the third experiment. Everything else is identical to the second anchoring experiment. The full description is provided in the appendix.

The descriptive statistics and the resulting illustration are presented in the following diagram:

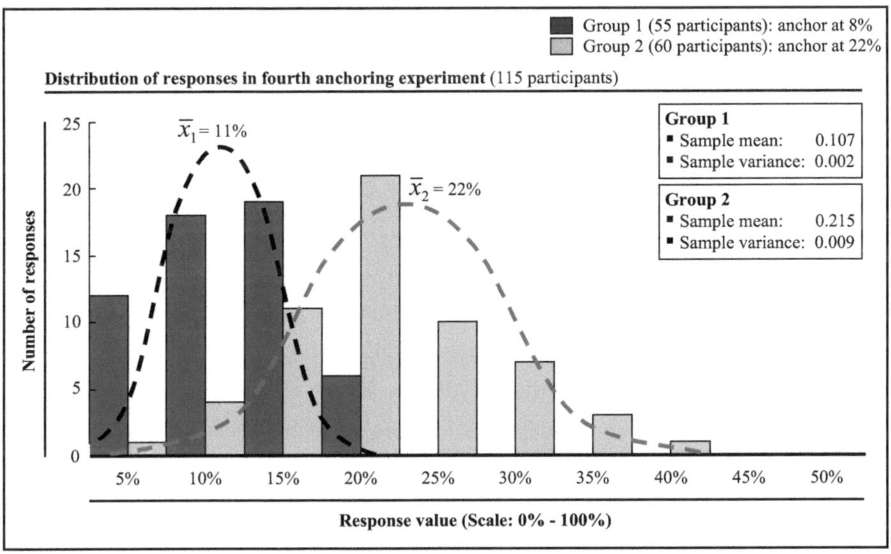

Illustration 12: Comparison of histograms for the fourth anchoring experiment

The figures and patterns in the above diagram resemble very closely those of experiment 2, despite the different incorporation of the anchor. The inferential statistics, both the two-tailed[403] and one-tailed[404] hypothesis tests, also produce identical results: the null hypothesis is rejected in favor of the alternative hypothesis, implying that the anchoring bias caused the deviations.

Conclusions

In summary, the null hypothesis – which claims that differing anchors do not affect the estimation judgment – is rejected in all four experiments in favor of the respective alternative hypotheses. This means that in all four experiments the average estimation judgments differ significantly between the two groups that were exposed to different anchors, and that the average estimates of the group with the higher anchor were significantly larger compared to the group that was exposed to the lower anchor, which is a clear violation of normative rationality.

The results obtained from the anchoring experiments are in line with the earlier derived research hypothesis[405]: The rejection of the null hypotheses implies that, at least in this particular case, there is a distortive effect due to anchoring, and that this effect biases the respective estimation judgment. Furthermore, the distortion is reproducible, as it emerges in all four cases. Finally, the biasing effect is systematic, meaning that it always works in the predicted direction: being exposed to a higher anchor leads to a higher average estimate compared to a lower anchor. Consequently, it can be concluded that the obtained results from

[403] The critical value ($t_{0.005,89} = \pm 2.632$) is far away from the observed value of the t-statistic ($t = -7.794$), the calculated p-value is $p < 10^{-10}$.

[404] The observed t-statistic value is lower than the critical value ($t_{0.01,89} = -2.369$), with $p < 10^{-11}$.

[405] This research hypothesis, derived in chapter 4.3.2.1, claims that anchoring biases exist and that they significantly influence and distort estimation judgments related to capital investments; moreover, it claims that this distortion is reproducible (it occurs in more than one experiment) and systematic (higher anchor leads to higher average estimate compared to lower anchor).

this series of anchoring experiments satisfy and underline the claims made earlier in the research hypothesis.

Furthermore, the fact that all four experiments lead to the same results, and that the level of statistical significance is extremely high in each case, gives a first indication that the distortive cognitive bias effect caused by anchoring might also be relevant in other capital investment contexts and maybe also for real life settings. However, this is only a first, very early indication – which could form the base for further research –, and several restrictions and limitations have to be considered with regard to the potential generalizability of the findings from the above experiments. These limitations, as well as possible conclusions and potential criticisms are addressed in detail in the overall discussion at the end of this main chapter.[406]

4.3.3 Empirical Experiments: Framing

The following part covers the two conducted empirical experiments related to framing, more precisely task framing. Subsequent to a summary of important theoretical aspects, the methodology and design of the two task framing experiments are described, followed by a detailed analysis of the respective results.

4.3.3.1 Underlying Theory

Framing[407] describes the distortion that different representations of the same problem can lead to differing preferences and choices, thus producing preference reversals. This constitutes a severe violation of normative rationality, in particular with regard to the invariance principle. Potential reasons for this phenomenon are for instance explained by the Prospect Theory: depending on the particular frame,

---

406 See chapter 4.4.

407 See chapter 3.3.1 for a detailed discussion of framing in general and the major aspects summarized in this paragraph.

different reference points are unconsciously established, and deviations are differently weighted, either as gains or losses, depending on the position of the respective reference point. Other potential explanations include the availability heuristic – information that is congruent with the particular frame might be more easily available than non-congruent pieces of information – and the 'confirmation trap' bias, which creates a tendency to primarily search for information that supports the particular frame and to neglect the search for disconfirming evidence.

Three types of framing are usually distinguished[408]: outcome framing[409], structure framing[410], and task framing, which means that the instruction specifying how the task is to be conducted is altered. For the intended empirical experiments, the task framing sub-type is selected, because this is adequately and reasonably implementable within the boundaries of the overall methodological approach and situational settings defined earlier for the total series of experiments, and it is expected to be of high relevance for the real life capital investment context: it happens rather quickly to accidentally frame a duty differently because a different frame might not be perceived as being a different task[411].[412] In addition, task framing is particularly influential if the amount or

408 See for instance Soman (2004: p382ff).

409 The verbal or numerical description of a problem is changed.

410 The structural format of the decision situation is adjusted.

411 In this context, 'task' is to be understood as the procedural approach used to address a specific problem or duty. Examples of tasks are for instance 'select one option' or 'reject one option'.

412 For example, if a manager assigns a duty to a subordinate with the target of deciding in which of two countries to invest, the manager (and the subordinate) might not think that 'select one country' is actually a different procedural approach (and hence a different task) compared to 'reject one country', because the overall target (have one country to invest in) is the same; thus, the tasks are perceived as the same, although they are not, and consequently both persons would not realize that 'select' and 'reject' actually establish different frames for the particular situation.

quality of available information differs among the respective options[413], which is not unusual in real life contexts.

The research hypothesis resulting from these considerations is that, at least in particular situations, task framing biases exist in a capital investment context and significantly distort the respective decision outcome, that these distortions are reproducible – meaning that task framing effects emerge in multiple situations – and that they then systematically affect capital investment decision making in a predictable direction: participants will tend towards the 'enriched' option for both tasks, thus producing a reversal of preferences, which constitutes a violation of normatively rational decision making theory. The following sections describe two experiments that test this research hypothesis.

4.3.3.2 Methodology and Preparation of Empirical Experiments

With regard to the general methodology and the overarching situational setting, both task framing experiments are based on the overall specifications described earlier.

Methodology and Design of the Experimental Situation

For the intended task framing experiments, a choice situation is required. This type of decision is very frequent in the capital investment context and applies for instance to all situations where one particular investment project is to be taken from a set of two or more available options. Given that no other research results about task framing in the capital investment context could be found, the decision

---

413 See for instance Soman (2004: p393ff) or Shafir (1993).

is to start with the simplest case of a choice set that contains only two options[414]. A two-item choice set is also not unusual in real life capital investment decision making, and can for example occur for mutually exclusive investment considerations or opportunities both in very early stages of the investment planning process – at a very general level, for instance deciding whether to invest rather in Asia or in South America – and in very late stages – at a very specific level, for instance the decision if a plant is built at a specific site near Guadalajara or near Bogota.

With regard to task types, the most frequent task framing variant is 'select versus reject'[415]. Given that selection is also a typical task in capital investment related activities, and rejection would not be seen as unusual or artificial by the participants either, the decision is to use this duality for the experiments. Moreover, task framing is fostered if the informational level of detail and the salience of the respective information differ between the options, for instance if an 'impoverished' option with no striking negative or positive features is contrasted with an 'enriched' option with both more positive and more negative features.[416] With regard to capital investments, although decision makers usually strive to have comparable levels of detail for each option, there are situations in which the actual amount and quality of information that is available for each option might differ considerably due to different reasons, especially for very early decisions. Accordingly, a set-up with an 'enriched' and an 'impoverished' option is selected. Finally, for the experiment it is also important that none of the two available options is clearly dominant, as this would reduce or impede the efficiency of task framing.

---

414 It is possible that task framing also occurs in situations with three or more available options, as for instance demonstrated by Shafir (1993). However, especially in the case of capital investments, this requires a more complex situation, and is also more difficult to analyze with the intended sample sizes for the 'select vs. reject' task framing that is chosen.

415 See for example Shafir (1993).

416 See Soman (2004: p394).

For the empirical experiments, two simplified capital investment situations have been devised that incorporate the above methodological considerations and are in line with the earlier developed overall boundaries. In the first situation, the CFO-participant has to help with a decision regarding an investment into the regionalization of one of the business unit's core products: this product should be improved and adapted to suit the needs of the respective local customers. However, the business unit can, for various reasons, only invest in adapting the product for one of the two regions, both consisting of several emerging countries. The CFO is provided with several pieces of qualitative information about the two regions, with region A being the 'enriched' option and region B being the 'impoverished' option. For instance, region A is characterized by an above-average population growth expectation with the per capita income being slightly substandard, while region B expects average population growth rates and customary per capita incomes. In total, region B is more or less average on all dimensions, and region A is either better or worse on each dimension, but with a similar number of positive and negative deviations.

In the second situation, the CFO helps to determine the location for a new production site abroad. The business unit management has compiled various relevant pieces of information, for instance regarding local infrastructure, availability of raw material and personnel, environmental requirements, granted governmental subsidies, etc. Analog to the first situation, one potential production site is presented as roughly average on all dimensions, while the other location is either better or worse on each criterion, but the number of pros and cons is balanced. However, in the second situation, location A is the 'impoverished' option and site B is the 'enriched' option, to counterbalance potential sequence effects on the results.

For each of the two situations two versions exist, which are identical apart from the change in the independent variable, which is the description of the task. In the 'select-version', the CFO has to choose a region for which the product is adapted – or respectively pick a location for the production facility in the second scenario –, and in the 'reject-version' the CFO has to state which one is eliminated. In order to avoid that participants accidentally confuse or misunderstand these tasks, it is very important to clearly highlight what needs to be done. In particular, it is vital that the participants realize that they have to eliminate an option in the 'reject-version'[417]. In addition, in cases where a partici-pant is presented with both task framing situations, it is important to ensure that he or she does not by an oversight miss the change in task definition.[418] Accor-dingly, the requirement to eliminate an option is highlighted in bold both in the description text and in the task text and is additionally rephrased again in the final task description.[419]

Preparatory Activities

The methodological and design-related set-up described above did not necessitate a quantitative scaling test. However, analogous to the other experiments, pre-tests were conducted in one-on-one situations, to test if the situational description is correctly understood and whether the task instruction is clear. In particular, it was

417 It is of course equally important that the participant properly understands the selection task. However, assuming that 'selection' is the natural, more intuitive frame, it is the exceptional, potentially surprising frame of 'rejection' or 'elimination' which requires more effort to ensure that the participant properly realizes this task.

418 In those cases, where the participant actually had to answer both of the two task framing situations, the 'select-version' was always presented before the 'reject-version', to avoid potential problems that could occur with switching the frame back from 'reject' to 'select'.

419 For instance, in the case of the production site situation, the situational description states (partly in bold) that the CFO has to decide *which location is rejected* and explains that this means at which site *NO investment* will take place. In addition, in the final task description at the very end, it states (again partly in bold) that the CFO must *eliminate one of the two site options* and asks which site that is, respectively *at which site NO investment is to be made*.

verified whether pre-test participants correctly realized the respective task type and the switch between 'select' and 'reject' tasks, by orally asking them about the nature of the task after they finished the pre-test. In summary, the results of the pre-test revealed no ambiguities and showed that the tasks were properly understood, also due to the measures taken to highlight the respective task[420]. Accordingly, no changes were found to be necessary.[421] Therefore, the pre-tested versions could be used for the actual experiments.

4.3.3.3 Analysis and Conclusions

The following sections describe and analyze in detail the two empirical experiments related to the effects of task framing in the context of capital investments, addressing the selected statistical test method, the descriptive and inferential analyses as well as the major conclusions.

Statistical Test Method

Given the binary decision situation, and considering the earlier stated research hypothesis, a statistical procedure is required that examines proportion differentces between two independent samples. In particular, the statistical method needs to test whether the observed preferences – measured as the percentage of participants who expressed a particular preference compared to all participants who

---

[420] Several participants actually stated that they would probably have missed the switch in task type if the respective task required had not been pointed out by highlighting it in bold and repeating it twice in the text.

[421] Apart from minimal layout adjustments and minor changes required with regard to punctuation.

took this decision – differ between the randomly assigned 'select-version' and 'reject-version' groups.[422]

With regard to large samples, the vast majority of authors in statistics[423] suggest a two-sample Normal distribution-based z-test, to test for the difference in population proportions as approximation[424], but the authors slightly differ with regard to which sample size per group is necessary to be considered as large enough.[425] However, as the empirical experiments are expected to yield a sufficiently large sample size, which satisfies and fulfills all definitions of 'large', the previously suggested statistical method is selected for the inferential analysis of the two task framing experiments.[426] Accordingly, assuming that '$p_{A,1}$' denotes the 'proportion of participants in group 1 that exhibited a preference for option A'[427], the respective statistic with the null hypothesis H_0: $p_{A,1} = p_{A,2}$[428] and the alternative hypothesis H_1: $p_{A,1} \neq p_{A,2}$ for a two-tailed test is:[429]

---

422 This must of course take into account that preferences are expressed differently in the two versions. For instance, if a participant's answer is option A in the 'select-version', then his or her preference is A, but if the participant's answer is option A in the 'reject-version', then his or her preference is B (because he or she rejected A, which implies a preference for B).

423 See for example Black (2008: p377ff), Montgomery/Runger (2007: p379ff), Matthäus (2007: p181ff), Schwarze (2006: p224f), or Vogel (1999: p237ff).

424 In the case of small samples, a statistical test method based on the Binomial distribution or the Hypergeometric distribution would be required, for example the Fisher exact test.

425 For instance, while Matthäus (2007: p181) generally demands a group sample size of each not less than n = 36, other authors provide relative definitions, referring to the central limit theorem, for instance Black (2008: p377): $n_1 * \hat{p}_1$, $n_2 * \hat{p}_2$, $n_1 *(1- \hat{p}_1)$, and $n_2 *(1- \hat{p}_2)$ must each be larger than 5 (a list of symbols with denotations is provided at the beginning of this thesis).

426 In contrast to the selected method, Shafir (1993) follows a slightly different test procedure for task framing experiments: he adds the corresponding preference percentages across the two groups and tests whether the sum significantly exceeds 100%.

427 This preference is exhibited differently in the two versions: in the 'select-version' a preference for A is exhibited by selecting option A, and in the 'reject-version' a preference for A is exhibited by rejecting option B.

$$z = \frac{(\hat{p}_{A,1} - \hat{p}_{A,2}) - (p_{A,1} - p_{A,2})}{\sqrt{p^* \times (1 - p^*) \times (\frac{1}{n_1} + \frac{1}{n_2})}} \quad \text{with} \quad p^* = \frac{n_1 \times \hat{p}_{A,1} + n_2 \times \hat{p}_{A,2}}{n_1 + n_2}$$

Analogous to the experiments on anchoring, the alpha value is set at the $\alpha = 0.01$ level, in order to reduce the likelihood of wrongly rejecting a true null hypothesis. Although this is an ambitious level for the first experiments in a new domain, a very low alpha value is intentionally used, for instance to reduce the susceptibility of the obtained results vis-à-vis critiques.

Task Framing Experiment 1

The first task framing experiment addresses the earlier described 'investment into the localization of a product' situation, with region A being the 'enriched' option and region B the 'impoverished' option. Participants were randomly assigned to two groups: group 1 received the 'reject' version and group 2 answered the 'select' version. The full description of the experiment is provided in the appendix.

In total, 303 participants took part in this experiment. In the first group, 36.7% of the participants expressed a preference for region A[430], in contrast to group 2, in which 60.3% preferred region A[431]. The following diagram summarizes the preferences expressed in the first task framing experiment:

[428] Which is equivalent to H_0: $p_{A;1} - p_{A;2} = 0$, meaning that the observed preferences are the same in both groups, thus implying that task framing has no effect.

[429] See for instance Black (2008: p378), Matthäus (2007: p182), Montgomery/Runger (2007: p380), or Vogel (1999: p238).

[430] They rejected option B in the 'reject-version', and thereby expressed a preference for option A.

[431] They selected option A in the 'select-version'.

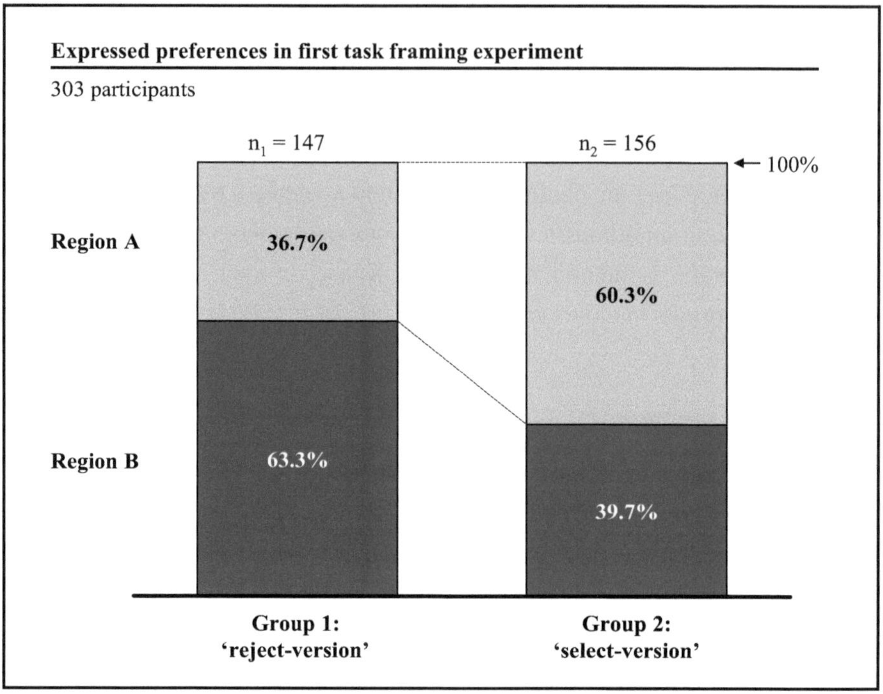

Illustration 13: Comparison of preferences in the first framing experiment

The above diagram contrasts the expressed preferences of participants across the two groups. The comparison of the 'reject-version' and the 'select-version' reveals a substantial shift of preferences: if asked to express one's preference via rejection (group 1), the majority of participants prefers to localize the product for region B, but if asked to express one's preference via selection (group 2), the majority of participants prefers to localize the product for region A. Furthermore, as predicted based on the theoretical considerations, in both groups the majority of participants tends towards the 'enriched' option: region A, the 'enriched' option, is both selected (group 2) and rejected (group 1) by the majority of participants of the respective groups. However, although the reversal of preferences – and hence the violation of normative rationality – seems substantial, only an inferential analysis can determine if this indication is statistically significant.

According to the above mentioned minimum sample size requirements, both groups' sample sizes are sufficiently large to apply the earlier selected inferential test method. As outlined before, the statistical hypothesis for this experiment consists of the null hypothesis H_0: $p_{A,1} = p_{A,2}$ and the alternative hypothesis H_1: $p_{A,1} \neq p_{A,2}$ for a two-tailed test, with $p_{A,1}$ denoting the percentage of participants in group 1 that expressed a preference for region A, and $p_{A,2}$ labelling the respective percentage in group 2. The selected two-sample z-test with $\alpha = 0.01$ yields a critical value of $z_{0.005} = \pm 2.576$. The observed z-statistic value is $z = -4.107$, which is less than -2.576, and accordingly the null hypothesis is rejected in favor of the alternative hypothesis. The calculated p-value for this test is $p < 0.00005$. This result means that there is a statistically significant difference between the proportions of the two samples. Accordingly, as the description of the task represents the only difference between the two groups in the experiment, it can be concluded that this task framing induced the distortive deviation and the resulting reversal of preferences, which palpably constitutes a violation of normative rationality with regard to the requirement of procedural invariance.

Task Framing Experiment 2

The second experiment related to task framing refers to the 'location of a new production site' scenario developed above. Opposite to the first task framing experiment, site A is the 'impoverished' option and site B is the 'enriched' option, to counterbalance potential sequence effects. The full description of the experiment is provided in the appendix.

61 of the 123 participants were randomly allocated to group 1 and received the 'select' version; the 'reject' version of the experiment was presented to the

remaining 62 participants, who formed group 2. However, while 54.1% of the participants in group 1 preferred site B[432], only 29.0% exhibited a preference for B[433] in group 2. A summary of the preferences exhibited in the second task framing experiment is provided in the following illustration:

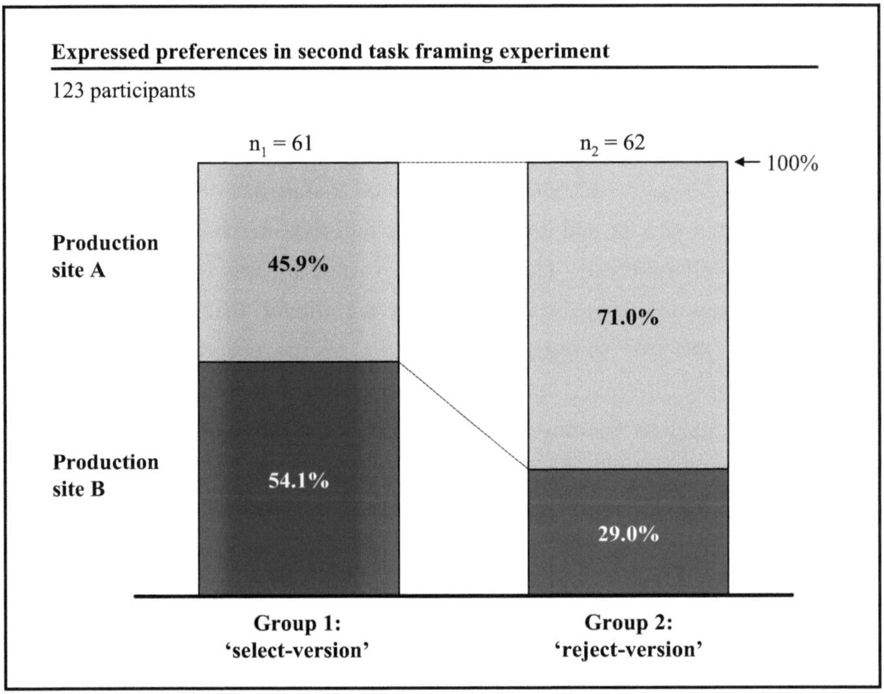

Illustration 14: Comparison of preferences in the second framing experiment

432 They chose B in the 'select-version'.

433 They eliminated option A in the 'reject-version', and hence expressed a preference for B.

The above comparison of the observed preferences in the two versions discloses that the majorities of both groups once again show a tendency towards the 'enriched' option[434] and indicates a strong preference reversal. On closer inspection, the descriptive diagram also illustrates a slightly skewed distribution of preferences. A potential explanation for this observation is that the two production site options might not be fully equally attractive and that the weights of the 'enriched' option's positive and negative aspects might not be fully balanced.[435] This has potentially caused a shift of the absolute preference levels, but the reversal of preferences still seems to take place and the biasing task framing effect still seems to have a highly distortive impact[436].

Despite being smaller than in the first experiment, the sample sizes of both groups satisfy the earlier stated minimum sample size requirements for the intended test method with the null hypothesis H_0: $p_{B,1} = p_{B,2}$ and the alternative hypothesis H_1: $p_{B,1} \neq p_{B,2}$.[437] The two-tailed, two-sample z-test with $\alpha = 0.01$ produces a z-statistic value of $z = 2.825$, which is larger than the critical value of $z_{0.005} = \pm 2.576$, and a p-value of $p < 0.005$. Consequently, the null hypothesis is rejected in favor of the alternative hypothesis and the observed difference

---

434 The 'enriched' option (production site B), is both selected (group 1) and rejected (group 2) by the respective majority of participants.

435 Based on a comparison of the observed preferences across both versions, it might be that the negative aspects of site B (for instance the 'occasional small political instabilities') slightly outweigh its positive aspects, which would shift the 'unbiased' a priori preference levels. Alternatively, the skewed distribution might also be simply due to a purely random effect. However, although the sample size in the second experiment is smaller than in the first experiment, the total sample size of 123 in this experiment indicates that the major reason for the shifted preferences lies in the characteristics of the two options, and is not a random effect.

436 However, if there actually was an a priori preference imbalance disfavoring option B, it would be likely that the task framing effect is slightly weaker. Similarly, if this imbalance had been so strong that option A would have been clearly dominant (which was not the case), then possibly no task framing effect might have occurred, as outlined in earlier considerations.

437 Given the binary format of the experiment, testing proportions of B is equivalent to testing proportions of A, but for consistency the test refers to the proportion of the 'enriched' option.

between the two groups' proportions is statistically significant. As in the first experiment, this represents a violation of the procedural invariance principle demanded by normative rationality.

Conclusions

In summary, the null hypothesis is rejected in both experiments, signifying that the different framing of the tasks – as selection or rejection – produced preference reversals and thus biased the decision outcome. These results clearly support the earlier derived research hypothesis[438]: rejecting the null hypotheses implies that a distortive effect due to task framing exits in these situations and biases the respective decision. Furthermore, the distortion emerged in more than one situation, which satisfies the reproducibility part of the research hypothesis, and it is systematic, as its effect always materialized in the predicted way: in both experiments, the results of both groups showed a tendency towards the 'enriched' option for both task versions. Accordingly, task framing seems to be highly relevant in the presented capital investment contexts, and possibly also for situations beyond the two particular examples. This issue of generalizability is, among others, addressed in more detail in the critical discussion at the end of this main chapter.[439]

[438] The research hypothesis derived in chapter 4.3.3.1 claims that task framing biases exist and considerably distort judgments in a capital investment context; moreover, this distortion is stated to emerge in more than one situation – it is reproducible – and to be systematic (it shows a tendency towards the 'enriched' option in both frames).

[439] See chapter 4.4.

4.3.4 Empirical Experiments: Asymmetric Dominance

The third and final series of empirical experiments is discussed in the following sections, which are analog – with regard to overall approach and structure – to the two previous sub-chapters on anchoring and framing experiments.

4.3.4.1 Underlying Theory

Asymmetric dominance[440] refers to the phenomenon that the relative preferences between two[441] existing options in a choice set are influenced and reversed if an additional, normatively irrelevant option is added to the choice set in such a way that this additional option is asymmetrically dominated, which means that the new option is dominated by one of the original options, but not by the other. As a result, the dominating original option is evaluated as considerably more desirable than before, in comparison to the second original option, which constitutes a violation of the 'independence of irrelevant alternatives' principle of normative rationality. Several potential explanations have been suggested for this cognitive bias, including for instance the Prospect Theory or the existence of unconsciously triggered, simplified evaluation processes that rely on pairwise comparisons.

In general, several different cases can be distinguished for the position of the newly-added third option – which is often referred to as the 'decoy' option – in relation to the dominating option. The following illustration schematically summarizes the most important decoy positions:

---

[440] See chapter 3.3.2 for a detailed discussion of asymmetric dominance in general and the major aspects summarized in this paragraph.

[441] Asymmetric dominance biases can also emerge in situations with a larger choice set. In this case, the same theoretical considerations apply. However, to avoid unnecessary complexity, the following considerations only focus on the simpler case of starting with two original options.

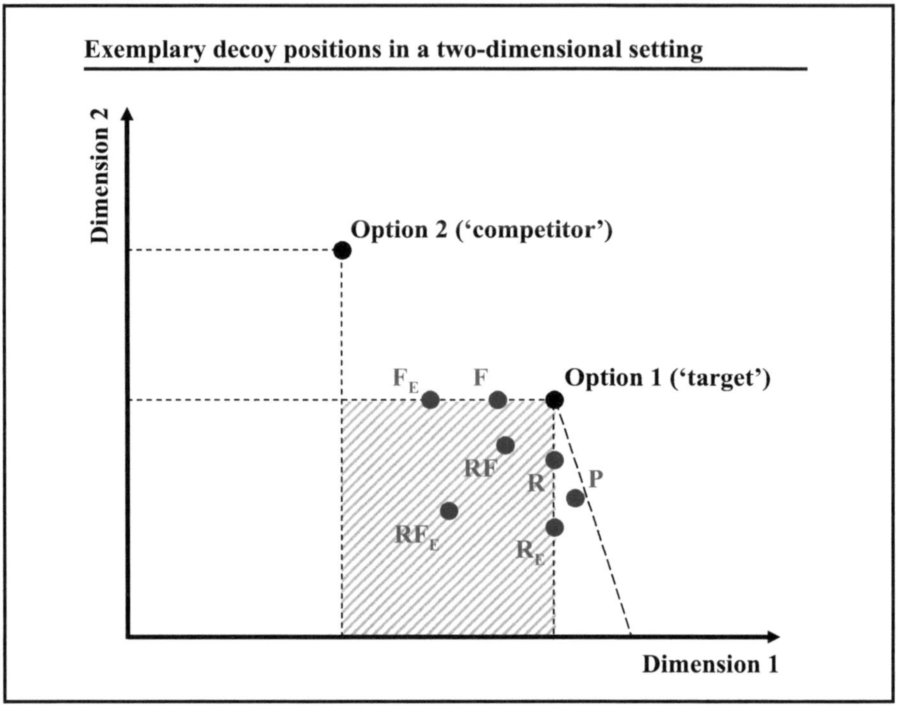

Illustration 15: Schematic illustration of potential decoy positions[442]

The above diagram depicts several potential decoy positions relative to option 1, which is the dominating option in the final three-item choice set, and is often referred to as the 'target'. An analogous set of decoy positions could also be constructed relative to option 2. In general, Huber et al. (1982) classify decoys according to the effect that they have on the perceived importance, or weight,

[442] Illustration based on discussions and illustrations in Huber et al. (1982) and Huber/Puto (1983), adapted and expanded by own considerations. Only 2 dimensions are applied for illustrative purposes and simplicity. Similar considerations are also possible if more dimensions are used.

related to the two dimensions. Accordingly, they distinguish between decoy positions that increase the range of the target's weaker dimension[443] – positions R and R_E –, positions that increase the frequency of the stronger dimension of the target[444] – positions F and F_E –, and combinations of both range and frequency: positions RF and RF_E. Furthermore, decoy positions could be distinguished according to the distance between the decoy and the target: while positions R, F, and RF are relatively close to the target, positions R_E, F_E, and RF_E are rather far away from it, and are thus often referred to as 'extreme' decoy positions.

Alternatively, decoy positions can be distinguished with regard to the type of dominance[445]: 'light' dominance, 'full' dominance, and 'pseudo' dominance. Position P is an example of 'pseudo' dominance: the decoy is, from a purely formal point of view, not dominated by the target, but it is in a highly inferior position[446]. In the case of 'light' dominance – which includes positions R, R_E, F, and F_E – the decoy is equally good compared to the target on one dimension, but worse on the second dimension. In contrast, 'full' dominance describes a situation in which the target is better than the decoy on both dimensions, which is the case for positions RF and RF_E in the above diagram.

---

443 The decoy is worse than the target on the target's weaker dimension (and thus the range of observed values on this dimension is enlarged), which makes the target's disadvantage look less intense (than without the decoy).

444 The decoy is weaker than the target (but still much better than the other option) on the target's stronger dimension, which increases the number of instances of good values on this dimension. Accordingly, the decoy 'strengthens' the advantage of the target and makes the other option look like a negative outlier on this dimension.

445 The terms 'light', 'full', and 'pseudo' dominance are not used in standard literature, but created by the author to describe the type of resulting dominance situation in a more structured way.

446 Decoy P is marginally better than the target on dimension 1 and considerably worse on dimension 2; hence, it is not formally dominated. However, the small advantage of the decoy on dimension 1 is more than outweighed by its large disadvantage on dimension 2 (there might be situations where the trade-off of gaining minimally on one dimension is worth the large loss on the second dimension, but this would require that one dimension is clearly superior to the other dimension in terms of value, which is not meant to be the case here), making the decoy inferior to the target.

In the capital investment context, the effects of asymmetric dominance might be relevant for a variety of choice situations, for instance when selecting between several mutually exclusive investment opportunities. However, as pointed out earlier[447], the strength of the indications which suggest that asymmetric dominance might also be relevant in the capital investment context is considerably weaker than for anchoring and framing. Nevertheless, based on the theoretical foundations of asymmetric dominance, the author believes that this distortive effect should also be influential in the capital investment environment.

Accordingly, the research hypothesis states that, in the context of capital investments, asymmetric dominance effects exist, that these significantly bias the respective decision outcome, that they are reproducible – meaning that the bias can be demonstrated in more than one experiment – and that they occur in a predictable fashion: depending on the position of the normatively irrelevant decoy option, the respective target is evaluated as significantly more desirable than in the situation where the other option assumes the dominating role, and preferences are reversed accordingly.

4.3.4.2 Methodology and Preparation of Empirical Experiments

The general setting and basic methodology for the asymmetric dominance experiments are in line with the previously established overall setting, deviations and specifications are discussed in the following sections.

---

[447] For more details see the discussion in the first step of the overall methodology and procedure for the empirical experiments, as outlined in chapter 4.3.1.

Methodology and Design of the Experimental Situation

As described above, the intended experiments on asymmetric dominance require a choice situation with several given options to select from. With regard to the number of options in the choice set, a three-item set with two 'base' options and one decoy option is selected[448], which is in line with the set-up used in the majority of asymmetric dominance experiments in other domains. This decision also makes sense when taking into account the limitations of the overall experimental set-up and the fact that no comparable research is known for asymmetric dominance in the capital investment context.

Each of the three options in the choice set is described along two distinctive dimensions. The reasons for opting for a two-dimensional set-up are similar to the ones for the choice-set size. However, given that in the real life capital investment environment most decisions include more than two variables, the description of the experimental situations will clearly state that the two given dimensions are the ones that are seen as most important for the respective decision problem, and that all options are roughly equal on all other important criteria, which can therefore be disregarded for this decision.[449] With regard to the two dimensions, it is of vital importance that these are sufficiently different from each other. If they were too similar – as for instance in the case of having two monetary dimensions like labor cost per unit and material cost per unit – the two dimensions could simply be combined or added up, and no real trade-off situation would occur. Moreover, for the same reason, it is imperatively necessary that the two dimensions are

---

448 However, experiments with larger choice sets would also be possible, from a theoretical point of view, and might be interesting areas for future research.

449 This might seem at first sight artificial. However, on closer observation, it is not extremely unusual in real life decisions that – although many criteria are taken into account during the decision making process – at the end of the decision it is actually a very limited number of criteria that tip the scales. Actually, from a purely methodological perspective, most capital investment appraisal procedures produce only one single output figure (for instance the NPV), and the methodology suggests that the decision is taken based on this one dimension.

independent of each other and that there is no obvious dominance of one dimension.

With regard to the different potential decoy positions discussed earlier, extreme decoy positions and 'pseudo' dominance decoys will not be used in the intended series of experiments.[450] Furthermore, the decision for the empirical experiments is to create one experiment with a 'light' dominance decoy and one experiment with a 'full' dominance decoy, because this covers two different important methodological variations and at the same time seems to be close to reality. For each of the two experiments, two different versions are created, which are identical apart from the independent variable: in one version the decoy is incorporated in such a way that the first 'base' option dominates the decoy, in the other version the decoy is dominated by the second 'base' option.[451]

In order to capture a large spectrum of potential capital investment contexts, one of the experimental situations describes a decision that is based on important content-related input variables or characteristics of the investment itself, and the second experimental situation simulates that an in-depth capital investment appraisal process has already taken place and therefore employs the outcome variables produced by the respective appraisal techniques as determinants of the decision problem.

In the first situation, the CFO has to take a capital investment decision for the pharmaceuticals business unit, which needs to invest into a new machine that produces pills. The two characteristics that have been identified as most important

---

450 Given that these experiments seem to be the first in the capital investment domain, focusing on using 'normal' decoy positions is the logical first step. However, other decoy positions might be interesting for future research.

451 This approach of comparing two three-item choice-sets is in line with the procedure used by many authors, for instance Hedgcock/Rao (2009) or Pettibone/Wedell (2000). However, others, for instance Huber et al. (1982), adopt a slightly different approach: they compare the three-item choice sets (with the decoy) to the respective two-item choice sets (without the decoy).

are flexibility – how many different types of pills the machine can create – and quantity or speed of production – how many pills the machine can produce in one hour. The CFO receives quantitative information regarding those two characteristics for each of the three short-listed machines, and is told that these machines are roughly equally good regarding all other potentially important criteria. Subsequently, the CFO has to decide in which machine the business unit should invest.

In the second experimental situation, the CFO supports the management of another business unit that wants to expand its activities and therefore seeks to invest into a new product segment. The business unit's controlling department has already conducted in-depth analyses for several options and accomplished the company's standard investment appraisal procedures, in particular the net present value[452] calculation and the utility value analysis[453]. Based on the results of this investment appraisal, the CFO has to determine into which of the three short-listed product segments the business unit will invest.

With regard to this second experimental situation, which includes two technical terms – 'net present value' and 'utility value analysis', it is important that the participants know what the two mentioned investment appraisal methods are about and how to understand the figures that result from both methods.[454] In order to ensure this – but at the same time avoid incomprehensible, lengthy technical definitions[455] – the description of the situation includes a short, non-technical explanation of the respective method's general aim and target, and how to read its quantitative output. Verifying if participants properly understand this explanation will be one of the key challenges for the pre-tests.

---

[452] See chapter 2.3.3 for detailed information on the net present value (NPV) method.

[453] See chapter 2.3.4 for further information on utility value analysis.

[454] It is not necessary that the participants have full knowledge about the respective methods and their detailed functioning, but they need to roughly understand the basic meaning and their output.

[455] Which might lead to participants 'giving up' the question before they even finished reading it.

Preparatory Activities: Scaling Test and Pre-Test

When preparing experiments on asymmetric dominance, some authors suggest conducting a scaling test before the final experiment, to calibrate the positions of the two 'base' options and obtain a more balanced set-up for the experiment.[456] However, this is absolutely optional, and no detrimental effect on the experiment or outcome is expected if the two 'base' options are not completely balanced – as long as no option is clearly dominant. Accordingly, the decision was to only conduct a scaling test for the first situation, the 'investment in a pharmaceutical machine' scenario[457], and skip this optional preparatory step for the second situation, the 'investment in a new product segment' scenario[458].

The scaling test for the first situation was conducted in the following way: the participants received the full description of the situation and were told that two machines are on the short-list, but that not all necessary pieces of information are available for both yet. Consequently, for the first machine the figures for both dimensions were provided, and for the second machine only the information regarding one dimension was given. Subsequently, the participants had to indicate

---

456 See for example Hedgcock/Rao (2009: p5) for an exemplary description of the scaling test procedure.

457 Given the nature of the investment situation and of the two dimensions, it is rather demanding to roughly balance them without a calibration test. Accordingly, the decision is to conduct a scaling test for this experiment in order to avoid a potentially highly unbalanced or unrealistic situational set-up.

458 The challenge of properly describing the technical investment appraisal terms is viewed as more important in this case. Accordingly, a scaling test would only make sense after the pre-test (if the scaling test participants didn't properly understand the description of the two appraisal methods, the results of the scaling test would be distorted or contain relatively low relevance). Therefore, the decision was to roughly estimate the two options' values for each dimension and only conduct a scaling test if pre-test participants stated that the options seem highly unbalanced or that one of the options is clearly dominant. Otherwise no scaling test is required.

which value they would demand for the second dimension in order to be completely indifferent between the two machines.

The scaling test was conducted with 16 participants. On average, they demanded a production speed of 14,176 pills per hour for the second machine, in order to be indifferent between the two machines. Accordingly, the respective value for the second machine's quantity dimension was set to 14,200[459] for the final experiment.

Subsequently, pre-tests have been conducted for both experimental situations, verifying if participants properly understand the explanations of technical terms and the description of the situation. Analog to the pre-tests for the other empirical experiments, one-on-one situations were employed to directly observe participants' reactions and obtain direct feedback afterwards. The pre-test for the 'investment in a pharmaceutical machine' scenario brought no indications of any unclarities. However, the pre-tests of the 'investment in a new product segment' scenario showed that the explanations of the net present value and utility value analyses were too technical in the early versions, and thus not properly understood by several participants. Consequently, these descriptions had to be adjusted. An additional series of pre-tests for this second situation found that the updated explanations were considerably better than before and seemed to be appropriate.[460] With regard to the balance of the two 'base' options in the second situation, for which no initial scaling test had been conducted, there were no indications for a highly unbalanced or unrealistic set-up, therefore it was decided that a subsequent, additional scaling test was not necessary. Similarly, no other aspects surfaced that would require a revision of the preliminary design of any of the two experiments.[461]

---

459 The figure was rounded to the nearest hundred, to be in line with the other figures in the description of the experimental situation.

460 Even if explicitly asked, no pre-test participant stated any issues with the updated explanations.

461 Apart from minor changes to adjust for accidental mistakes in spelling.

4.3.4.3 Analysis and Conclusions

The following sub-chapter discusses the statistical test procedure and the analyses and conclusions with regard to the two empirical experiments on asymmetric dominance in a capital investment related setting.

Statistical Test Method

The statistical situation and considerations for the asymmetric dominance experiments are similar to the earlier case of task framing. The target is to contrast the proportions of a parameter across two samples. However, the choice set for the asymmetric dominance experiments contains three items, in contrast to only two items in the case of task framing. Accordingly, two different approaches seem possible[462], given that primarily the two 'base' options are of interest, and that the share of the decoy option[463] is expected to be relatively low:[464] remove and ignore the decoy option answers from the analysis, thus creating a true binary situation, or define the binary variables for the analysis as 'share of participants

[462] A third approach is also imaginable, which is not discussed in literature so far: if one would assume that decoy choices are random errors – for instance caused by inattentiveness – then one could argue that a similar number of random errors has also occurred for the actual choices of the other two options. Therefore, one might not only remove the decoy answers from the analysis, but also an equal number of instances for both 'base' options. However, this approach would potentially inflate the observed magnitude of an existing gap or tendency (as the absolute difference between the two base options is still the same, but from a relative perspective the gap is larger).

[463] Although the decoy is normatively irrelevant and should thus not be selected from the pure perspective of normative rationality, the actual share of the decoy in empirical experiments is typically not zero. For instance, Hedcock/Rao (2009: p7) report decoy selection rates of 4% and 12% – which is rather high –, and Huber et al. (1982: p94) indicate rates of about 2%.

[464] See for instance Huber et al. (1982: p94).

choosing option A' versus 'share of participants not choosing option A'[465]. However, applying the first approach proportionally increases the respective shares of the two base options, thereby slightly inflates the relative size of a possible gap and therefore potentially influences the test result. Consequently, the decision is to apply the second approach and not remove and ignore the decoy choices.

Based on the above considerations, the same two-tailed, two-sample z-test for comparing population proportions that was applied for the task framing analyses is also applied for examining the asymmetric dominance experiments. Consequently, with '$p_{1,A}$' denoting the 'proportion of participants in group 1 that selected option A'[466], the test statistic[467] is the following:[468]

$$z = \frac{(\hat{p}_{1,A} - \hat{p}_{2,A}) - (p_{1,A} - p_{2,A})}{\sqrt{p^* \times (1 - p^*) \times (\frac{1}{n_1} + \frac{1}{n_2})}} \quad \text{with} \quad p^* = \frac{n_1 \times \hat{p}_{1,A} + n_2 \times \hat{p}_{2,A}}{n_1 + n_2}$$

The respective alpha value is again set at the $\alpha = 0.01$ level, which decreases the probability of falsely rejecting a true null hypothesis and increases the validity of the obtained findings.

Asymmetric Dominance Experiment 1

The first experiment on asymmetric dominance concerns the 'investment in a pharmaceutical machine' situation. Participants were randomly allocated to the

---

465 This complementary event ('not A') includes all participants that choose either option B or the decoy option.

466 The denomination for the asymmetric dominance experiments ($p_{1,A}$) is on purpose reversed, compared to the denomination for the task framing experiments ($p_{A,1}$), to avoid confusions.

467 For the null hypothesis H_0: $p_{1,A} = p_{2,A}$ and the alternative hypothesis is H_1: $p_{1,A} \neq p_{2,A}$.

468 See for instance Black (2008: p378), Matthäus (2007: p182), Montgomery/Runger (2007: p380), or Vogel (1999: p238).

two versions of the experiment, which are identical apart from the values provided for the third option, the decoy. In group 1, the decoy is set in such a way that it is asymmetrically dominated by machine A, in the second group machine B asymmetrically dominates the decoy. For this experiment, the decoy is set in a 'light' dominance position: it is equal to the respective target A or B on one dimension, and worse on the other. The following diagram schematically illustrates these points:

Choice set for group 1

Machine	Flexibility: no. of different pills	Quantity: no. of pills/hour
A	64	5,900
B	27	14,200
C	64	5,300

Choice set for group 2

Machine	Flexibility: no. of different pills	Quantity: no. of pills/hour
A	64	5,900
B	27	14,200
C	24	14,200

Schematic overview and comparison

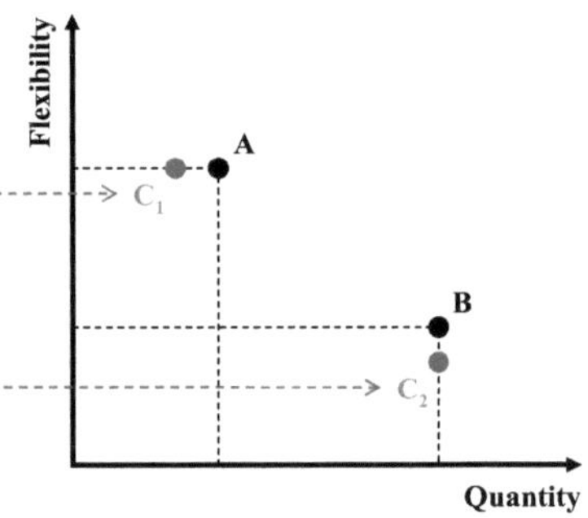

Illustration 16: Schematic representation of the first decoy experiment

The above illustration schematically depicts the situation in the 'investment in a pharmaceutical machine' scenario. The left side displays the quantitative data that the respective groups received with regard to the three machines available[469]. On the right side, the overall situation across the two groups is summarized, in order to clarify the positions of the respective decoys. In both cases, according to the

[469] The grey rectangles are added to improve the clarity of this illustration; they were not part of the participants' original situation descriptions, nor was the illustration at the right side.

earlier mentioned classification of Huber et al. (1982), the decoy increases the range of the target's weaker dimension. The appendix contains a full description of the experiment.

The following diagram summarizes the two groups' choices:

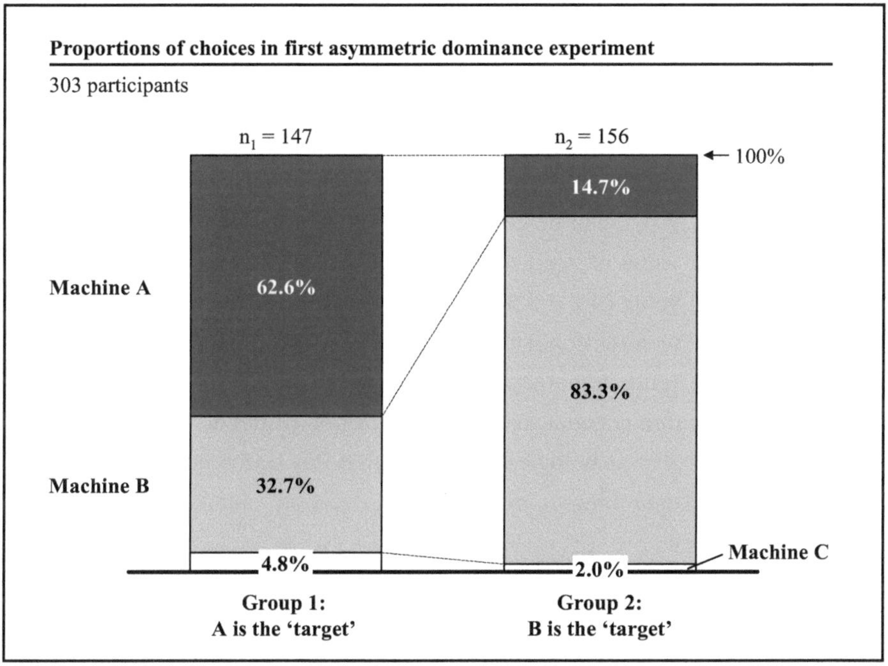

Illustration 17: Comparison of choices in the first asymmetric dominance experiment

The above illustration shows that out of the 303 participants, 147 participants were assigned to group 1, the remaining 156 to group 2. In the first group[470], 62.6% of the participants decided to invest in machine A, while only 14.7% of the

[470] In which the normatively irrelevant decoy is asymmetrically dominated by option A.

participants opted for machine A in group 2[471]. The diagram also depicts the two groups' choice patterns[472] and indicates a substantial reversal of preferences: if the normatively irrelevant decoy option is asymmetrically dominated by – and hence similar to – machine A, then the majority of participants decide to invest in machine A and only a minority prefers machine B. However, if, ceteris paribus, the decoy option is asymmetrically dominated by machine B, then the largest part of the participants opts for the investment in machine B, and only very few decide to invest in machine A. This is not compatible with normatively rational behavior.

Given the sufficiently large sample sizes, the earlier described two-tailed, two-sample z-test with the null hypothesis H_0: $p_{1,A} = p_{2,A}$ and the alternative hypothesis H_1: $p_{1,A} \neq p_{2,A}$ can be conducted.[473] Setting an alpha level of $\alpha = 0.01$ results in a critical value of $z_{0.005} = \pm 2.576$. This is considerably lower than the observed z-statistic value of $z = 8.588$, meaning that the difference is statistically significant, which is also confirmed by a very small p-value of $p < 10^{-15}$. Consequently, the null hypothesis is rejected in favor of the alternative hypothesis. Taking into account that only the position of the decoy option varied across the two versions, it is logical to reason that this difference – and thus the asymmetric dominance bias – distorted the decision outcome and violated normative rationality.

Asymmetric Dominance Experiment 2

In the second asymmetric dominance experiment, the 177 participants had to take a capital investment decision based on the output of an in-depth investment

471 In which option B asymmetrically dominates the decoy.

472 The observed proportions of participants selecting the decoy (option C) are in line with the findings of the majority of other asymmetric dominance experiments, as outlined earlier.

473 With $p_{1,A}$ being the share of participants in group 1 that selected machine A, and $p_{2,A}$ describing the respective proportion in group 2.

appraisal[474] in the previously developed 'new product segment' scenario. This time, the decoy is located in a 'full' dominance position: it is weaker than the target on both dimensions. The decoy is asymmetrically dominated by product B in the first group (85 participants), and by product A in the second group (92 participants).[475] The following illustration displays the detailed values and positions:

Choice set for group 1

Product	Net present value (NPV) in EUR mill.	Utility value, scale: 0 - 100
A	58.7	82.4
B	65.9	73.5
C	65.7	73.2

Choice set for group 2

Product	Net present value (NPV) in EUR mill.	Utility value, scale: 0 - 100
A	58.7	82.4
B	65.9	73.5
C	58.6	82.1

Schematic overview and comparison

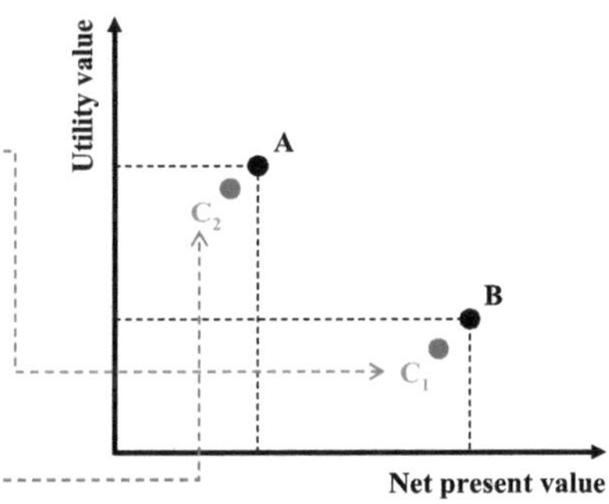

Illustration 18: Schematic representation of the second decoy experiment

The results are similar to the first asymmetric dominance effect: 67.1% of the participants in the first group opted for investment B, compared to only 30.4% in the second group 2. The following diagram summarizes the observed choices and reveals a substantial reversal of preferences that is consistent with the previously predicted pattern, stating that the judgments of the majorities in both groups would be influenced drastically by the position of the normatively irrelevant

[474] Including a net present value calculation and an utility value analysis.

[475] The complete description of the experiment is provided in the appendix.

decoy and that they would select the investment option which asymmetrically dominates the decoy in the respective situation:

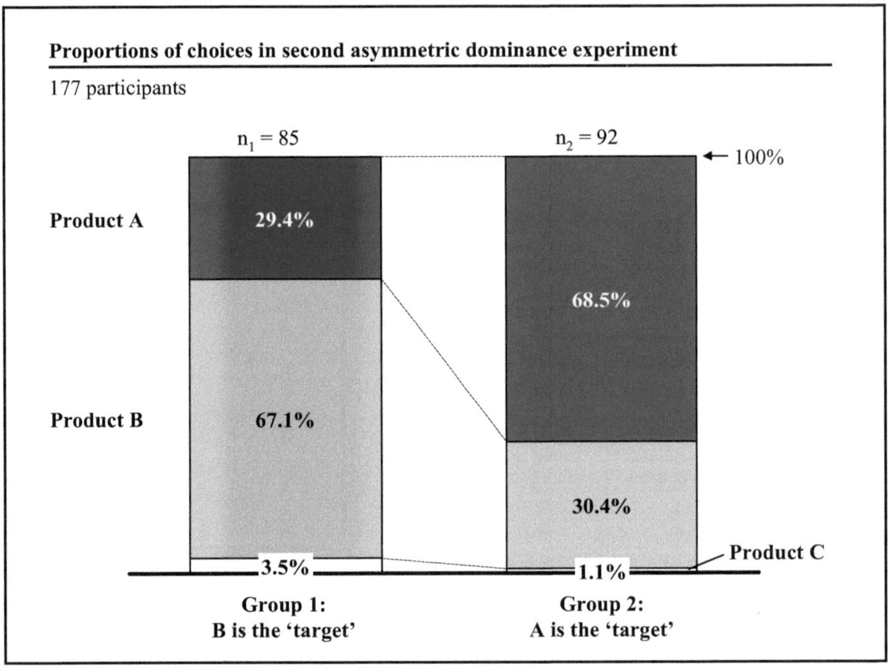

Illustration 19: Comparison of choices in the second asymmetric dominance experiment

Conducting the two-tailed, two-sample z-test[476] for this experiment yields a p-value of $p < 10^{-5}$ and an observed z-statistic value of $z = 4.992$ being larger than

[476] Using the null hypothesis H_0: $p_{1,B} = p_{2,B}$ and the alternative hypothesis H_1: $p_{1,B} \neq p_{2,B}$ as well as an alpha level of $\alpha = 0.01$.

the critical value of $z_{0.005} = \pm 2.576$.[477] This result signifies that there is a statistically significant difference between the proportions of the two samples, and thus an obvious violation of normative rationality, which is again attributable to the existence of the asymmetric dominance bias.[478]

Conclusions

Summing up, the null hypothesis – stating that no cognitive bias exists – is rejected twice in favor of the alternative hypothesis. Altering the decoy positions caused substantial, and statistically highly significant, reversals of preferences in both investment contexts, which clearly violates the 'independence of irrelevant alternatives' principle of normative rationality.

With regard to the previously developed research hypothesis[479], the observed results clearly support all its aspects: The existence of asymmetric dominance biases and their distortive effects is confirmed by the twofold, and thus reproducible, rejection of the null hypotheses, at least in the respective settings analyzed. Moreover, the observed choices exactly reflect the predicted patterns and thus satisfy the research hypothesis' requirement of being systematic: the results of both experiments revealed a clear tendency towards the respective target option. Accordingly, the observed results from the asymmetric dominance experiments fulfill and support the claims established in the research hypothesis.

---

477 The fact that the observed z-statistic value is lower than in the first experiment – and consequently the calculated p-value is higher – is presumably due to the considerably lower sample size of the second experiment, compared to the first experiment. Nevertheless, even with the smaller sample size, the results for this experiment are statistically highly significant.

478 Because the varying decoy positions are the only difference between the two groups.

479 See chapter 4.3.4.1 for the full research hypothesis, which claims that asymmetric dominance biases exist and systematically (tendency towards the respective target option) and reproducibly (more than one situation) distort judgments related to capital investments.

In summary, the previous sections described three experimental series and demonstrated effects of different cognitive biases on particular capital investment decisions. However, these findings so far only relate to the specific situation and set-up in the experiment. With regard to their potential generalizability, a critical discussion is required. This is the focus of the next sub-chapter.

4.4 Critical Discussion of Conclusions and Limitations

The theoretical considerations at the beginning of this main chapter as well as the empirical findings in the subsequent parts all indicate that cognitive biases are relevant in the particular capital investment contexts that they relate to. Moreover, the consistency of the findings across a large variety of different areas of capital investments and the uniformly high levels of their respective statistical relevance provide further indications that the findings could potentially also apply to other capital investment situations, including real life contexts. This sub-chapter addresses this issue and critically discusses the most important limitations that have to be considered in relation to the potential generalizability.

In the first step, the preliminary conclusions that could be drawn from the theoretical and empirical parts as a whole are briefly highlighted, as foundation for the following discussions. Afterwards, potential critical arguments with regard to the general approach and the overall methodological set-up and the corresponding constraints are addressed. Subsequently, the focus is on potential limitations inherent in the incongruity between participant population and relevant real life population, which is expected to be one of the major critiques that could be brought up against the conducted series of empirical experiments. Finally, the results of a replication study with more experienced participants, which was conducted in order to test the validity of the raised critiques, are presented.

4.4.1 Preliminary Conclusions

The discussion of analogies to the widely accepted relevance of cognitive biases in other business domains, like marketing and HR, and with regard to financial investments – the so-called behavioral finance – demonstrated that cognitive biases might also be relevant for the capital investment environment. The two fictitious case examples further fostered this hypothesis by illustrating in more detail how cognitive biases could affect particular capital investment related decision making situations. With regard to an empirical perspective, the eight con-ducted empirical experiments demonstrated, for very different types of capital investment decisions[480] and activities across a large number of differing situations, that cognitive biases did have a significant impact on the particular situations. In addition, the magnitude of the statistical significance levels was far beyond any expectations, and the experiments consistently showed the theoretically derived patterns and outcomes.

In the second chapter[481], four defining characteristics of cognitive biases were introduced[482]: *deviations* from the normative standard, which affect outcomes in a *systematic* and predictable way, appear *involuntarily* and are *hard to avoid*. The empirically observed effects possess these defining characteristics[483]: in all experiments, the null hypothesis – which stated that the respective cognitive bias has no effect and that normative rationality is not violated – was rejected in favor of the

---

480 Including estimation judgments as well as different types of selection decisions in a capital investments related environment.

481 See chapter 3.2.1 for details on the named characteristics and further definitions of cognitive biases in general.

482 See Pohl (2004: p2f).

483 In line with the intention of the research, the experimental set-up was focused on the first three aspects, and covered a broad variety of cognitive biases across different situations. However, the selected methodology and set-up are not adequate to properly prove the fourth aspect: 'hard to avoid'. This would be a potential area for future research. However, the consistency of the observed distortions across many situations, the demonstrated reproducibility, and the high level of statistical significance at least indicate that these distortions are probably hard to avoid.

respective alternative hypothesis, which demonstrates a deviation from the normative standards of rationality. Moreover, the distortions occurred in a systematic way, biasing the outcomes not randomly, but consistently in the direction that was predicted beforehand in the respective research hypothesis. Finally, the biases emerged involuntarily, that is without deliberate will of the participant, and without the participant realizing that his or her decisions were being distorted.

All the above aspects indicate that the observations are not just accidental effects or random artifacts, but systematic distortions. Their functioning and their impact are highly similar to those of cognitive biases in other domains, for instance everyday judgments or financial investment decision making, where the existence and effects of cognitive biases were also first demonstrated in similar experiments and afterwards observed in innumerous real life situations and generalized far beyond the particular laboratory setting. Drawing on this analogy, and on the earlier mentioned similar indications, it seems coherent to conclude that the existence and relevance of cognitive biases for the capital investment domain could also be generalizable beyond the specific experimental situations,[484] at least to a certain extent and subject to potential limitations. These are discussed in the following sections.

4.4.2 Limitations inherent in the General Approach and Methodological Set-Up

Given that the theoretical considerations and the conducted research are based on the fundamentals of the 'heuristics and biases' approach, the majority of potential criticisms and resulting limitations related to the selected approach and the applied methodology are expected to reflect the arguments and critiques raised

---

[484] This would of course not mean that cognitive biases always occur in each and every situation related to capital investments, but only in certain situations – just as it has already been pointed out for all other domains.

against the 'heuristics and biases' in general, which have already been discussed in detail earlier[485]. Many of these critiques are highly general and do not focus on this particular study, but rather only on the fact that the study includes arguments and findings developed in the 'heuristics and biases' tradition. Consequently, repeating and reconsidering these general arguments would not add any additional insights and is seen as redundant. Therefore, only those major arguments that are specific to the particular study conducted are addressed in the following paragraphs, focusing in particular on the 'artificiality' critique.

However, before addressing the criticism of 'artificiality', an additional aspect is to be pointed out concerning the earlier addressed general discussion related to the 'one-sided view' critique of the 'heuristics and biases' approach. With regard to the business context in general, but especially for larger capital investment decisions, a single instance of a distortion can potentially have a very high impact on the company. Accordingly, the criticized primary focus of the 'heuristics and biases' approach on 'faulty cases' need not be seen as a negative argument concerning the domain of capital investments. Contrarily, for companies in today's highly competitive environment it is not enough to be right 'most of the time'[486], but rather they must strive to be right as often as possible, and therefore explicitly concentrate on reducing the 'faulty' cases.

With regard to the conducted research, the key aspect concerning the overarching question "whether or not one can generalize from observed behavior in the laboratory to natural behavior in the world" (Schmuckler, 2001: p419)[487] is

---

485 See chapter 3.4 for a detailed discussion of key critiques and arguments that support and/or refute the individual aspects.

486 In contrast, with regard to simple everyday judgments – which were the focus of cognitive bias research so far, and thus also the reference point for the 'focus on faulty cases only' critique – it is usually sufficient to be right most of the time, because being misled due to simplifying heuristics has often no severe consequences in everyday judgments (but saves a lot of time).

487 This questions is sometimes paraphrased under the term 'ecological validity'. See for instance Neisser (1976), Schmuckler (2001), or Cole et al. (1997) for detailed discussions of ecological validity from different perspectives.

the earlier raised critique of 'artificiality', claiming that the observed biases would not be applicable to the real world at all, because they were only due to the artificial laboratory circumstances and to the highly simplified set-up. This reproach of over-simplicity might for example argue that the selected scenarios were far too simple and not representative of actual decision situations and that no detailed analysis was possible for the participant given the unrealistically low amount of information provided. Admittedly, these issues are rightfully brought up, and consequently they need to be addressed.

It is undoubtedly true that the laboratory conditions are not fully representative of the real life settings and that the selected experimental situations are simplified[488]. However, this has never been denied, nor was it ever claimed that the experiments would provide a complete picture of the reality of capital investment decisions. Instead, it was even pointed out several times that the experiments create simplified situations and that the findings can therefore not be translated universally to real life decisions, but that the respective limitations inherent in the selected approach must be taken into account. Nevertheless, having used a simplified set-up for the experiments does by no means signify that the observed findings can under no circumstances apply to real life settings – it 'just' means that one has to be aware of the restrictions related to the generalizability of laboratory experiments, and that further indications are needed – beyond the findings from an individual experiment – to infer that cognitive biases could also be relevant for other, real life capital investments decisions.

Some aspects that could serve as additional indications have already been summarized earlier, for instance the consistency of the findings across many different types of capital investment decisions and the high level of statistical significance. Also, one might argue that in real life there are also very simple, small, low-involvement business decisions that possess similar features as the

[488] Which applies, to varying degrees, to every model used in all sciences.

decisions presented in the experiments[489]. In addition, time pressure and very limited knowledge are also aspects that could apply to real life capital investment decisions, for instance in a very early stage of the investment process when selecting which investment opportunities might be worth to take a deeper look at[490], or when quickly estimating and justifying the value of a particular input variable while reading a capital investment opportunity business case under time pressure[491]. Furthermore, some experiments might, upon investigation, be actually closer to reality than it seems at first sight: the second experiment on asymmetric dominance simulates a situation in which considerable time and effort has already been invested in the analysis of three different investment options in order to calculate two classical investment appraisal figures: the net present value and the utility value. Both, in the experiment and in real life, the final decision might at the end come down to a trade-off between these two figures. Also, it is probably not unrealistic to assume that the person who takes the final decision – for instance a senior manager – has not conducted the preparatory analyses himself or herself, but that someone else did these analyses, and that the final decision maker's knowledge is therefore to a certain extent limited and does not include all details of the prior analyses. Admittedly, the situation in the experiment is still more simplified than the above described real life situation; however, the 'gap' between experiment and reality is probably not as large as it seemed to be at first sight, though it still exists.

In summary, the above stated aspects do of course not mean that the findings from the experiments apply equally to real life settings. However, they provide

---

[489] The 'content' of such decisions is of course different: they are not about the future location of a production site or a large machine, but concern rather small, low-involvement decisions like which screen to purchase for the office desktop computer. However, the essential features and the applied decision process of the investment decision are comparable.

[490] This could lead to situations with features that are essentially similar to the asymmetric dominance or task framing experiments.

[491] Thereby potentially creating a situation with similar characteristics as in the anchoring experiments.

additional indications of an increased likelihood that the relevance of cognitive biases, which was demonstrated to exist in simplified experimental capital investment situations, could also be applicable in real life capital investment settings. In order to create further insights, it will be necessary to conduct comparable field studies, which complement the conducted laboratory experiments[492], but go far beyond the scope and initial intention of this thesis. Furthermore, given that the conducted research was the first to apply cognitive biases to the domain of capital investments, the logical decision was to conduct laboratory experiments as a first step, and thereby create a solid foundation for extended future studies that might follow afterwards.

Another aspect that should be addressed concerning the general approach and methodological set-up of the conducted research are potential limitations that would result from methodological mistakes. Having committed such mistakes would drastically reduce the generalizability of the findings; actually, this would already reduce or even eradicate the validity of the experiments themselves and the respective findings. Therefore, this aspect has already been addressed and discussed in detail in the sections describing the preparations of the empirical experiments.[493] In particular, in line with best practice methodology for experiments, the precautionary measures of random assignment – to eliminate the influence of participant variables like for instance a priori preferences of participants with regard to risk, personality, sex, etc. – and holding constant of environmental variables have been applied. In combination with the sufficiently large sample size and the selection of adequate statistical test methods, these measures

492 See for instance Esgate et al. (2005: p5ff) or Sternberg (2009: p15ff) for comparative discussions and information on field studies and laboratory experiments.

493 See chapter 4.3.1, and in particular the third step for a detailed discussion of the methodology and potential methodological mistakes, for instance not taking care of participant or environmental variables.

do in general eliminate the risk that the observed findings are pure artifacts of methodological mistakes.

4.4.3 Limitations inherent in the Incongruity between Participant Population and Relevant Real Life Population

Further limitations concerning the generalizability might arise from another major critique that the conducted research could potentially be confronted with: the incongruity between participant population and relevant real life population. This argument might raise two different main areas of critiques: firstly, one might argue that capital investment decisions are not made by individuals, but by groups, and that the cognitive biases would disappear in the case of groups taking the decisions. Secondly, one might argue that students are per se the wrong participant population, and that the cognitive bias would be non-existent if the 'proper' population was addressed. Both parts of this potential critique towards the conducted empirical research seem at first sight obvious and imaginable, and accordingly both need to be addressed in more detail.

The first part of the above critique consists itself of two components: the question whether groups or individuals are the right 'actor' for taking capital investment decisions, and the question if group decisions would eliminate the observed effects of cognitive biases on capital investments. It is undoubtedly true that there are capital investment decisions, which are not taken by individuals, but by teams or so-called buying centers. However, there are certainly also many capital investment decisions that are taken by individuals, for instance smaller decisions, judgments with lower importance, or capital investment decisions in small and medium-sized companies. Consequently, it is probably not possible to universally state whether individuals or groups are the appropriate population.

However, with regard to the above claim that the biases would disappear if the decisions were taken by groups, extensive research[494] in many domains has demonstrated that this is usually not the case: cognitive biases do not per se disappear in group settings[495]; sometimes they are even amplified[496], and, on top, additional biases can occur in group settings[497]. Accordingly, it seems that the first part of the 'incongruity of participant population and relevant population' critique is rather weak, as the distortive effects are not expected to generally disappear, even if groups would take the decisions instead of individuals.[498] Nevertheless, strictly considered, with regard to a potential generalization of the observed findings from the conducted experimental research, one needs to take into account the limitation that they formally only apply to individuals, not to groups, although the research results from other domains suggest that this constraint is relatively weak.

Concerning the second part of the 'incongruity of participant population and relevant population' critique, one has to admit that students are not the perfect participant group. Undoubtedly, experienced capital investment practitioners would be a better fit, from the theoretical perspective.[499] However, besides the practical problem of getting practitioners to take part in the experiments, and

494 See for instance Tenbrunsel et al. (1996: p326), Eliaz et al. (2006), or Montier (2007: p209ff) for discussions of the relevance of individual biases in group settings and for several additional references to empirical research that demonstrates that the cognitive biases do not disappear.

495 See for instance Kerr et al. (1996).

496 See for example Montier (2007: p101).

497 See for instance Bazerman (2006: p176f) for examples of group biases with regard to information sharing and decision making.

498 Nevertheless, this could be another very informative area for future research.

499 Taking into account the earlier discussion on 'artificiality', and combining the arguments, the ideal research set-up would be to conduct proper field experiments with capital investment practitioners. However, this was not feasible for this thesis, especially given that this was the first research in this domain, and that the willingness of companies to participate was therefore, and for several other reasons, very low.

taking into account the fact that the vast majority of research on cognitive biases in many domains is conducted with students, the selected students for the conducted experiments might not have been as unsuitable to function as participants as it seems at first sight. All students that took part in the experiment studied business sciences[500] and the majority was in their third year of studies[501]; accordingly, it can be expected that they have at least adequate some theoretical experience related to and relevant for capital investment decisions. In addition, most students were familiar with similar scenario games or role plays from their studies.

Consequently, taking into account all the above arguments, it can be argued that the selected participant group was not inappropriate for the conducted experiments. Nevertheless, the obvious lack of practical experience of the participating undergraduate students can not be denied, and definitely constitutes a restricting factor for the question of generalizability. However, being aware of this potential limitation, a small replication study was conducted with professionally experienced participants, which is described in the following subchapter.

4.4.4 Replication Study with Professionally Experienced Participants

In contrast to the main series of experiments described so far, the replication study is conducted with post-graduate students. The target of this small-scale study is to obtain a first indication concerning the above discussed potential critique, which claims that the observed findings are only due to the low practical experience of the participants in the main study and that the biasing effects would disappear if participants were more experienced. Accordingly, the research hypo-

---

500 Some participants majored in business-related studies, for example 'industrial engineering', but attended the respective business course – in which the experiments took place – as part of their regular curriculum.

501 In addition, the group of participants included no first-year students at all.

thesis for this replication study is that the distortive effects are also present in the experiments with professionally experienced participants.

For the replication study, a representative subset of four experiments from the main study was selected: one experiment on task framing, one experiment on asymmetric dominance, and two experiments on anchoring[502]. The replication study was conducted in exactly the same way as the main study. Apart from the experience of the participants, all other factors were identical.

In total, in two course sessions at two German universities[503], 73 post-graduate students took part in the replication study. The vast majority of the participating students obtained significant professional experience before their post-graduate studies. On average, the professionally experienced students stated that they have worked for 4 years prior to their post-graduate studies, which is considerably more than the participants in the main study. In addition, the majority of participants were between 26 and 30 years old[504], which is about 5 years older than the participants in the main study.

For all experiments, the 73 participants were randomly assigned to one of two groups[505]. The subsequent analyses of the results correspond to the particular procedures outlined in the main study. Accordingly, the following descriptions of the statistical tests and results are shortened considerably and focus only on the major numbers and aspects.

---

[502] Given that the two anchoring experiments are linked, it was easier to conduct both anchoring experiments instead of having to slightly adapt the instructions and carve out one experiment.

[503] ESB Reutlingen Business School (MBA class) and University of Applied Sciences Hof (Master in marketing management class).

[504] Although participants were not directly quoted for their age, but only marked their age group, it is reasonable to assume – analogously to the reasoning described for the undergraduates – that the average ages is roughly around 28 to 29 years.

[505] Group 1 consisted of 37 participants, group 2 encompassed 36 participants.

Anchoring

Both anchoring experiments were conducted with the 'random-generator' version of presenting the anchor. In the 'likelihood of completion on time' experiment, the sample mean of the first group (high anchor) is 73.2%, in contrast to 43.4% in the second group (low anchor). Due to the results of the respective two-tailed two-sample t-test for unequal variances[506], the null hypothesis (H_0: $\mu_1 = \mu_2$) is rejected in favor of the alternative hypothesis (H_1: $\mu_1 \neq \mu_2$) at the 1% significance level.

In the second anchoring experiment, the 'market share after one year' scenario, the sample means are 9.0% (group 1, low anchor) and 20.0% (group 2, high anchor). The two-tailed two-sample t-test for unequal variances[507] with $\alpha = 0.01$ again resulted in a rejection of the null hypothesis in favor of the alternative hypothesis.

Task Framing

In this experiment, the 'investment into the localization of a product' scenario was again tested empirically, with region A being the 'enriched' option. In the first group ('reject-version'), only 40.5 % of the participants expressed a preference for region A, in contrast to 72.2% in the second group ('select-version'). The results of the two-tailed two-sample z-test[508] imply that the task framing bias leads to a statistically significant reversal of preferences: the null hypothesis is dismissed in favor of the alternative hypothesis.

---

506 The observed t-statistic value of $t = 6.239$ exceeds the critical value of 2.658; $p < 10^{-7}$.

507 The obtained t-statistic value of $t = -6.008$ is below the critical value of -2.658; $p < 10^{-6}$.

508 The observed z-statistic value of $z = -2.729$ is below the critical value of -2.576; p-value is $p < 0.007$.

Asymmetric Dominance

For asymmetric dominance, the 'investment in a new product segment' scenario, in which the decision is taken based on the results of a net present value calculation and an utility value analysis, was selected, due to its proximity to reality. In the first group[509], 64.9% decided to invest in product B, while only 22.2% selected option B in the second group[510]. According to the results of the respective two-tailed two-sample z-test[511], at the 1% significance level the null hypothesis is again dismissed in favor of the alternative hypothesis.

In total, all four experiments of the replication study with professionally experienced participants result in statistically significant violations of normative rationality due to the distortive effects of cognitive biases. The observed findings are completely in line with the earlier findings from the main study with less experienced participants. Moreover, the observed average judgment values for the particular experiments are roughly the same across both groups of participants.[512] Accordingly, the findings indicate that the effects of cognitive biases do by no means disappear if the participants are more experienced. This actually confutes the second claim of the previously addressed 'incongruity of participant population and relevant population' limitation.

509 The decoy is asymmetrically dominated by B

510 Option A asymmetrically dominates the decoy.

511 The observed z-statistic value of $z = 3.676$ exceeds the critical value of 2.576; p-value is $p < 0.0003$.

512 The level of statistical significance in the replication study is lower than in the respective main study experiment. However, given similar judgmental values and averages, this reduced level is presumably due mainly to the considerably lower sample size. Nevertheless, the observed findings of all experiments in the replication study are statistically significant at least at the 1% level, which is already very impressive.

Overall, the above discussions illustrated that the potential generalization of the observed findings from the conducted research is subject to restrictions. In particular, when adopting a formally strict interpretation, the findings are limited to similar artificial laboratory settings with the respective participant population and for individual decision makers. However, the above discussions also illustrated that there are many arguments which indicate that the observed findings might also apply beyond the respective limitations. For instance, the experimental set-up is in fact by no means as far away from reality as it might have seemed at first sight. Furthermore, the results of the replication study indicate that cognitive biases also affect professionals with more experience. All these aspects signify that the distortive effects of cognitive biases, which could be demonstrated in a broad series of experiments in this thesis, also seem to be relevant for other capital investment situations and for real life capital investment contexts. However, further research[513] is needed to generate deeper insights in this area and fortify this indication.

In summary, the theoretical considerations, the observed empirical findings and the critical discussions support the initial research hypothesis of this thesis and provide solid indications that cognitive biases do exist in a capital investment environment – at least in particular settings – and violate in a systematic and reproducible way several fundamental principles of normative rationality. These considerations suggest that the respective decisions are negatively affected and that accordingly countermeasures are required to reduce potential detrimental effects. The following chapter addresses this issue.

[513] There is a large variety of potential areas for research. See chapter 6.2 for a discussion of potential set-ups and content-related foci for these.

5 Debiasing and Potential Countermeasures against Cognitive Biases

This chapter describes potential actions that could be undertaken to reduce the negative effects of cognitive biases. The first part points out that cognitive biases are usually rather robust. Subsequently, the second part discusses a selection of countermeasures that potentially attenuate their detrimental effects. The last part finally introduces a general approach for companies to create of a strategy that mitigates cognitive biases in a business context, and addresses factors that might inhibit the adoption of particular debiasing techniques.

This chapter primarily wants to provide a high-level overview of debiasing and the related techniques, and does not intend to discuss particular countermeasures in full detail or provide an in-depth recommendation for a universal counterstrategy.[514]

5.1 Robustness of Cognitive Biases

One of the earlier discussed[515] key characteristics of cognitive biases is their persistency and robustness: they are hard to avoid[516] and subjectively nearly incorrigible up to a certain point[517]. Approaching this from a theoretical perspective, Bazerman (2006: p194) argues that "many behaviors at the individual, group, and organizational level are ingrained, or part of a standard repertoire, and are therefore quite difficult to change". In addition, given that cognitive biases

---

514 On the one hand, because this would go far beyond the intention and also the scope of this thesis, and on the other hand, because no simple, universal solution exists. Accordingly, developing counterstrategies against cognitive biases in a particular company context would have to go beyond the general approach introduced in a later part of this chapter: it is partly very individual and requires customized considerations.

515 See chapter 3.2.1.

516 See for instance Pohl (2004: p2f).

517 See Piatelli-Palmarini (1994: p140).

affect decision making unconsciously, it is very hard for the decision maker to detect their effects. However, even if one is aware of a bias and tries to avoid it, the bias usually remains.[518]

A large body of studies in different domains and concerning different cognitive biases confirms this persistency. For instance, Fischhoff's (1982b) meta analysis impressively describes the extreme robustness of two biases: the 'hindsight bias' and the 'overconfidence bias'. Similarly, extensive empirical research has demonstrated the persistency of many other cognitive biases, for example asymmetric dominance[519] or anchoring biases, which occur in a large variety of different domains[520], are not reduced if payments are rewarded for accuracy[521] and even emerge if participants are explicitly made aware of the anchor's effects[522]. In addition, research shows that cognitive biases also affect experts[523] and likewise occur in professional contexts[524].

With regard to the empirical experiments conducted in the previous chapter[525], the fact that comparable anchoring effects occurred consistently and systematically for different versions of presenting the anchor value – in particular also for the 'roll-the-dice' version, which made the irrelevant nature of the anchor value extremely obvious – could also be seen as another indication for the robustness of the particular cognitive bias. In addition, the results of the

518 See Bazerman (2006: p194).

519 See for example Colman et al. (2007), Park/Kim (2005), or Hedgcock/Rao (2009).

520 See for instance Mussweiler et al. (2004: p185f) for an extensive list of research examples.

521 See for example Tversky/Kahneman (1974: p1130) or Chapman/Johnson (2002: p125).

522 See for instance Chapman/Johnson (2002: p125) or Wilson et al. (1996).

523 See for example Shafir/Tversky (1995: p84) for framing effects observed in physicians.

524 See for instance Joyce/Biddle (1981) for empirical examples of practicing auditors being influenced by the anchoring effects.

525 The demonstration of robustness was not among the intentions of this empirical research. Accordingly, the selected set-up of the conducted experiments considerably limits potential insights on the persistency of cognitive biases.

replication study with professionally experienced participants further support the impression that the particular cognitive biases examined in the empirical experiments are rather robust.

In summary, the above arguments indicate that it is probably nearly impossible to fully eliminate cognitive biases. Based on these examples from various domains, there is no indication or any other reason to believe that this should be different when it comes to the effects of cognitive biases in a capital investment environment. Accordingly, given the high importance of many capital investment decisions, it is necessary to find measures to at least attenuate the respective negative effects. The major ones are introduced in the following sections.

5.2 Debiasing Techniques

In this sub-chapter, the term 'debiasing' is briefly defined and a selection of counteracting techniques[526] from three areas is introduced and evaluated at a basic level[527]: 'knowledge, experience, and expertise', 'incentives and accountability', and 'training and tools'.[528]

---

[526] Including both countermeasures that – based on research – seem to be suitable as well as strategies which are frequently believed to be appropriate, although actually they are usually not.

[527] With regard to countermeasures, there is a very large variety of different – partly ambiguous and contradictory – approaches, arguments, findings, and understandings. The intention here is to briefly address the most important and most frequently stated areas of potential countermeasures and provide, on a basic level, a selection of general arguments and research results in line with the major opinions and findings of the respective literature. An in-depth discussion of all aspects and facets would go far beyond this thesis's scope and intention.

[528] The aspects discussed in this and the following chapter apply not only to capital investments, but also to most other types of important business decisions. Accordingly, despite the frequent use of the superordinate term 'business context' in the remaining part of this chapter, all considerations equally apply to the capital investment context as well.

5.2.1 Definition of Debiasing in General

Bazerman (2006: p193) defines debiasing as "a procedure for reducing or eliminating biases from the cognitive strategies of the decision maker". In general, it consists of three steps or components[529]: unfreezing, change, and refreezing.[530] The first step – unfreezing – requires that one realizes the deviation from the normative standard and is willing to act on this insight. Subsequently, the next step – change – means that one understands the bias and the underlying rationales and develops strategies to counteract them. The third step, refreezing, finally demands that one repeatedly applies the new strategies until they have fully replaced the earlier ones: "Refreezing involves integrating the changes into the personality or cognitive make-up of the individual" (Arnott, 2006: p63).

However, although this might give the impression that debiasing is a simple, quick and easy procedure, the opposite is actually often the case. As pointed out earlier, cognitive biases are usually very robust and persistent, and accordingly successful debiasing requires considerable time and effort.[531] In addition, being aware of the biases, accepting their existence and being willing to act and change are vital prerequisites for applying the countermeasures that are introduced in the following sections. In fact, these countermeasures – also referred to as debiasing techniques – actually constitute already the second step in the unfreezing-change-refreezing framework presented above: they facilitate the change. The stated prerequisites represent in effect the first step of the framework.

---

529 See Bazerman (2006: p194ff), whose approach actually builds on a more general model of social change, which was initially developed by Lewin (1947) and subsequently refined by Schein (1996).

530 The presented unfreezing-change-refreezing framework summarizes the essential features of debiasing in a comprehensible and general way. A considerably more complex and detailed framework of debiasing and debiasing methods is for instance presented by Fischhoff (1982b).

531 See for example Keren (1990) for additional information on debiasing in general and on debiasing processes, including procedural and structure modifying elements.

5.2.2 Knowledge, Experience, and Expertise

A frequently stated claim, which is also brought up regularly by critics of the 'heuristics and biases' approach, is that knowing about a bias or having experience in a certain content area will eliminate the bias. Accordingly, acquiring knowledge and experience is often proposed as one potential technique that counteracts the effects of cognitive biases.

However, it seems that this is not the case. Although knowledge about the existence of judgmental heuristics and the resulting biases could help to avoid some specific types of errors[532], this is usually only the case for rather simple errors, and does not hold for the majority of distortions in question. For example, research demonstrates that anchoring even occurs if participants are specifically made aware of the anchor's effects[533] and that the 'hindsight bias' remains even if it is explicitly described to participants[534].

Similarly, experience does not automatically reduce or eliminate cognitive biases. For instance, although mathematically sophisticated people can avoid simple, statistically elementary errors like the gambler's fallacy[535], they still commit the same judgmental errors like others in less elementary cases.[536] Moreover, having experience in a particular professional domain usually does not make one immune against the effects of cognitive biases in this area, which is for instance demonstrated by Fennema/Perkins (2008) for experienced chartered accountants with regard to finance-related biases, by Shafir/Tversky (1995: p84) for framing effects observed in physicians, or by McCarthy et al. (1993) for

532 See Gerrig/Zimbardo (2008: p263).

533 See for instance Chapman/Johnson (2002: p125) or Wilson et al. (1996).

534 See for example Mandel (2006) or Harley et al. (2004).

535 Falsely believing that past events influence independent future events, for instance believing that past outcomes at a roulette table (for example 4 times red in a row) influence the likelihood of an independent future event (for example to have red again in the next turn).

536 See for instance Tversky/Kahneman (1974: p1130).

investment behavior biases of entrepreneurs.[537] The results of the replication study conducted for this thesis also support this notion: although the participants in the second study were considerably more experienced[538], the effects of the cognitive biases were still highly distortive and indicated the same violations of normative rationality as in the first study with less experienced participants. One potential explanation for this frequently found ineffectiveness of experience as debiasing technique is suggested by Brehmer (1980: p223): people are subject to "a number of biases which prevent them from using the information which experience provides".

However, other findings[539] indicate a less negative and more ambiguous picture with regard to experience, for example concerning the 'sunk cost' bias[540]: although the above addressed type of experience – in the respective study measured as years of financially related work experience – had no effect on the particular cognitive bias, another type of more specific experience – in the respecttive study the number of accounting courses attended – seemed to have a counteracting effect[541] on the 'sunk cost' bias. As a consequence, it might be necessary to distinguish between experience and expertise[542], with expertise meaning "the development of a schematic principle that involves conceptual

---

537 Further cases are for instance described by Staw/Hoang (1995) for sports-related sunk cost effects found in professional sports decision makers or by Kidd (1970) in relation to engineers' judgments regarding technical projects.

538 They had obtained considerably more professional experience as well as academic experience compared to the participants in the first study.

539 See for instance Garland et al. (1990) on experimental behavior related to oil exploration.

540 See Fennema/Perkins (2008).

541 The authors argue that this is presumably because approaches to properly address the issue of sunk costs are usually taught in accounting classes, and that the participants with many accounting courses had therefore acquired the appropriate expertise to spot and overcome this particular bias.

542 See for instance Bereby-Meyer/Grosskopf (2008) or Neale/Northcraft (1990) for discussions of experience and expertise.

understanding of the problem" (Bereby-Meyer/Grosskopf, 2008: p24), which in turn enables the decision maker to recognize particular biases[543]. However, using expertise as countermeasure necessitates more than just being familiar with the situational content or being an expert in a particular domain. It requires that one fully understands the underlying rationale of the respective bias, is able to spot it in the particular setting, and also has the appropriate tools[544] at hand to counteract the bias.[545]

Nevertheless, despite some interesting and promising findings for very specific and rather simple biases, and given the highly specific character of expertise, its general usefulness as potential counteracting strategy is also expected to be constrained due to transferability limitations, both across different content areas as well as across different types of cognitive biases. Furthermore, the hitherto research findings are far from being clear and coherent concerning the above aspects.[546] Accordingly, considerably more research is needed to further clarify the suitability – or inadequacy – of knowledge, experience and expertise as possible countermeasures.

5.2.3 Incentives and Accountability

The second area of potential debiasing techniques is based on another frequently stated claim of many critics: biases can be eliminated by properly motivating decision makers. If they were correct, then the impact of cognitive biases could be drastically reduced, or even eradicated, by applying motivational strategies like offering incentives or establishing accountability.

---

543 See Bazerman (2006: p193).

544 For instance those tools that are referred to in chapter 5.2.4.

545 Accordingly, acquiring relevant expertise is very closely linked to training, which is addressed in the next but one section.

546 See for instance Hinds (1999), who presents studies in which expertise actually amplified the observed distortive effects.

With regard to providing incentives, which is probably the most frequently used motivational strategy, a large body of research[547] indicates that these usually do not reduce the effects of cognitive biases. Although there are also few instances where incentives slightly improved decision making for particular tasks, the general opinion to date is that incentives do not systematically make decisions better with regard to the effects of cognitive biases.[548] For instance, early research already indicated that biases occur even if subjects are encouraged to be accurate and are rewarded for correct answers[549]. Recent research further supports this notion that biases are usually not reduced even if payments are offered for accuracy.[550] In some cases, introducing incentives can even lead to a deterioration of decision making quality and judgmental performance.[551]

Another motivational strategy that is frequently suggested as potential countermeasure to reduce the detrimental effects of cognitive biases is assigning accountability. Accountability is very closely linked to justification – which describes the process of explaining a decision or a judgment –, because accountability usually means that one has to or at least must be prepared to justify one's judgments.[552] In general, having to justify a decision[553] is expected to increase self-criticisms and thus to improve the likelihood of detecting potential flaws in one's reasoning. However, actual findings are less clear: the effects of accountability on judgments involving cognitive biases seem highly variable across tasks and

547 See for example Hsee et al. (2004), Camerer/Hogarth (1999), or Larrick (2004).

548 Camerer/Hogarth (1999: p33) even state that "there is no replication study in which a theory of rational choice was rejected at low stakes in favor of a well-specified behavioral alternative, and accepted at high stakes". Although this is probably a bit too pessimistic, it probably fits for the majority of cases.

549 See Tversky/Kahneman (1974: p1130).

550 See for example Chapman/Johnson (2002: p125) on anchoring biases.

551 See for instance Arkes et al. (1986) or Hogarth et al. (1991).

552 See Johnson/Kaplan (1991).

553 Or alternatively expecting that one will have to justify one's decision,

individuals, and are found – depending on the study – to slightly improve, or deteriorate, or even not at all affect the respective violation of rationality.[554] Furthermore, due to its social component, accountability can produce unwanted side-effects and, in particular situations, eventually amplify existing biases and even create additional biases.[555] For instance, being accountable and having to justify decisions to an audience with known preferences can lead to a behavior consistent with the 'confirmation trap' bias. Similarly, some biases like asymmetric dominance or the 'compromise effect' are fostered and amplified by the need to provide justification.

In summary, the adequacy and effectiveness of these motivational strategies is highly ambiguous. Although there seem to be a few cases where they did reduce the effect of a particular cognitive bias, the majority of findings indicate that incentives and accountability do not systematically and significantly reduce the impact of these distortions. Furthermore, motivational strategies implicitly require that the decision maker actually has the ability to take a better and unbiased decision[556]; if he or she does not have adequate competencies or tools at hand, all strategies based on motivation are doomed to fail. Accordingly, this again points towards training as a potential solution – and in this case as a prerequisite – to counteracting the effects of cognitive biases.

5.2.4 Training and Tools

One quintessence of the above discussions of the two most frequently suggested areas of potential countermeasures is that training might play a key role for debiasing efforts.[557] In general, training can take different forms, ranging from

---

554 See for instance Lerner/Tetlock (1999), Simonson/Nye (1992), or Fennema/Perkins (2008).

555 See Larrick (2004: p322f).

556 See Fennema/Perkins (2008: p232ff).

557 Both, as a means by itself, but also as necessary precondition for being able to apply other debiasing techniques.

simple techniques – for example 'consider the opposite'[558], which directs attention to contrary evidence, 'ask an outsider'[559], which supports a change of perspective, or 'analysis of competing hypotheses'[560], which helps to align multiple hypotheses with observed data – over general training in relevant areas – for instance in reasoning and statistics – to advanced procedures like 'analogical reasoning', 'examining the difference'[561], or 'reference class analysis'[562].

Although the general focus of debiasing shifted only recently towards examining training in more depth as a potential countermeasure against the effects of cognitive biases, several research findings indicate that specific training and the application of the respective techniques can help to reduce the distortive effects of particular biases.[563] However, research also indicates that even the simplest techniques – for instance actively seeking disconfirming evidence, or giving dissenting voices the opportunity to properly express themselves – are to date only applied by a minority of companies.[564]

---

558 See for example Soll/Klayman (2004) or Larrick (2004: p323f).

559 See for instance Kahneman/Lovallo (1993) or Bazerman (2006: p198f).

560 See for example Heuer (1999: p95ff9 or Wheaton/Chido (2006).

561 See for instance Bazerman (2006: p196f): both tools incorporate the use of different learning exercise techniques and environments – for instance cases, simulations, and real-world experiences – in combination with a subsequent reflection and focus on linking the learning between several exercises through analogies, which can help to improve debiasing and generate overarching insights. 'Examining the difference' is essentially similar to 'analogical reasoning', but focuses on the differences instead of the similarities and common aspects.

562 See Horn et al. (2005) for a detailed description of 'reference class analysis', which involves looking at a group of similar business situations and draw conclusions from analyzing them.

563 See for example Mussweiler et al. (2000) for examples of positive effects due to the 'consider the opposite' training strategy or Thompson et al. (2000) for examples of successful efforts on debiasing via 'analogical reasoning'.

564 See Dye et al. (2009: p2), who report that only about a third of all survey companies (n = 2.207) "actively sought evidence contrary to initial plan". Similarly, for the majority of decisions, dissenting opinions were not given adequate possibilities to express their concerns.

In addition, the above referred to studies all focused on very specific, usually simple biases. How effective training is for more complex and demanding biases is not clear yet. For instance, Sanna et al. (2002) report that using a simple technique – to think about and list possible alternative outcomes – actually increased the distortive effect of the respective cognitive bias in many cases.[565] In addition, the transferability across domains and especially across biases is expected to be limited. Furthermore, other findings point out that training often only improves the performance of a share of participants, not of all, and that the positive effect can disappear after some time. Moutier/Houdé (2003), for example, conducted experiments with participants who received intensive conjunction fallacy inhibition training. Participants were tested before and after the training. However, only a share of the participants improved their decision making for the particular type of task, but the majority did not improve. Furthermore, delayed post-tests indicated that the improvement was reduced and disappeared over time. Nevertheless, training could be a potential countermeasure against cognitive biases, but further research is needed.

A similar debiasing approach is the use of statistical tools. During the past years and decades, the combination of technological progress and theoretical advancements fostered the development of highly sophisticated techniques to assist in decision making. These include a large variety of different methods like simple linear models, various decision analysis techniques, for instance based on multi attribute decision making theory, or comprehensive decision support systems that incorporate highly sophisticated statistical procedures.[566] Empirical

---

565 Sanna et al. (2002: p497) argue that this presumably happened because "listing many counterfactual thoughts was experienced as difficult and [...] the experienced difficulty suggested that there were not many ways in which the event might have turned out otherwise".

566 See for instance Larrick (2004: p327ff) for an overview of and introduction to various tools, including among others decision analysis, methods based on multi attribute utility, and decision support systems.

findings[567] available to date suggest that applying these statistical techniques does improve decision making with regard to specific cognitive biases, in particular biases linked to probability, for instance 'neglect of base rates', 'insensitivity to sample sizes', or the 'regression to the mean' bias.

The use of these tools is very closely linked to training: the user must understand the tool, know how it works and how to properly apply it, understand its respective constraints and limitations, and be able to select the appropriate tool for the respective situation. This requires extensive training and significant efforts, at least for the more sophisticated tools. Furthermore, given that applying sophisticated techniques is often time consuming, it is impossible to base every single potentially biased decision on these techniques. This, in turn, means that the decision maker has to decide if an advanced decision tool is to be applied – and if yes which one –, which could again open the door for cognitive biases. Moreover, the seeming suitability of advanced decision tools for mitigating some distortions could potentially lead to an overreliance on these tools. In addition, despite their intuitive appeal as countermeasure, every tool has its particular limitations and constraints[568], which need to be taken into account, and even the most sophisticated tools are not per se immune against methodology-based effects

---

567 See for example Payne et al. (1999) for respective applications of decision analysis techniques, Arnott (2006) with regard to decision support systems, or Dawes (1971) for very early examples of success with linear models.

568 One needs to take into account that these statistical tools have originally not been developed to counter cognitive biases, but for other purposes. Accordingly, they can only be properly applied as a countermeasure for the respective cases and for specific biases.

that are similar to the impact of cognitive biases.[569] Accordingly, one needs the right tools at the right time and must be able to apply them in the right way to the right problem. In addition, "it takes time, effort, and courage for an organization to move from relying on faulty intuition to carefully assessing data and using appropriate statistical techniques" (Bazerman, 2006: p190). However, this effort might be worthwhile, as the selective application of simple techniques and statistical methods, accompanied by adequate training – both to understand the tool and know how to use it as well as to decide when to use it – seems to be a promising starting point to reduce the detrimental effects of cognitive biases.[570]
In summary, the previous parts briefly introduced several potential debiasing techniques and illustrated that this aspect of cognitive biases is still in an early phase and thus highly ambiguous. The most promising approach to date seems to be a combination of training and tools. Despite some limitations, and although this is not expected to completely eliminate all biases, it could at least help to reduce the magnitude of the detrimental effects.

5.3 Counterstrategies

With regard to the distortions addressed throughout this thesis, companies simply "cannot trust [...] biases to be inconsequential, and accordingly, strategies for the detection and correction of biased inferences are needed" (Taylor, 1982: p200).

---

569 Although sophisticated tools can help to reduce certain biases, the biases of human beings on the individual level that the tool helps to avoid might be reproduced on the methodological level of the tool itself. For instance, in the case of the 'analytical hierarchy protocol' (AHP), a multi-attribute decision making tool, in particular circumstances preference reversals can occur when adding additional options. This is, to a certain extent, similar to the asymmetric dominance bias observed in human beings.

570 However, as pointed out in the final chapter, further research is required to obtain a more detailed picture of the cases and conditions under which training and tools properly counteract the effects of cognitive biases.

However, given the diversity of companies' capital investment activities, and the large variety of potentially influential cognitive biases, companies have to develop an individualized counterstrategy that considers their particular situation. This sub-chapter outlines a general framework that can serve as a foundation for this purpose and briefly addresses factors that potentially inhibit the adoption of countermeasures in general.

Serfas (2008: p13ff) suggests a comprehensive general approach for developing a counterstrategy against cognitive biases in a business context. It consists of five distinct elements, which are depicted in the following illustration:

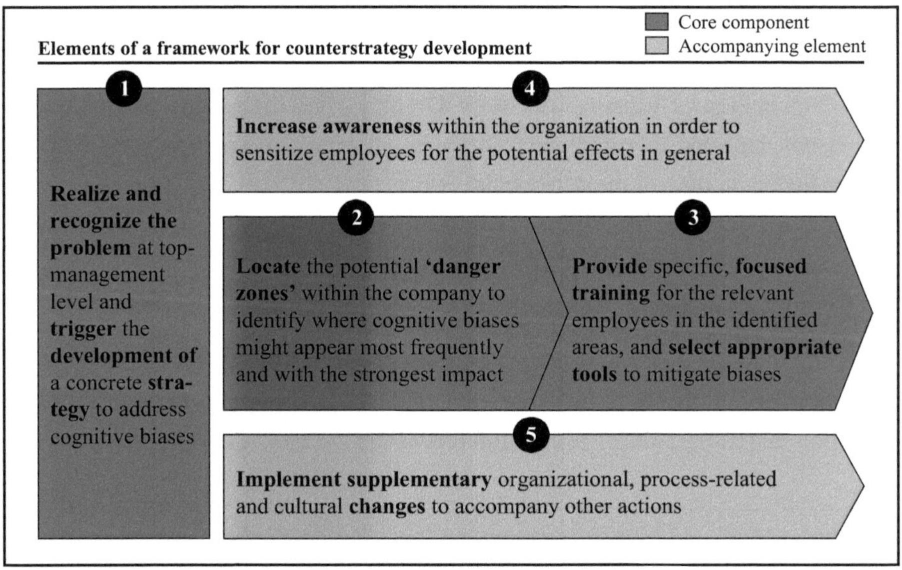

Illustration 20: Potential approach for developing a counterstrategy[571]

[571] Based on the description and discussion in Serfas (2008: p13ff).

The above illustrated approach[572] distinguishes between three core steps and two accompanying – but by no means less important – components. It highlights, from a generic perspective, the key steps and activities a company has to undertake in order to develop a suitable counterstrategy against the distortions addressed earlier.

The first step is to become aware of the existence of cognitive biases and to realize that their effects can be harmful in a business context, in order to subsequently trigger the development of a counterstrategy. It is absolutely vital that the top management is heavily involved in this step and that the process of finding ways to reduce the organization's vulnerability with regard to the impact of cognitive biases is driven and backed by senior managers.[573] However, to obtain their support, these managers first have to be made aware that important business decisions could be subject to particular unconscious distortions and they have to realize their potential detrimental impact. Accordingly, the target of this first step is to obtain a clear commitment from the top management to address cognitive biases and to develop a respective counterstrategy.

The next step is to locate the potential 'danger zones' within the organization. One has to identify those areas and types of decisions within the company where the effects of cognitive biases potentially have the strongest negative impact. Accordingly, it is advisable to focus first of all on these 'danger zones'. Typical 'danger zones' include for instance activities related to the preparation and analysis of business cases for capital investments[574] – for example an investment in a new production facility, the expansion of an existing plant, or the development of a new product –, high-level strategic decisions, or risk manage-

[572] Although the following part builds primarily on the original approach, the respective description goes partly beyond the original concept and refines it where suitable.

[573] If this initiative is not supported by the top managers, it will likely not be sufficiently paid attention to by all other employees, and is therefore doomed to fail.

[574] See the discussion in chapter 4.2.2 for detailed examples of the potential impact of cognitive biases on these decisions.

ment related considerations[575]. The end product of this second step is a clear, prioritized list containing the most important 'danger zones' for the particular company.[576]

The third step subsequently focuses on mitigating and reducing the effect that cognitive biases could have in each of the identified 'danger zones'. Accordingly, every affected member of staff receives adequate training that focuses on the individual area, duties, and working environment, and increases the ability to spot and cope with cognitive biases. Depending on the situation, different training elements have to be selected and tailored.[577] For example, if the previous analysis revealed that the 'confirmation trap' bias could be highly relevant for a particular business decision that is frequently taken, then the simple technique 'consider the opposite' could be one suitable remedy. In addition, where appropriate, employees could be provided with adequate tools, for instance decision support systems or statistical programs, as well as with the necessary knowledge to properly handle these tools. Accordingly, the aim of this third step is to have identified a tailored set of debiasing techniques for each 'danger zone' and to have trained the respective employees in using these countermeasures.

However, just following the three steps described above is likely not enough. Although the areas and decisions that currently seem to be the most important ones are covered, only a small set of people in the organization are addressed so far. This is not sufficient in the long run, for instance because other endangered areas could exist that have been understated or overlooked, or new 'danger zones' could emerge somewhere else without being noticed. Accordingly, a counter-strategy against cognitive biases must be accompanied by actions that increase the general awareness within the organization and sensitize a substantially larger

---

[575] See chapter 4.2.1 for an illustrative case addressing the effects of cognitive biases in this context.

[576] The content of this list is expected to vary between companies, for example due to different business models or industry environments.

[577] See chapter 5.2.4 for a discussion of training and tools as debiasing techniques.

number of employees. In addition, the above described steps have to be supplemented by organizational, process-related, and cultural changes. For instance, the management should encourage everyone to seek and openly discuss disconfirmatory information with the same vigor as supporting evidence. Accordingly, the managers have to foster "an organizational environment that promotes and rewards the kind of critical thinking [...] for example, analysis on difficult issues that considers in depth a series of plausible hypotheses rather than allowing the first credible hypothesis to suffice" (Heuer, 1999: pxxiv). Additionally, introducing the four-eye-principle[578] for specific sets of decisions can also be a simple measure to mitigate some biases, in particular those related to a decision maker's individual experiences that impact availability. With regard to the earlier mentioned example of capital investment business cases, potential changes could for instance include institutionalized investment procedures, a central, standardized database for investment proposals with a shared data pool, or explicit, overarching guidelines for the preparation and evaluation of these business cases.[579]

Implementing these two accompanying elements in addition to the three previously described core activities enables companies to develop comprehensive counterstrategies against the most severe effects of cognitive biases. However, one has to be aware that this must not be a one-off exercise; instead, frequent attention and continuous improvement are necessary to reduce the detrimental impact that cognitive biases can have on business decisions in general and capital investment decisions in particular.

---

578 Meaning in this case that at least two persons take a specific decision together, instead of one person deciding alone.

579 See Serfas (2008: p15).

A similar approach, consisting of four steps, is suggested by Lovallo/Sibony (2010: p41ff):[580] The first step consists of selecting which decisions are worth the effort. The authors argue that two types of relevant decisions exist – rare, one-of-a-kind strategic decision and repetitive high-stake decisions – and that "in most companies, there are generally no more than one or two such critical processes" (Lovallo/Sibony, 2010: p42). In the second step, the cognitive biases that are most likely to affect these selected critical decision are identified. Subsequently, in the third step, practices and tools are determined that could be used to counter the most relevant biases. Finally, these practices have to be embedded in the formal processes of the organization.

In contrast to the earlier described counterstrategy framework, the second approach focuses strongly on mitigation through formal procedures and processes, and concentrates on a small set of highly influential decisions. A common element of both counterstrategy approaches presented above is the bias-specific selection of debiasing techniques. Accordingly, companies also need to address the issue of ensuring that the selected countermeasures and the developed strategy are properly implemented and that the intended results materialize.

However, although some potential measures – for instance simple training techniques like 'consider the opposite' – are relatively easy to implement, there are several factors that inhibit individuals from changing their decision making behavior and from appropriately adopting countermeasures. These factors also favor a – maybe partly conscious, but potentially mainly unconscious – resistance against debiasing and debiasing strategies.[581] One potential reason for this lies in the 'overconfidence bias', which is intrinsic to most human beings: a deep-rooted

---

580 As this approach ('four steps to adopting behavioral strategy') is only rather briefly sketched by Lovallo/Sibony (2010) themselves, and given that it is to a certain extent similar to the earlier described approach by Serfas (2008), this second approach is only outlined very briefly here.

581 See for example Larrick (2004: p331ff) or Bazerman (2006: p194f) for further information on the mentioned inhibiting factors.

believe that one is a very good judge. In addition, many decision makers are satisfied with the status quo – for instance because they do not realize or do not want to accept that they are subject to certain biases, as this would mean to admit that they did it 'wrong' in the past, or because they fail to understand the benefits of debiasing – and are risk averse when it comes to relinquishing control over the decision process. Accordingly, they prefer the certain outcome of known behavior to the uncertain outcome of innovate behavior.

These factors also have to be taken into account when discussing potential measures to reduce the effects of cognitive biases, and they especially have to be taken care of and addressed when developing and implementing counter-strategies, because, as pointed out earlier, awareness and willingness to change are vital prerequisites for the success of any approach to counteracting cognitive biases.

6 Conclusion

This chapter summarizes the major aspects addressed in each of the preceding chapters and identifies possible approaches and relevant fields for additional research.

6.1 Overall Summary

The overall target of this thesis was to look for indications – both from a theoretical and from an empirical perspective – that signify whether or not cognitive biases can emerge in a capital investment context and systematically violate normative rationality then. In total, the obtained findings from the theoretical considerations and the empirical experiments constitute solid indications for affirming the above research question.

Following an introductory first chapter covering the origin and academic relevance of this research question, the *second chapter* introduced the properties and characteristics of capital investments and their appraisal, in order to build a common basis for the discussions in later chapters. The first part focused on investments in general and capital investments in particular. Following a description of several potential approaches to defining investments in general – the major one being based on sequences of cash inflows and cash outflows over time –, a classification into financial and capital investments has been introduced and the major characteristics of capital investments – in particular the high initial investment and the long-run time horizon – have been addressed. Subsequently, the major phases of a typical capital investment project have been described and key activities named.

The second part of this chapter introduced decision theory and decision models, which form the base for decision making, also in the context of capital investments. The description of the fundamentals of decision theory revealed two approaches: descriptive models explain how decisions are actually taken in real life, and normative models prescribe how decisions should be made. The foundation for many normative models is the basic concept of rationality, which has been addressed subsequently, including a short discussion of three exemplary postulates that are part of its underlying axiomatic system: comparability, transitivity and invariance. The last section finally outlined the key components of decision models – acts, states, and outcomes, as well as a system of goals and preferences – and introduced different types of uncertainty.

The third part finally described the investment appraisal process in general and introduced selected appraisal models, beginning with two static tools – the accounting rate of return method and the payback period approach – that do not take into account the time value of money. Subsequently, two frequently used dynamic methods – the NPV method and the IRR approach – were presented, which overcome this deficiency of static models. The last section finally highlighted several sophisticated techniques, focusing on methods that incorporate uncertainty into the decision making process and on approaches for multiple attribute decision making.

The intention of the *third chapter* was to give an introduction to and provide a basic understanding of the 'heuristics and biases' approach and several cognitive biases, in order to establish the foundation for the following theoretical discussions and empirical analyses. The first part covered the fundamentals of psychology in general and cognitive psychology in particular. Having defined psychology and distinguished several of its contemporary perspectives and approaches, the subsequent sections focused on cognitive psychology – one of the major sub-disciplines of psychology –, which studies mental information processing activities and the resulting behavioral consequences. The final sections then briefly addressed content-related subjects and major sub-disciplines of cognitive psychology.

The second part of this third chapter focused primarily on the 'heuristics and biases' approach initiated by Daniel Kahneman and Amos Tversky in the 1970s. Following a short introduction to heuristics – 'mental shortcuts' to information processing –, cognitive biases have been defined as mental errors caused by the unconscious use of these simplified information processing strategies by human beings, and their characteristics have been discussed. Subsequently, three fundamental heuristics – availability, representativeness, and anchoring – were introduced and the cognitive biases that result from each of them have been described and discussed in detail.

The third part of this chapter introduced a selection of further relevant cognitive biases that go beyond the three fundamental heuristics. Each of the selected four groups of distortions – framing effects, irrational relativity, action and inaction preferences, and overconfidence effects – was described and the respective cognitive biases were explained, in order to illustrate the multitude and diversity of cognitive biases and the large variety of different ways in which they can distort decision making.

The last part of the third chapter finally addressed several frequently raised critiques faced by the 'heuristics and biases' approach – for instance the allegation of 'artificiality' with regard to its underlying research –, and critically discussed the major arguments and issues. This resulted in the conclusion that although some of the critical arguments are valid to a certain extent, many of the key criticisms are not fully justified and can be rebutted.

The overall aim of the fourth chapter was to combine the considerations and concepts of the two preceding chapters and to examine whether cognitive biases are relevant in the context of capital investments. Accordingly, the first part addressed preparatory considerations from a theoretical perspective. It started with a description of the widely accepted and repeatedly demonstrated existence of cognitive biases in several general business contexts – for example in marketing, human resource management and negotiations –, and their effects. Subsequently, the focus was on investment-related activities and decisions. A short excursus on 'behavioral finance' addressed theoretical implications and empirical evidence with regard to cognitive biases and demonstrated that their effects are very relevant for financial investment decision making. Subsequently, analogies between financial and capital investment were discussed, which indicated several impediments to empirically testing potential hypotheses about cognitive biases in the capital investment context, but also found that the basic concept and rationale of both types of investments are quite similar, which favors the underlying hypothesis that cognitive biases could also be relevant for capital investments. Finally, it was established that cognitive biases are expected to be primarily relevant in the stimulation and decision phases of the capital investment life cycle, and also to a certain extent in the disinvestment phase.

The fourth chapter's second part complemented the earlier considerations by presenting two illustrative, fictitious case examples that demonstrated the potentially distortive impact of cognitive biases on capital investment related decisions. The first example illustrated in detail how several cognitive biases could influence activities related to identifying and evaluating risks for a capital investment project, focusing on biases that stem from the availability and representativeness heuristics. The second case example described in detail the potential influence of cognitive biases when preparing and analyzing business cases for capital investment opportunities, focusing exemplarily on the 'confirmation trap', anchoring biases, and distortions related to interrelations. In total, both case examples illustrated that cognitive biases could potentially affect capital investment related decisions.

The third and major part of this chapter addressed the design, execution and analysis of eight empirical experiments covering a broad range of different capital investment decision making situations. Following a detailed description of the overall approach and methodology of the conducted experiments – which focused on three distinct cognitive biases: anchoring, task framing, and asymmetric dominance –, each one was described in detail, including a refinement of the underlying theory and an in-depth analysis of the respective results. Every single experiment yielded statistically significant results and demonstrated the hypothesized distortive effects, which resulted in clear violations of various principles of normative rationality. In total, the results of the experimental series strongly support the research hypothesis and indicate that cognitive biases are relevant for capital investments.

The last part of this chapter finally addressed the question regarding the possibility of generalizing the obtained results and outlined potential restrictions. On the one hand, it was pointed out that, strictly interpreted, the potential generalization is subject to some limitations, inherent in the selected approach and methodological set-up, and in the incongruity of participant population and relevant real life population. On the other hand, the discussion highlighted many aspects that considerably relativized and attenuated the respective limitations. In addition, several potential critiques concerning the conducted research were addressed, critically discussed in detail and largely refuted. Furthermore, in reaction to the possible critique that the distortive effects would disappear if more experienced participants had been selected, a replication study was conducted with professionally experienced participants. This yielded equally significantly distorted results and revealed the same violations of normative rationality. Finally, it was argued that despite some limitations that need to be considered, there is a large number of indications which suggest that the observed findings can to a certain extent be generalized beyond the particular experimental context.

Based on the findings of the fourth chapter, it seemed likely that cognitive biases do affect capital investment decisions. Accordingly, the *fifth chapter* gave a general overview of debiasing concepts. The first part provided a variety of examples, which all demonstrated that most cognitive biases are in general very robust and that they can hardly be eliminated completely. The second part addressed debiasing in general and introduced three areas of potential counter-measures: 'knowledge, experience and expertise', 'incentives and accountability', and 'training and tools'. Despite a few promising indications, the respective discussions revealed a rather ambiguous and unclear picture for all three areas. Nevertheless, they also highlighted that training seems to be a key factor for all three approaches. The third part of the fifth chapter introduced a general framework that companies can use as a foundation for the development of a counterstrategy against cognitive biases, and finally described aspects that might unconsciously deter people from adopting and implementing countermeasures.

In summary, the declared purpose of this thesis – to look for, and find, indications for or against the existence and the impact of cognitive biases in a capital investment context – has clearly been achieved. Based on the fundamentals of capital investments and cognitive biases discussed in the first part of this thesis, the second part combined the two concepts through theoretical discussions, illustrative case examples and a large series of empirical experiments, which clearly showed statistically highly significant violations of normative rationality in simplified capital investment contexts. Summing up, based on the multitude of obtained indications, the theoretical considerations as well as the empirical findings in this thesis strongly suggest that capital investment decisions are affected by cognitive biases.[582]

Nevertheless, this new scientific field of cognitive biases in the context of capital investments is still relatively young, similar to the status of behavioral finance a few decades ago, and would greatly benefit from additional research. The final sub-chapter therefore proposes several areas for further research.

6.2 Areas for Future Research

Despite the presented findings in this thesis, the conducted research constitutes only the very first step into this new research area at the intersection of capital investment related decision making and cognitive psychology. However, additional research is necessary to validate the findings, clarify existing open questions, explore new issues and generate deeper insights into this field.

With regard to future research, four different directions can be distinguished: approaches that expand the 'breadth' of the field by extending research to other

582 Note that the obtained indications 'only' suggest this conclusion, but do of course not prove it. However, as discussed in the introduction, an ultimate proof was neither the target of this thesis, nor was it deemed possible given the point of departure and the actual circumstances.

cognitive biases, approaches that explore the 'depth' of the field by focusing in detail on a particular bias, approaches that address overarching aspects of methodology and set-up, and approaches that examine potential countermeasures and their effectiveness. The following illustration schematically summarizes these four directions:

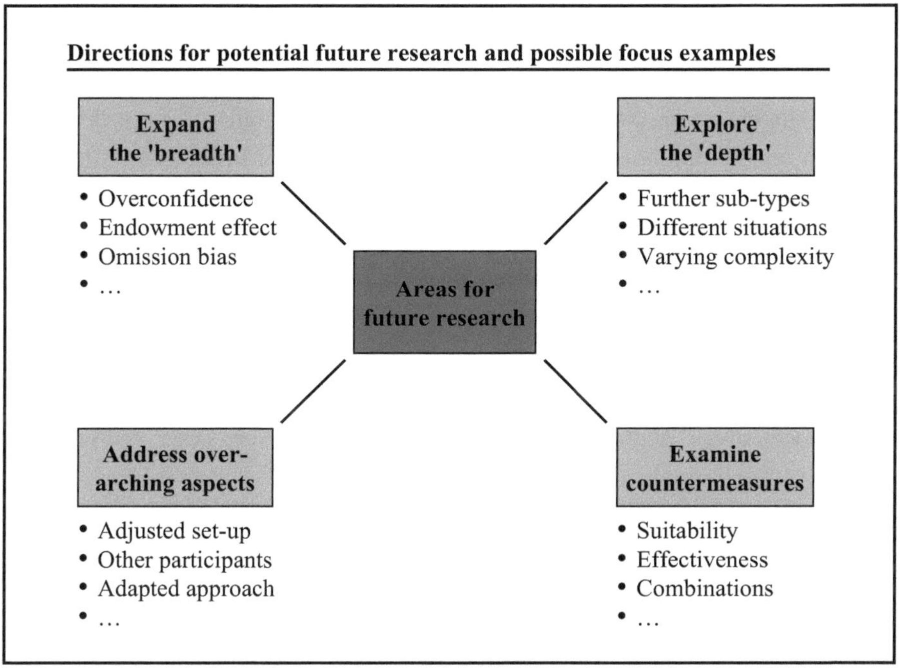

Illustration 21: Overview of potential areas for future research

Concerning the first approach, expanding the 'breadth' by extending research to include other cognitive biases, there is a huge range of further cognitive biases. However, it is important to focus research activities on those cognitive biases that are expected to be potentially applicable and relevant for capital investment decisions, including for instance overconfidence, the 'endowment effect', or the 'omission bias'. The discussions in the third chapter already addressed several of these potentially relevant biases, but there are significantly more. Drawing on the analogy to financial investments, and analyzing which cognitive biases have been addressed in behavioral finance might also help to identify potentially relevant biases.

With regard to the second approach, exploring the 'depth' by focusing in detail on a particular bias, the conducted research might already provide several starting points. Deep-dives on anchoring could for instance focus on different types of anchor values, different ways of incorporating the anchor, different content-related situations, or different levels of complexity. Similarly, deep-dives for research on framing could for example include different tasks, other situations with varying levels of complexity, different ways of data representation – for instance displaying data as text, table, or graphically –, or other sub-types of framing like structure framing or outcome framing. With regard to asymmetric dominance, potential starting points could for example include other decoy positions, the use of phantom decoys, larger choice sets, or more attribute dimensions. In addition, all other cognitive biases could also be the subject for similar deep-dives. Accordingly, this area of research is very large, and provides innumerous opportunities to generate further insights.

Concerning the third approach, addressing overarching aspects of methodology and set-up, there is also a large variety of potential starting points. In particular, one could address the potential critiques and the identified limitations of the research presented in this thesis, and accordingly conduct for instance experiments with 'real' professionals instead of students and with groups instead of individuals, or use considerably more complex role play situations or even real-life field studies and observations instead of laboratory experiments. Furthermore, research could also address more general aspects like the identification of specific factors that provoke or favor the emergence of cognitive biases. Moreover, in addition to the various empirical research aspects that need to be addressed, the theoretical foundations also have to be explored and improved in parallel, in order to better understand cognitive biases and their effects.

The fourth research area, examining potential countermeasures, addresses the question of how to avoid particular cognitive biases and how to set up counter-acting strategies, and analyzes factors that amplify or reduce the magnitude and strength of cognitive biases' effects. The earlier parts on debiasing techniques and counterstrategies have clearly illustrated that considerable research is still needed in this area. Accordingly, future efforts for example need to identify which debiasing techniques are suitable to mitigate which particular bias, clarify how effective each particular countermeasure is, determine how the combined use of several techniques influences the impact of cognitive biases, etc. Accordingly, future research could employ a within-subject design for experiments, in contrast to the between-subjects design that was used for the experiments conducted in this thesis. For instance, the magnitude of the impact of a bias could be tested for the same participant before and after a particular training.

Summing up, the above part showed the high diversity of the possible research areas and illustrated that this new scientific domain addressing cognitive biases in a capital investment context is still in a very early stage. Nevertheless, the research conducted in this thesis, including the theoretical considerations as well as the observed empirical findings, constitutes a significant scientific contribution to the initiation and development of this new research field. Moreover, given the high importance of capital investments for companies and the large potential impact of cognitive biases on the respective decisions, this new domain is expected to receive considerable attention in the future.

Appendices

Appendix I: Introductory description of the situation[583]

The following information was provided to all participants prior to each experiment. It consists of a short oral introduction to the general background and a brief written explanation of the overall situation in the role play experiment.

Oral background information

The participants are told – either by the experimenter or by their course supervisor together with the experimenter – that the university's business faculty is currently developing a business game for its students and that it needs the student's help for testing and trying out some of the questions and exercise formats. The students are also told that this task is not linked to their course performance rating and that it is anonymous and not marked.

Written introduction to the pen and paper experiment

You are the chief financial officer (CFO) of X-Inc., a multinational conglomerate corporation with several business units that operate in different business areas various market segments. One of your key duties as CFO is to support and advise the managers of the various business units with regard to their capital investment decisions. For today, several business units require your support for decisions that have to be taken at short notice.

---

583 Translated from German (original language of experiments) to English.

Appendix II: Anchoring experiment 1[584]

Current situation

X-Inc. has just acquired a smaller company named N-Ltd., and wants to integrate N-Ltd. as additional business unit alongside its existing units. N-Ltd. operates in a sector in which X-Inc. is not active. Shortly before the acquisition, N-Ltd. has launched an important capital investment project to build a production and distribution facility for a new product, which will be introduced to the market once the facility is finished. The investment is planned to be completed in about one year from now.

You are asked to quickly assess the current situation at N-Ltd. with regard to this capital investment project, in particular concerning the probability that the project will be completed on time (i.e. finished without delay).

Task: Determination of likelihood of completion on time

Unfortunately, you do not have the time and resources to conduct a detailed analysis of the project plan and the progress. Instead, you have to make your own judgment based on the information you have. You recall that, in the past, N-Ltd. has usually finished its investment projects on time. However, you reckon that the take-over might potentially have implied some delays, but it seems, compared to the original plan, as if additional resources has been allocated to the project, as counter-measure. In documents you received earlier from N-Ltd. you see that they usually build-in a small time buffer or cushion for small delays into their project schedules. However, you also heard rumors that one of the many sub-contractors involved in the project might be in danger of becoming insolvent, which could entail some problems.

Do you estimate that the likelihood of this project being completed on time (i.e. finished without delay) is higher or lower than 84% [36%] ?
(Please note that the number 84% [36%] was generated randomly during the process of printing by a random generator, and is thus completely irrelevant for your task and contains no informational value at all!)

The likelihood that the project is completed on time is:

Higher than
84 % [36%]

Lower than
84 % [36%]

What do you estimate is the likelihood that this investment project is completed on time (i.e. finished without delay)? Please provide a value between 0% and 100%.

The likelihood that the project is completed on time is:

_________ %

---

[584] Translated from German (original language of experiments) to English. The following text is the version presented to group 1. The changes for group 2 are displayed in [squared brackets].

Appendix III: Anchoring experiment 2[585]

Current situation

X-Inc. has just acquired a smaller company named N-Ltd., and wants to integrate N-Ltd. as additional business unit alongside its existing units. N-Ltd. operates in a sector in which X-Inc. is not active. Shortly before the acquisition, N-Ltd. has launched an important capital investment project to build a production and distribution facility for a new product, which will be introduced to the market once the facility is finished. The investment is planned to be completed in about one year from now.

You are asked to quickly assess the current situation at N-Ltd. with regard to this capital investment project, in particular concerning the future market share of the respective new product that will be produced and distributed in the facility.

Task: Estimate of future market share

The available information regarding the future market share of N-Ltd.'s new product is rather sparse, and you don't have the time to wait for a detailed analysis. In a discussion with the responsible product manager you receive the following information: the respective market is quite fragmented and highly competitive. According to the documentation available there are apparently 5 major competitors, whose market shares seem to be roughly equal, as well as several other smaller market players. N-Ltd. does not operate in this segment yet (nor does X-Inc.). A test of the new product with potential customers went positively. According to your research department, the new product will be highly superior to the majority of other products currently on the market. It is not known if the competitors already develop advanced products, but there are rumors that some market players will launch slightly improved products soon.

?	Do you estimate that the market share of the new product will be higher or lower than 8% [22%] one year after its introduction to the respective market? (Please note that the number 8% [22%] was generated randomly during the process of printing by a random generator, and is thus completely irrelevant for your task and contains no informational value at all!)	The market share of the new product after one year in the market is: Higher than 8 % [22%] Lower than 8 % [22%]
?	What do you estimate will be the market share of the new product after being in the market for one year? Please provide a value between 0% and 100%.	The market share of the new product after one year in the market is: ________ %

[585] Translated from German (original language of experiments) to English. The following text is the version presented to group 1. The changes for group 2 are displayed in [squared brackets].

Appendix IV: Anchoring experiment 3[586]

Current situation

X-Inc. has just acquired a smaller company named N-Ltd., and wants to integrate N-Ltd. as additional business unit alongside its existing units. N-Ltd. operates in a sector in which X-Inc. is not active. Shortly before the acquisition, N-Ltd. has launched an important capital investment project to build a production and distribution facility for a new product, which will be introduced to the market once the facility is finished. The investment is planned to be completed in about one year from now.

You are asked to quickly assess the current situation at N-Ltd. with regard to this capital investment project, in particular concerning the probability that the project will be completed on time (i.e. finished without delay).

Task: Determination of likelihood of completion on time

Unfortunately, you do not have the time and resources to conduct a detailed analysis of the project plan and the progress. Instead, you have to make your own judgment based on the information you have. You recall that, in the past, N-Ltd. has usually finished its investment projects on time. However, you reckon that the take-over might potentially have implied some delays, but it seems, compared to the original plan, as if additional resources has been allocated to the project, as countermeasure. In documents you received earlier from N-Ltd. you see that they usually build-in a small time buffer or cushion for small delays into their project schedules. However, you also heard rumors that one of the many sub-contractors involved in the project might be in danger of becoming insolvent, which could entail some problems.

N-Ltd.'s new assistant spontaneously guessed 84% [36%]. However you did accidentally observe that he simply rolled two (ten-sided) dices, resulting in exactly this number. Thus you know that this 'guess' is irrelevant and does not contain any informative value for you.
Do you estimate that the likelihood of this project being completed on time (i.e. finished without delay) is higher or lower than 84% [36%] ?

The likelihood that the project is completed on time is:

Higher than 84 % [36%]

Lower than 84 % [36%]

What do you estimate is the likelihood that this investment project is completed on time (i.e. finished without delay)? Please provide a value between 0% and 100%.

The likelihood that the project is completed on time is:

_________ %

---

586 Translated from German (original language of experiments) to English. The following text is the version presented to group 1. The changes for group 2 are displayed in [squared brackets].

Appendix V: Anchoring experiment 4[587]

Current situation

X-Inc. has just acquired a smaller company named N-Ltd., and wants to integrate N-Ltd. as additional business unit alongside its existing units. N-Ltd. operates in a sector in which X-Inc. is not active. Shortly before the acquisition, N-Ltd. has launched an important capital investment project to build a production and distribution facility for a new product, which will be introduced to the market once the facility is finished. The investment is planned to be completed in about one year from now.

You are asked to quickly assess the current situation at N-Ltd. with regard to this capital investment project, in particular concerning the future market share of the respective new product that will be produced and distributed in the facility.

Task: Estimate of future market share

The available information regarding the future market share of N-Ltd.'s new product is rather sparse, and you don't have the time to wait for a detailed analysis. In a discussion with the responsible product manager you receive the following information: the respective market is quite fragmented and highly competitive. According to the documentation available there are apparently 5 major competitors, whose market shares seem to be roughly equal, as well as several other smaller market players. N-Ltd. does not operate in this segment yet (nor does X-Inc.). A test of the new product with potential customers went positively. According to your research department, the new product will be highly superior to the majority of other products currently on the market. It is not known if the competitors already develop advanced products, but there are rumors that some market players will launch slightly improved products soon.

The assistant's 'guess' is this time 8% [22%], but you observed that he again simply rolled dices to obtain exactly this figure. Thus you know that this 'guess' is uninformative and useless; hence, you have to make your own estimate.
Do you estimate that the market share of the new product will be higher or lower than 8% [22%] one year after its introduction to the respective market?

The market share of the new product after one year in the market is:

Higher than
8 % [22%]

Lower than
8 % [22%]

What do you estimate will be the market share of the new product after being in the market for one year? Please provide a value between 0% and 100%.

The market share of the new product after one year in the market is:

________ %

---

587 Translated from German (original language of experiments) to English. The following text is the version presented to group 1. The changes for group 2 are displayed in [squared brackets].

Appendix VI: Task framing experiment 1[588]

Task: Investment in the regionalization of a product

The management of another business unit of X-Inc. needs your help concerning an important investment decision. This business unit wants to further increase its sales abroad by selling one of its core products also in emerging markets in the future. This requires that the product is enhanced and adapted to the respective conditions in order to suit the needs of the local customers. Two potential regions, each consisting of several emerging countries, have been identified for which the product could be regionalized. However, for various reasons, the business unit can only invest in adapting the product for one of the two regions, but not for both. You have to select in which alternative the business unit should invest [You have to eliminate one of the two investment alternatives and decide which region is rejected] , i.e. you need to decide for which region the product will [NOT] be regionalized. For that purpose, the business unit management has provided you with the following information regarding the two regions:

For region A, an above-average positive demographic development is expected. The regional population's per capita income is slightly below average. The brand of X-Inc.'s business unit is already very well-known by the local consumers. The analysts at X-Inc. expect a very tough and fierce competition in the market. The business unit management succeeded in negotiating very favorable tax conditions with the local state authorities. The technical experts at X-Inc. expect that the cost and difficulty of adapting the product to the regional conditions and needs will be higher than usual.
For region B, an average demographic development is expected and the regional per capita income is also average. The local brand awareness of the business unit is normal. X-Inc.'s analysts expect a medium level of competition. Tax conditions are typical for the region. The cost and difficulty of adapting the product is usual.

?

You have to select [reject] one of the two regions. Which region do you choose for the investment [Which region do you eliminate, i.e. in which region do you NOT invest]?

Region A ☐

Region B ☐

588 Translated from German (original language of experiments) to English. The following text is the 'select-version', which was presented to group 2. The changes for group 1, which received the 'reject-version', are marked in [squared brackets].

Appendix VII: Task framing experiment 2[589]

Task: Investment in a new production site

You are asked to support the management of one of X-Inc.'s business units with regard to an important capital investment decision. The business unit plans to invest in building a new production site abroad. A preliminary analysis of interesting locations has been conducted, and two potential sites are on the final short-list. You have to select one of the two investment alternatives [You have to eliminate one of the two investment alternatives and decide which location is rejected], i.e. you need to decide at which site the business unit will [NOT] invest. For that purpose, the management of the business unit has provided you with the following information regarding the two potential locations:

The infrastructure at site A is typical for the region. The availability of raw materials for the production and of personnel is at an average level. The political situation is stable. Legal environmental and safety requirements are normal. Authorities have granted an average level of subsidies and other means of public support.
Site B possesses a very well developed infrastructure. Due to the geographic location, it is more costly and time-consuming to obtain particular raw materials for the production. The availability of skilled workers and other personnel is very high in the surrounding area. The political situation in the country is characterized by occasional small instabilities. An analysis of the legal safety and environmental requirements revealed high standards. Government and local authorities have granted very attractive subsidies and a high level of other public support activities.

?	You have to select [reject] one of the two production sites. Which site do you choose for the investment [Which site do you eliminate, i.e. in which site do you NOT invest]?	Site A	☐
		Site B	☐

[589] Translated from German (original language of experiments) to English. The following text is the 'select-version', which was presented to group 1. The changes for group 2, which received the 'reject-version', are marked in [squared brackets].

Appendix VIII: Asymmetric dominance experiment 1[590]

Task: Investment in a new machine to produce pills

The pharmaceuticals business unit is about to take an important capital investment decision and asks for your support. The business unit has to invest in a new machine to produce pills. Based on a detailed analysis, two characteristics have been identified as most important: flexibility (i.e. how many different pills the machine can produce) and quantity or speed of production (i.e. how many pills the machine can produce in one hour). The available machines partly differ considerably with regard to the two above named characteristics. Concerning all other important criteria, all proposed machines are roughly equally good. The following three machines are on the short-list, and you have to select exactly one of them:

Machine	Flexibility: number of different producible pills	Quantity: number of pills produced per hour
A	64	5,900
B	27	14,200
C	64 [24]	5,300 [14,200]

?

In which machine do you want to invest? Please select exactly one of the three machines:

Machine A ☐

Machine B ☐

Machine C ☐

[590] Translated from German (original language of experiments) to English. The following text is the version presented to group 1. The changes for group 2 are displayed in [squared brackets].

Appendix IX: Asymmetric dominance experiment 2[591]

Task: Investment in a new product segment

One of X-Inc.'s business units has asked for your support with regard to an important capital investment decision. The respective business unit wants to increase its assortment of products and therefore plans to invest in a new product segment. Three possible base products from different segments are on the final short-list. The financial controlling and product development departments have already analyzed each option in detail and have accomplished two important standard investment appraisal procedures: a *net present value* calculation (evaluates the monetary 'attractiveness' of an investment, i.e. its financial 'value'; the net present value, also called NPV, is expressed in Euros: the higher the value the better) and an *utility value* analysis (evaluates the non-monetary 'benefit' or 'attractiveness' of an investment, based on several non-financial factors and targets; the utility value is expressed as a number on a scale between 0 and 100, with 100 being the positive maximum). The results of both analyses are provided in the following table. You need to trade off both measures and have to decide in which of the three short-listed products the business unit should invest:

Product	**Net present value (NPV) in EUR millions**	**Utility value, scale: 0 - 100**
A	58.7	82.4
B	65.9	73.5
C	65.7 [58.6]	73.2 [82.1]

?

In which product do you want to invest? Please select exactly one of the three products:

Product A ☐

Product B ☐

Product C ☐

591 Translated from German (original language of experiments) to English. The following text is the version presented to group 1. The changes for group 2 are displayed in [squared brackets].

Appendix X: Demographic information collection[592]

Final demographic information (collected for statistical reasons and completely anonymous)

☐	I'm a student	Study major: Years of study: University:	________________ ______ years ________________
☐	I'm working	Occupation: Experience:	________________ ______ years
☐	I'm an MBA, Master, or PhD student	Study major: Years of study: University: Occupation: Experience:	________________ ______ years ________________ ________________ ______ years

Gender: I am … ☐ male ☐ female

Age: I belong to the following age group:

☐	20 years or younger	☐	41-45 years
☐	21-25 years	☐	46-50 years
☐	26-30 years	☐	51-55 years
☐	31-35 years	☐	56-60 years
☐	36-40 years	☐	61 years or older

Further comments: ____________________________

____

! **Thank you very much for your support!**

[592] Translated from German (original language of experiments) to English.

References

Adam, D. (1996): Planung und Entscheidung: Modelle – Ziele – Methoden, 4th edition, Gabler, Wiesbaden.

Agans, P. and Shaffer, L. (1994): The Hindsight Bias: The Role of the Availabilityy Heuristic and Perceived Risk, Basic and Applied Social Psychology, Vol. 15, pp. 439-449.

Allsopp, V. (1995): Understanding economics, Routledge, London.

Alpert, M. and Raiffa, H. (1982): A Progress Report on the Training of Probability Assessors, In Kahneman, D., Slovic, P. and Tversky, A. (eds.), Judgment under Uncertainty: Heuristics and Biases (Cambridge University Press, 1982), pp. 294-305.

Anderson, J. (2007): Kognitive Psychologie, 6th edition, Springer, Berlin.

Andrade, J. and May, J. (2004): Cognitive psychology, Garland Science/BIOS Science, Abingdon.

Ariely, D. (2008): Predictably Irrational: The Hidden Forces that Shape our Decisions, HarperCollins, London.

Arkes, H., Dawes, R. and Christensen, C. (1986): Factors influencing the Use of a Decision Rule in Probabilistic Tasks, Organizational Behavior and Human Decision Processes, Vol. 37, pp. 93-110.

Arnott, D. (2006): Cognitive Biases and Decision Support Systems Development: a Design Science Approach, Information Systems Journal, Vol. 16, pp. 55-78.

Atrill, P. and McLaney, E. (2002): Management Accounting for Non-specialists, Pearson Education, Harlow.

Aumann, R. (1994): Rationality and Bounded Rationality, Games and Economic Behavior, Vol. 21, pp. 2-14.

Baker, H. and Nofsinger, J. (2002): Psychological Biases of Investors, Financial Services Review, Vol. 11, pp 97-116.

Balota, D. and Marsh, E. (2004): Cognitive Psychology: An Overview, In Balota, D. and Marsh, E. (eds.), Cognitive Psychology: Key Readings (Psychology Press, New York).

Bamberg, G. and Baur, F. (1991): Statistik, 7th edition, Oldenbourg, Munich.

Bamberg, G. and Coenenberg, A. (2002): Betriebswirtschaftliche Entscheidungslehre, 11th edition, Vahlen, Munich.

Barber, B. and Odean, T. (2000): Trading is hazardous to your Wealth: the Common Stock Investment Performance of individual Investors, Journal of Finance, Vol. 55, pp. 773-806.

Bar-Hillel, M. (1982): Studies of Representativeness, In Kahneman, D., Slovic, P. and Tversky, A. (eds.), Judgment under Uncertainty: Heuristics and Biases (Cambridge University Press, 1982), pp. 69-98.

Baron, J. (2007): Thinking and Deciding, 4th edition, Cambridge University Press, Cambridge.

Barrow. M. (2006): Statistics for Economics, Accounting, and Business Studies, 4th edition, Pearson Education, Harlow.

Barucci, E. (2003): Financial Markets Theory: Equilibrium, Efficiency, and Information, Springer, London.

Baumol, W. and Blinder, A. (2009): Economics: Principles and Policy, 11th edition, South-Western Cengage Learning, Mason.

Bazerman, M. (2006): Judgment in Managerial Decision Making, 6th edition, John Wiley & Sons, Hoboken.

Beach, L. (1990): Image Theory: Decision Making in Personal and Organizational Contexts, Wiley, Chichester.

Bell, D., Raiffa, H. and Tversky, A. (1988): Descriptive, Normative and Prescriptive Interactions in Decision Making, In Bell, D., Raiffa, H. and Tversky, A. (eds.), Decision Making: Descriptive, Normative and Prescriptive Interactions (Cambridge University Press, Cambridge), pp. 9-31.

Benartzi, S. (2001): Excessive Extrapolation and the Allocation of 401(k) Accounts to Company Stock, Journal of Finance, Vol. 56, pp. 1747-1764.

Bereby-Meyer, Y and Grosskopf, B. (2008): Overcoming the Winner's Curse: an Adaptive Learning Perspective, Journal of Behavioral Decision Making, Vol. 21, pp. 15-27.

Bernoulli, D. (1738): Specimen theoriae novae de mensura sortis, translated, Bernoulli, D. (1954): Exposition of a new Theory on the Measurement of Risk, Econometrica, Vol. 22, pp. 22-36.

Bhimani, A., Horngren, C., Datar, S. and Foster, G. (2008): Management and cost accounting, 4th edition, Pearson Education, Harlow.

Bhushan, N. and Rai, K. (2004): Strategic Decision Making: Applying the Analytic Hierarchy Process, Springer, London.

Bickhard, M. and Terveen, L. (1995): Foundational Issues in Artificial Intelligence and Cognitive Science, Elsevier, Amsterdam.

Binmore, K. (2009): Rational decisions, Princeton University Press, Princeton.

Black, K. (2008): Business Statistics for Contemporary Decision Making, 5th edition, Wiley & Sons, Hoboken.

Blohm, H., Lüder, K. and Schaefer, C. (2006): Investition, 9th edition, Vahlen, Munich.

Bosch, K. (1993): Statistik-Taschenbuch, 2nd edition, Oldenbourg, Munich.

Brans, J. and Mareschal, B. (2005): PROMETHEE Methods, In Figueira, J., Greco, S. and Ehrgott, M. (eds.), Multiple Criteria Decision Analysis: State of the Art Surveys (Springer, New York), pp. 163-195.

Brehmer, B. (1980): In one Word: Not from Experience, Acta Psychologica, Vol. 45, pp. 223-241.

Brown, C. (2006): Cognitive Psychology, Sage Publications, London.

Bruner, J., Postman, L. and Rodrigues, J. (1951): Expectations and the perception of color, American Journal of Psychology, Vol. 64, pp. 216-227.

Buehler, R., Griffin, D. and Ross, M. (1994): Exploring the Planning Fallcy: Why People underestimate their Task Completion Times, Journal of Personality and Social Psychology, Vol. 67, pp. 366-381.

Buehler, R., Griffin, D. and Ross, M. (2002): Inside the Planning Fallacy: The Causes and Consequences of Optimistic Time Predictions, In Gilovich, T., Griffin, D. and Kahneman, D. (eds.), Heuristics and Biases: The Psychology of Intuitive Judgment (Cambridge University Press, 2002), pp. 250-270.

Bukszar, E. (2003): Does Overconfidence Lead to Poor Decisions? A Comparison of Decision Making and Judgment under Uncertainty, Journal of Business and Management, Vol. 9, pp. 33-43.

Calver, G. (2004): What is Packaging Design?, RotoVision, Hove.

Camerer, C. and Hogarth, R. (1999): The Effects of Financial Incentives in Experiments: a Review and Capital-Labor-Production Framework, Journal of Risk and Uncertainty, Vol. 19, pp. 7-42.

Camerer, C., Loewenstein, G. and Weber, M. (1989): The Curse of Knowledge in Economic Settings: an experimental Analysis, Journal of Political Economy, Vol. 97, pp. 1232-1254.

Cann, A., Sigfried, W. and Pearce, L. (1981): Forced Attention to specific Application Qualifications: Impact on Physical Attractiveness and Sex of Applicant Biases, Personnel Psychology, Vol. 34, pp. 65-75.

Chadwick, L. (1998): Management Accounting, 2nd edition, Thomson, London.

Chapman, G. and Johnson, E. (1994): The Limits of Anchoring, Journal of Behavioral Decision Making, Vol. 7, pp. 223-242.

Chapman, G. and Johnson, E. (2002): Incorporating the Irrelevant: Anchors in Judgments of Belief and Value, In Gilovich, T., Griffin, D. and Kahneman, D. (eds.), Heuristics and Biases: The Psychology of Intuitive Judgment (Cambridge University Press, 2002), pp. 120-138.

Chapman, L. and Chapman, J. (1969): Illusory Correlation as an Obstacle to the Use of valid Psychodiagnostic Signs, Journal of Abnormal Psychology, Vol. 74, pp. 271-280.

Cole, M., Hood, L. and McDermott, R. (1997): Concepts of Ecological Validity: Their differing Implications for comparative Cognitive Research, In Cole,

M., Engeström, Y. and Vasquez, O. (eds.), Mind, Culture, and Activity: seminal Papers from the Laboratory of comparative Human Cognition (Cambridge University Press, 1997), pp. 49-56.

Colman, A., Pulford, B. and Bolger, F. (2007): Asymmetric Dominance and Phantom Decoy Effects in Games, Organizational Behavior and Human Decision Processes, Vol. 104, pp. 193-206.

Damodaran, A. (2008): Strategic Risk Taking: a Framework for Risk Management, Pearson Education, New Jersey.

Das, T. and Teng, B. (1999): Cognitive Biases and Strategic Decision Processes: an Integrative Perspective, The Journal of Management Studies, Vol. 36, pp. 757-778.

Dayananda, D., Irons, R., Harison, S., Herbohn, J. and Rowland, P. (2002): Capital Budgeting: Financial Appraisal of Investment Projects, Cambridge University Press, Cambridge.

De Bondt, W. and Thaler, R. (1985): Does the Stock Market Overreact?, Journal of Finance, Vol. 40, pp. 793-808.

Diekhoff, G. (1992): Statistics for the Social and Behavioral Sciences: Univariate, Bivariate, Multivariate, Wm. C. Brown Publishers, Dubuque.

Dipboye, R. and Macan, T. (1988): A Process View of the Selection/Recruitment Interview, In Schuler, R., Yougblood, S. and Huber, V. (eds.), Readings in Personnel and Human Resource Management, 3rd edition (West Publishing, 1988), pp. 217-232.

Drury, C. (2004): Management and Cost Accounting, 6th edition, Thomson Learning, London.

Drury, C. (2008): Management and Cost Accounting, 7th edition, Cengage Learning, London.

Dye, R., Sibony, O. and Truong, V. (2009): Flaws in strategic Decision Daking: McKinsey Global Survey Results, The McKinsey Quarterly, Online Edition, pp. 1-6.

Dyer, J. (2005): MAUT – Multiple Attribute Utility Theory, In Figueira, J., Greco, S. and Ehrgott, M. (eds.), Multiple Criteria Decision Analysis: State of the Art Surveys (Springer, New York), pp. 265-296.

Eliaz, K., Ray, D. and Razin, R. (2006): Choice Shifts in Groups: A Decision-Theoretic Basis, American Economic Review, Vol. 96, pp. 1.321-1.332.

Epley, N. and Gilovich, T. (2001): Putting Adjustment Back in the Anchoring and Adjustment Heuristic: Differential Processing of Self-Generated and Experimenter-Provided Anchors, Psychological Science, Vol. 12, pp. 391-396.

Epley, N. and Gilovich, T. (2006): The Anchoring-and-Adjustment Heuristic: Why the Adjustments are Insufficient, Psychological Science, Vol. 17, pp. 311-318.

Esgate, A., Groome, D., Baker, K., Heathcote, D., Kemp, R., Maguire, M. and Reed, C. (2005): An Introduction to Applied Cognitive Psychology, Psychology Press, Hove.

Ewert, R. and Wagenhofer, A. (2008): Interne Unternehmensrechnung, 7th edition, Springer, Berlin

Eysenck, M. (2004): Psychology: An International Perspective, Psychology Press, Hove.

Eysenck, M. (2006): Fundamentals of Cognition, Psychology Press, Hove.

Eysenck, M. and Keane, M. (2005): Cognitive Psychology: a Student's Handbook, 5th edition, Psychology Press, Hove.

Fennema, M and Perkins, J. (2008): Mental Budgeting versus Marginal Decision Making: Training, Experience and Justification Effects on Decisions involving Sunk Costs, Journal of Behavioral Decision Making, Vol. 21, pp. 225-239.

Fiedler, K. (2004): Illusory correlation, In Pohl, R. (eds.), Cognitive Illusions: A Handbook on Fallacies and Biases in Thinking, Judgment and Memory (Psychology Press, 2004), pp. 97-114.

Figueira, J., Mousseau, V. and Roy, B. (2005): ELECTRE Methods, In Figueira, J., Greco, S. and Ehrgott, M. (eds.), Multiple Criteria Decision Analysis: State of the Art Surveys (Springer, New York), pp. 133-162.

Fischhoff, B. (1975): Hindsight is not equal to Foresight: The Effects of Outcome Knowledge on Judgment under Uncertainty, Journal of Experimental Psychology: Human Perception and Performance, Vol. 1, pp. 288-299.

Fischhoff, B. (1982a): For those condemned to Study the Past: Heuristics and Biases in Hindsight, In Kahneman, D., Slovic, P. and Tversky, A. (eds.), Judgment under Uncertainty: Heuristics and Biases (Cambridge University Press, 1982), pp. 335-351.

Fisher, I. (1928): The Money Illusion, Adelphi, New York.

Fisk, J. (2004): Conjunction Fallacy, In Pohl, R. (eds.), Cognitive Illusions: A Handbook on Fallacies and Biases in Thinking, Judgment and Memory (Psychology Press, 2004), pp. 23-42.

Flyvbjerg, B., Garbuio, M. and Lovallo, D. (2009): Delusion and Deception in large Infrastructure Projects: Two Models for explaining and preventing Executive Disaster, Californian Management Review, Vol. 51, pp. 170-193.

Friedenberg, J. and Silverman, G. (2006): Cognitive science: an introduction to the study of mind, Sage Publications, London.

Galbraith, R. and Underwood, B. 81973): Perceived Frequency of Concrete and Abstract Words, Memory and Cognition, Vol. 1, pp. 56-60.

Garland, H., Sandefur, C. and Rogers, A. (1990): De-escalation of Commitment in Oil Exploration: when Sunk Costs and Negative Feedback coincide, Journal of Applied Psychology, Vol. 75, pp. 721-727.

Garnham, A. and Oakhill, J. (1994): Thinking and reasoning, Blackwell, Oxford.

Geldermann, J. and Rentz, O. (2007): Multi-Criteria Decision Support for integrated Technique Assessment, In Kropp, J. and Scheffran, J. (eds.), Advanced Methods for Decision Making and Risk Management in Sustainability Science (Nova Science Publishers, New York), pp. 257-273.

Gerrig, R. and Zimbardo, P. (2008): Psychology and Life, 18th edition, Pearson Education, Boston.

Gigerenzer, G. (1991): How to make Cognitive Illusions Disappear: Beyond 'Heuristics and Biases', In Stroebe, W. and Hewstone, M. (eds.), European Review of Social Psychology Vol. 2 (Wiley, 1991), pp. 83-115.

Gigerenzer, G. (1994): Why the Distinction between Single-Event Probabilities and Frequencies is important for Psychology (and vice versa), In Wright, G. and Ayton, P. (eds.), Subjective Probability (Wiley, 1994), pp. 129-161.

Gigerenzer, G. (1996): On narrow Norms and Vague Heuristics: A Rebuttal to Kahneman and Tversky, Psychological Review, Vol. 103, pp. 592-596.

Gigerenzer, G. (2008): Gut Feelings: Short Cuts to better Decision Making, Penguin Books, London.

Gigerenzer, G., Todd, P. and the ABC Research Group (eds.) (1999): Simple Heuristics that make us Smart, Oxford University Press, New York.

Gilovich, T. and Griffin, D. (2002): Introduction – Heuristics and Biases: Then and Now, In Gilovich, T., Griffin, D. and Kahneman, D. (eds.), Heuristics and Biases: The Psychology of Intuitive Judgment (Cambridge University Press, 2002), pp. 1-18.

Gilovich, T. and Medvec, V. (1995): The Experience of Regret: What, When, and Why, Psychological Review, Vol. 102, pp. 379-395.

Gilovich, T., Griffin, D. and Kahneman, D. (eds.) (2002a): Heuristics and Biases: The Psychology of Intuitive Judgment, Cambridge University Press, New York.

Gilovich, T., Vallone, R. and Tversky, A. (2002b): The Hot Hand in Basketball: On the Misperception of Random Sequences, In Gilovich, T., Griffin, D. and Kahneman, D. (eds.), Heuristics and Biases: The Psychology of Intuitive Judgment (Cambridge University Press, 2002), pp. 601-616.

Glaser, M., Nöth, M. and Weber, M. (2004): Behavioral Finance, In Koehler, D. and Harvey, N. (eds.), Blackwell Handbook of Judgment & Decision Making (Blackwell Publishing, 2004), pp. 527-546.

Goldstein, W. and Hogarth, R. (1997): Judgment and Decision Research: Some historical context, In Goldstein, W. and Hogarth, R. (eds.), Research on Judgment and Decision Making: Currents, Connections, and Controversies (Cambridge University Press, 1997), pp. 3-65.

Götze, U. (2006): Investitionsrechnung, 5th edition, Springer, Berlin.

Götze, U., Northcott, D. and Schuster, P. (2007): Investment Appraisal: Methods and Models, Springer, Berlin.

Graves, L. and Powell, G. (2006): The effect of Sex Similarity on Recruiters' Evaluations of Actual Applicants: A Test of the Similarity-Attraction Paradigm, Personnel Psychology, Vol. 48, pp. 85-98.

Gravetter, F. and Wallnau, L. (2009): Statistics for the Behavioral Sciences, 8th edition, Wadsworth Cengage Learning, Belmont.

Griffin, D. and Brenner, L. (2004): Perspectives on Probability Judgment Calibration, In Koehler, D. and Harvey, N. (eds.), Blackwell Handbook of Judgment & Decision Making (Blackwell Publishing, 2004), pp. 177-199.

Griffin, D. and Buehler, R. (1999): Frequency, Probability, and Prediction: Easy solutions to Cognitive Illusions?, Cognitive Psychology, Vol. 38, pp. 48-78.

Griffin, D. and Tversky, A. (2002): The Weighing of Evidence and the Determinants of Confidence, In In Gilovich, T., Griffin, D. and Kahneman, D. (eds.), Heuristics and Biases: The Psychology of Intuitive Judgment (Cambridge University Press, 2002), pp. 230-249.

Groppelli, A. and Nikbakht, E. (2006): Finance, 5th edition, Barron's Educational, New York.

Groves, T. and Loeb, M. (1979): Incentives in a Divisionalized Firm, Management Science, Vol. 25, pp. 221-230.

Guthrie, G. (2009): Real Options in Theory and Practice, Oxford University Press, New York.

Hansen, H., Huhn, W., Legrand, O., Steiners, D. and Vahlenkamp, T. (2009): Capex Excellence: Optimizing Fixed Asset Investments, John Wiley & Sons, Chichester.

Hardaker, J., Huirne, R., Anderson, J. and Lien, G. (2004): Coping with risk in agriculture, 2nd edition, CABI Publishing, Wallingford.

Harley, E., Carlsen, K. and Loftus, G. (2004): The "Saw-It-All-Along" Effect: Demonstrations of Visual Hindsight Bias, Journal of Experimental Psychology: Learning, Memory, and Cognition, Vol. 30, pp. 960-968.

Hastie, R. and Dawes, R. (2001): Rational Choice in an uncertain World: The Psychology of Judgment and Decision Making, Sage, Thousand Oaks.

Hawkins, S. and Hastie, R. (1990): Hindsight: Biased Judgments of Past Events after the Outcomes are Known, Psychological Bulletin, Vol. 107, pp. 311-327.

Hedgcock, W. and Rao, A. (2009): Trade-Off Aversion as an Explanation for the Attraction Effect: a Functional Magnetic Resonance Imaging Study, Journal of Marketing Research, Vol. 46, pp. 1-13.

Heinen, E. (1957): Zum Begriff und Wesen der betriebswirtschaftlichen Investition, Betriebswirtschaftliche Forschung und Praxis BFuP, No. 9, pp. 16-31 & pp. 85-98.

Heuer, R. (1999): Psychology of Intelligence Analysis, Center for the Study of Intelligence, Central Intelligence Agency, Washington, D.C.

Heun, M. (2007): Finanzmarktsimulation mit Multiagentensystemen, DUV, Wiesbaden

Hinds, P. (1999): The Curse of Expertise: The Effects of Expertise and Debiasing Methods on Predictions of Novice Performance, Journal of Experimental Psychology: Applied, Vol. 5, pp. 205-221.

Hoffrage, U. (2004): Overconfidence, In Pohl, R. (eds.), Cognitive Illusions: A Handbook on Fallacies and Biases in Thinking, Judgment and Memory (Psychology Press, 2004), pp. 235-254.

Hogarth, R., Gibbs, B., McKenzie, C. and Marquis, M. (1991): Learning from Feedback: Exactingness and Incentives, Journal of Experimental Psychology: Learning, Memory, and Cognition, Vol. 17, pp. 734-752.

Horn, J., Lovallo, D. and Viguerie, S. (2005): Beating the Odds in Market Entry, The McKinsey Quarterly, Vol. 52, No. 4, pp. 34-45.

Hsee, C., Zhang, J. and Chen, J. (2004): Internal and Substantive Inconsistencies in Decision Making, In Koehler, D. and Harvey, N. (eds.), Blackwell Handbook of Judgment & Decision Making (Blackwell Publishing, 2004), pp. 360-378.

Huber, J. and Puto, C. (1983): Market Boundaries and Product Choice: Illustrating Attraction and Substitution Effects, Journal of Consumer Research, Vol. 10, pp. 31-44.

Huber, J., Payne, J. and Puto, C. (1982): Adding Asymmetrically Dominated Alternatives: Violations of Regularity and the Similarity Hypothesis, Journal of Consumer Research, Vol. 9, pp. 90-98.

Huberman, G. (2001): Familiarity breeds Investment, Review of Financial Studies, Vol. 14, pp. 659-680.

Johnson, V. and Kaplan, S. (1991): Experimental Evidence on the Effects of Accountability on Auditor Judgments, Auditing: a Journal of Practice & Theory, Vol. 10, pp. 96-107.

Joyce, E. and Biddle, G. (1981): Anchoring and Adjustment in Probabilistic Inference in Auditing, Journal of Accounting Research, Vol. 19, pp. 120-145.

Jungermann, H., Pfister, H. and Fischer, K. (2005): Die Psychologie der Entscheidung: Eine Einführung, 2nd edition, Elsevier Spektrum, Heidelberg.

Kahneman, D. and Lovallo, D. (1993): Timid Choices and bold Forecasts: a cognitive Perspective on Risk Taking, Management Science, Vol. 39, pp. 17-31.

Kahneman, D. and Tversky, A. (1973): On the Psychology of Prediction, Psychological Review, Vol. 80, pp. 237-251.

Kahneman, D. and Tversky, A. (1979): Prospect Theory: An Analysis of Decision under Risk, Econometrica, Vol. 47, pp. 263-291.

Kahneman, D., Knetsch, J. and Thaler, R. (2000): Anomalies: The Endowment Effect, Loss Aversion, and Status Quo Bias, In Kahneman, D. and Tversky, A. (eds.), Choices, Values, and Frames (Cambridge University Press, 2000), pp. 159-170.

Kahneman, D., Knetsch, J. and Thaler, R. (2000): Experimental Tests of the Endowment Effect and the Coase Theorem, In Thaler, R. (eds.), Quasi Rational Economics (Russell Sage Foundation, 1994), pp. 167-188.

Kahneman, D., Slovic, P. and Tversky, A. (eds.) (1982): Judgment under Uncertainty: Heuristics and Biases, Cambridge University Press, New York.

Kelman, M., Rottenstreich, Y. and Tversky, A. (2004): Context-Dependence in Legal Decision Making, In Tversky, A. and Shafir, E. (eds.), Preference, Belief, and Similarity: Selected Writings (Massachusetts Institute of Technology, 2004), pp. 963-993.

Keren, G. (1990): Cognitive Aids and Debiasing Methods: Can Cognitive Pills cure Cognitive Ills?, In Caverni, J., Fabre, J. and Gonzalez, L. (eds.), Cognitive Biases (Elsevier, 1990), pp. 523-552.

Kern, W. (1974): Investitionsrechnung, Poeschel, Stuttgart.

Kerr, N., MacCoun, R. and Kramer, G. (1996): Bias in Judgment: Comparing Individuals and Groups, Psychological Review, Vol. 4, pp. 687-719.

Kidd, J. (1970): The Utilization of subjective Probabilities in Production Planning, Acta Psychologica, Vol. 34, pp. 338-347.

Kinney, M. and Raiborn, C. (2009): Cost Accounting: Foundations and Evolutions, 7th edition, Thomson South-Western, Mason.

Kleindorfer, P., Kunreuther, H. and Schoemaker, P. (1993): Decision Sciences: an Integrative Perspective, Cambridge University Press, Cambridge.

Knetsch, J. (2000): The Endowment Effect and Evidence of Nonreversible Indifference Curves, In Kahneman, D. and Tversky, A. (eds.), Choices, Values, and Frames (Cambridge University Press, 2000), pp. 171-179.

Knetsch, J. and Sinden, J. (1984): Willingness to Pay and Compensation Demanded: Experimental evidence of an unexpected Disparity in Measures of Value, Quarterly Journal of Economics, Vol. 99, pp. 507-521.

Kozielecki, J. (1981): Psychological decision theory, revised edition, Kluwer Acadmic Publishers, Dordrecht.

Kruschwitz, L. (2007): Investitionsrechnung, 11th edition, Oldenbourg, Munich.

Kühberger, A. (1997): Theoretical Conceptions of Framing Effects in Risky Decisions, In Ranyard, R., Crozier, W. and Svenson, O. (eds.), Decision making: Cognitive Models and Explanations (Routledge, 1997) , pp. 128-144.

Laffont, J. and Martimort, D. (2002): The Theory of Incentives: the Principal-Agent Model, Princeton University Press, Princeton

Larrick, R. (2004): Debiasing, In Koehler, D. and Harvey, N. (eds.), Blackwell Handbook of Judgment & Decision Making (Blackwell Publishing, 2004), pp. 316-337.

Laux, H. (2005): Entscheidungstheorie, 6th edition, Springer, Berlin.

Lax, D. and Sebenius, J. (2004): Anchoring Expectations, Negotiation, September issue, Harvard Business Publishing Newsletters, pp. 9-11.

Lerner, J. and Tetlock, P. (1999): Accounting for the effects of Accountability, Psychological Bulletin, Vol. 125, pp. 255-275.

Lewin, K. (1947): Group Decision and Social Change, In Newcomb, T. and Hartley, E. (eds), Readings in Social Psychology (Holt, 1947), pp. 330-344.

Lichtenstein, S., Fischhoff, B. and Phillips, L. (1982): Calibration of Probabilities: The State of the Art to 1980, In Kahneman, D., Slovic, P. and Tversky, A. (eds.), Judgment under Uncertainty: Heuristics and Biases (Cambridge University Press, 1982), pp. 306-334.

Lilien, G. and Rangaswamy, A. (2004): Marketing Engineering: Computer-assisted Marketing Analysis and Planning, 2nd edition, Trafford, Victoria.

Lovallo, D. and Sibony, O. (2010): The Case for Behavioral Strategy, The McKinsey Quarterly, Vol. 47, pp. 30-43.

Lovallo, D., Viguerie, P., Uhlaner, R. and Horn, J. (2007): Deals without Delusions, Harvard Business Review, Vol. 85, pp. 92-99.

Luce, M., Payne, J. and Bettman, J. (1999): Emotional Trade-Off Difficulty and Choice, Journal of Marketing Research, Vol. 36, pp. 143-159.

Lucey, T. (2002): Quantitative Techniques, 6th edition, Thomson Learning, London.

Lucey, T. (2003): Management accounting, 5th edition, Thomson Learning, London.

Lücke, W. (1991): Investitionslexikon, 2nd edition, Vahlen, Munich.

Lumby, S. (1988): Investment appraisal and financing decisions, 3rd edition, Van Nostrand Reinhold, Workingham.

Madura, J. (2006): International Financial Management, 8th edition, Thomson South-Western, Mason.

Malhotra, D. and Bazerman, M. (2007): Negotiation Genius: How to overcome Obstancles and achieve brilliant Results at the Bargaining Table and Beyond, Bantam, New York.

Mandel, G. (2006): Patently Non-Obvious: Empirical Demonstration that the Hindsight Bias Renders Patent Decisions Irrational, Ohio State Law Journal, Vol. 67, pp. 1.391-1.463.

Mankiw, N. (2009): Principles of Economics, 5th edition, South-Western Cengage Learning, Mason.

Manktelow, K. (1999): Reasoning and thinking, Psychology Press, Hove.

Martel, J. and Matarazzo, B. (2005): Other Outranking approaches, In Figueira, J., Greco, S. and Ehrgott, M. (eds.), Multiple Criteria Decision Analysis: State of the Art Surveys (Springer, New York), pp. 197-262.

Matthäus, W. (2007): Statistische Tests mit Excel leicht Erklärt, Teubner, Wiesbaden.

McCarthy, A., Schoorman, F. and Cooper, A. (1993): Reinvestment Decisions by Entrepreneurs: Rational Decision Making or Escalation of Commitment?, Journal of Business Venturing, Vol. 8, pp. 9-24.

McClave, J. and Benson, P. (1991): Statistics for Business and Economics, 5th edition, Dellen Publishing, San Francisco.

McCray, G., Purvis, R. and McCray, C. (2002): Project Management under Uncertainty: The Impact of Heuristics and Biases, Project Management Journal, Vol. 33, pp. 49-57.

McKelvie, S. (1997): The Availability Heuristic: Effects of Fame and Gender on the Estimated Frequency of Male and Female Names, The Journal of Social Psychology, Vol. 137, pp. 63-78.

McLaney, E. (2006): Business finance: Theory and Practice, 7th edition, Pearson Education, Harlow.

McLaney, E. (2009): Business finance: Theory and Practice, 8th edition, Pearson Education, Harlow.

Metcalfe, J. (1998): Cognitive Optimism: Self-Deception or Memory-Based Processing Heuristics?, Personality and Social Psychology Review, Vol. 2, pp. 100-110.

Mokdad, A., Marks, J., Stroup, D. and Gerberdind, J. (2004): Actual Causes of Death in the United States 2000, Journal of the American Medical Association, Vol. 291, pp. 1239-1245.

Montgomery, D. and Runger, G. (2007): Applied Statistics and Probability for Engineers, 4th edition, Wiley & Sons, Hoboken.

Montier, J. (2007): Behavioural Investing: a Practitioner's Guide to applying Behavioural Finance, Wiley & Sons, Chichester.

Moutier, S. and Houdé, O. (2003): Judgement under Uncertainty and Conjunction Fallacy Inhibition Training, Thinking and Reasoning, Vol. 9, pp. 185-201.

Müller-Lyer, F. (1889): Optische Urteilstäuschungen, Archiv für Anatomie und Physiologie: Physiologische Abteilung 2 (Supplement), pp. 263-270.

Mun, J. (2006): Real Options Analysis: Tools and Techniques for Valuing Strategic Investments and Decisions, 2nd edition, John Wiley & Sons, Hoboken.

Mussweiler, T., Englich, B. and Strack, F. (2004): Anchoring Effect, In Pohl, R. (eds.), Cognitive Illusions: A Handbook on Fallacies and Biases in Thinking, Judgment and Memory (Psychology Press, 2004), pp. 183-200.

Mussweiler, T., Strack, F. and Pfeiffer, T. (2000): Overcoming the inevitable anchoring effect: Considering the Opposite compensates for selective Accessibility, Personality and Social Psychology Bulletin, Vol. 26, pp. 1142-1150.

Neale, N. and Northcraft, G. (1990): Experience, Expertise, and Decision Bias in Negotiation: The Role of Strategic Conceptualization, In Sheppard, B., Bazerman, M. and Lewicki, R. (eds.) Research on Negotiation in Organizations II (JAI Press, 1990), pp. 55-75.

Neisser, U. (1976): Cognition and Reality: Principles and Implications of Cognitive Psychology, W. H. Freeman, New York.

Nevid, J. (2009): Psychology: Concepts and Applications, 3rd edition, Cengage Learning, Boston.

Nijhawan, R. (1997): The Müller-Lyer Illusion Reexamined, In Rock, I. (eds.), Indirect perception (Massachusetts Institute of Technology Press, 1997), pp. 315-333.

Nisbett, R. and Ross, L. (1980): Human Inference: Strategies and Shortcomings of Social Judgment, Prentice Hall, Englewood Cliffs.

Nofsinger, J. (2008): The Psychology of Investing, 3rd edition, Pearson Education, New Jersey.

Over, D. (2004): Rationality and the Normative/Descriptive Distinction, In Koehler, D. and Harvey, N. (eds.), Blackwell Handbook of Judgment & Decision Making (Blackwell Publishing, 2004), pp. 3-18.

Park, J. and Kim, J. (2005): The Effects of Decoys on Preference Shifts: The Role of Attractiveness and Providing Justification, Journal of Consumer Psychology, Vol. 15, pp. 94-107.

Payne, J., Bettman, J. and Schkade, D. (1999): Measuring constructed Preferences: Towards a Building Code, Journal of Risk and Uncertainty, Vol. 19, pp. 243-270.

Pettibone, J. and Wedell, D. (2000): Examining Models on nondominated Decoy Effects across Judgment and Choice, Organizational Behavior and Human Decision Processes, Vol. 81, pp. 300-328.

Piatelli-Palmarini, M. (1994): Inevitable Illusions: How Mistakes of Reason rule our Minds, John Wiley & Sons, New York.

Pinker, S. (1997): How the Mind works, Norton, New York.

Pohl, R. (2004): Introduction: Cognitive Illusions, In Pohl, R. (eds.), Cognitive Illusions: A Handbook on Fallacies and Biases in Thinking, Judgment and Memory (Psychology Press, 2004), pp. 1-20.

Pompian, M. (2006): Behavioral Finance and Wealth Management: How to Build Optimal Portfolios that account for Investor Biases, Wiley & Sons, Hoboken.

Proctor, R. (2006): Managerial Accounting for Business Decisions, 2nd edition, Pearson Education, Harlow.

Rapopport, A. (1989): Decision Theory and Decision Behaviour: Normative and Descriptive Approaches, Kluwer Acadmic Publishers, Dordrecht.

Read, D., Loewenstein, G. and Rabin, M. (1999): Choice bracketing, Journal of Risk and Uncertainty, Vol. 19, pp. 171-197.

Reber, R. (2004): Availability, In Pohl, R. (eds.), Cognitive Illusions: A Handbook on Fallacies and Biases in Thinking, Judgment and Memory (Psychology Press, 2004), pp. 147-163.

Resnik, M. (1987): Choices: an introduction to decision theory, University of Minnesota Press, Minneapolis.

Ritov, I. and Baron, J. (1990): Reluctance to Vaccinate: Omission bias and Ambiguity, Journal of Behavioral Decision Making, Vol. 3, pp. 263-277.

Röhrich, M. (2007): Fundamentals of Investment Appraisal: An Illustration based on a Case Study, Oldenbourg, Munich.

Rosenzweig, P. (2007): The Halo Effect, and the Eight Other Business Delusions That Deceive Managers, Free Press, New York.

Ross, M. and Sicoly, F. (1982): Egocentric Biases in Availability and Attribution, In Kahneman, D., Slovic, P. and Tversky, A. (eds.), Judgment under Uncertainty: Heuristics and Biases (Cambridge University Press, 1982), pp. 179-189.

Russo, J. and Shoemaker, P. (1989): Decision Traps, Simon & Schuster, New York.

Saaty, T. and Vargas, L. (2001): Models, Methods, Concepts & Applications of the Analytic Hierarchy Process, Kluwer Academic Publishers, Dordrecht.

Salinger, E. (1994): Betriebswirtschaftliche Entscheidungstheorie, 3rd edition, Oldenbourg, Munich.

Samuelson, W. and Zeckhauser, R. (1988): Status Quo Bias in Decision Making, Journal of Risk and Uncertainty, Vol. 1, pp. 7-59.

Sanna, L., Schwarz, N. and Stocker, S. (2002): When Debiasing Backfires: Accessible Content and Accessibility Experiences in Debiasing Hindsight, Journal of Experimental Psychology: Learning, Memory, and Cognition, Vol. 28, pp. 497-502.

Savage, L. (1954): The Foundations of Statistics, John Wiley & Sons, New York.

Schäfer, H. (2005): Unternehmensinvestitionen: Grundzüge in Theorie und Management, 2nd edition, Physica, Heidelberg.

Schein, E. (1996): Kurt Lewin's Change Theory in the Field and in the Classroom: Notes toward a Model of managed Learning, Systems Practice, Vol. 9, pp. 27-47.

Schmuckler, M. (2001): What Is Ecological Validity? A Dimensional Analysis, Infancy, Vol. 2, pp. 419-436.

Schwarze, J. (2006): Grundlagen der Statistik II: Wahrscheinlichkeitsrechnung und Induktive Statistik, 8th edition, Verlag Neue Wirtschafts-Briefe, Herne.

Segall, M., Campbell, D. and Herskovits, M. (1966): The Influence of Culture on Visual Perception, Bobbs-Merrill, New York.

Serfas, S. (2008): How Unconscious Information Processing-Related Biases affect the Generation of Knowledge in SMEs: An Exemplary Illustration focusing on Cognitive Biases resulting from the Availability Heuristic, Research Paper, 2nd International Scientific Conference on Knowledge Economy, pp. 1-19.

Shafir, E. (1993): Choosing versus Rejecting: Why some Options are both Better and Worse than Others, Memory & Cognition, Vol. 21, pp. 546-556.

Shafir, E. and Tversky, A. (1995): Decision Making, In Osherson, D. and Smight, E. (eds.), An Invitation to Cognitive Science: Thinking, 2nd edition (Massachusetts Institute of Technology, 1995), pp. 77-100.

Shafir, E., Diamond, P. and Tversky, A. (2000): Money Illusions, In Kahneman, D. and Tversky, A. (eds.), Choices, Values, and Frames (Cambridge University Press, 2000), pp. 335-355.

Shampanier, K., Mazar, N. and Ariely, D. (2007): Zero as a Special Price: the True Value of Free Products, Marketing Science, Vol. 26, pp. 742-727.

Shefrin, H. (2002): Beyond Greed and Fear: Understanding Behavioral Finance and the Psychology of Investing, Oxford University Press, New York.

Shugan, S. (1980): The Cost of Thinking, The Journal of Consumer Research, Vol. 7, pp. 99-111.

Sierke, B. (1990): Investitions-Controlling im Controlling-System, Bing, Korbach.

Simonson, I. (1989): Choice base on Reasons: The Case of Attraction and Compromise Effects, Journal of Consumer Research, Vol. 16, pp. 158-174.

Simonson, I. and Nye, P. (1992): The Effect of Accountability on Susceptibility to Decision Errors, Organizational Behavior and Human Decision Processes, Vol. 51, pp. 416-446.

Slovic P. and Fischhoff, B. (1977): On the Psychology of Experimental Surprises, Journal of Experimental Psychology: Human Perception and Performance, Vol. 3, pp. 544-551.

Slovic, P. (2000): The Construction of Preference, In Kahneman, D. and Tversky, A. (eds.), Choices, Values, and Frames (Cambridge University Press, 2000), pp. 489-502.

Slovic, P. and Lichtenstein, S. (1971): Comparison of Bayesian and Regression Approaches to the Study of Information Processing in Judgment, Organizational Behavior and Human Performance, Vol. 6, pp. 649-744.

Smith, H. (1998): Misconceptions of Chance: Developmental Differences and Similarities in Use of the Representativeness Heuristic, Psychological Reports, Vol. 83, pp. 703-707.

Soll, J. and Klayman, J. (2004): Overconfidence in Interval Estimates, Journal of Experimental Psychology: Learning, Memory, and Cognition, Vol. 30, pp. 299-314.

Soman, D. (2004): Framing, Loss Aversion, and Mental Acounting, In Koehler, D. and Harvey, N. (eds.), Blackwell Handbook of Judgment & Decision Making (Blackwell Publishing, 2004), pp. 379-398.

Spranca, M., Minsk, E. and Baron, J. (1991): Omission and Commission in Judgment and Choice, Journal of Experimental Social Psychology, Vol. 27, pp. 76-105.

Stalmeier, P., Wakker, P. and Bezembinder, T. (1997): Violations of Unidimensional Procedure Invariance, Journal of Experimental Psychology, Vol. 23, pp. 1196-1205.

Staw, B. and Hoang, H. (1995): Sunk Costs in the NBA: why Draft Order affects Playing Time and Survival in Professional Basketball, Administrative Science Quarterly, Vol. 40, pp. 474-494.

Sternberg, R. (2009): Cognitive Psychology, 5th edition, Wadsworth Cengage Learning, Belmont.

Strack, F. and Mussweiler, T. (1997): Explaining the Enigmatic Anchoring Effect: Mechanisms of Selective Accessibility, Journal of Personality and Social Psychology, Vol. 73, pp. 437-446.

Taylor, S. (1982): The availability bias in social perception and interaction, In Kahneman, D., Slovic, P. and Tversky, A. (eds.), Judgment under Uncertainty: Heuristics and Biases (Cambridge University Press, 1982), pp. 190-200.

Teigen, K. (2004): Judgements by Representativeness, In Pohl, R. (eds.), Cognitive Illusions: A Handbook on Fallacies and Biases in Thinking, Judgment and Memory (Psychology Press, 2004), pp. 165-182.

Tenbrunsel, A., Glavin, T., Neale, M. and Bazerman, M. (1996): Cognitions in Organizations, In Clegg, S., Hard, C. and Nord, W. (eds.), Handbook of Organization Studies (Sage Publications, 1996), pp. 313-337.

Thaler, R. (1980): Toward a positive Theory of Consumer Choice, Journal of Economic Behavior and Organization, Vol. 1, pp. 39-60.

Thaler, R. (1994): Quasi Rational Economics, Russell Sage Foundation, New York.

Thompson, L., Gentner, D. and Loewenstein, J. (2000): Analogical training more powerful than Individual Case Training, Organizational Behavior and Human Decision Processes, Vol. 82, pp. 60-75.

Tversky, A. and Kahneman, D. (1974): Judgment under Uncertainty: Heuristics and Biases: Biases in Judgments reveal some Heuristics of Thinking under Uncertainty, Science, Vol. 185, pp. 1124-1131.

Tversky, A. and Kahneman, D. (1981): The Framing of Decisions and the Psychology of Choice, Science, Vol. 211, pp. 453-458.

Tversky, A. and Kahneman, D. (1982): Availability: A Heuristic for Judging Frequency and Probability, In Kahneman, D., Slovic, P. and Tversky, A. (eds.), Judgment under Uncertainty: Heuristics and Biases (Cambridge University Press, 1982), pp. 163-178.

Tversky, A. and Kahneman, D. (1983): Extensional versus Intuitive Reasoning: The Conjunction Fallacy in Probability Judgment, Psychological Review, Vol. 90, pp. 293-315.

Tversky, A. and Kahneman, D. (1992): Advances in Prospect Theory: Cumulative Representation of Uncertainty, Journal of Risk and Uncertainty, Vol. 5, pp. 297-323.

Tversky, A. and Kahneman, D. (2000): Rational Choice and the Framing of Decisions, In Kahneman, D. and Tversky, A. (eds.), Choices, Values, and Frames (Cambridge University Press, 2000), pp. 209-240.

Tversky, A. and Simonson, I. (2000): Context-Dependent Preferences, In Kahneman, D. and Tversky, A. (eds.), Choices, Values, and Frames (Cambridge University Press, 2000), pp. 518-527.

Van Horne, J. and Wachowicz, J. (2008): Fundamentals of Financial Management, 13th edition, Pearson Education, Harlow.

Vogel, F. (1999): Beschreibende und Schließende Statistik, 11th edition, Oldenbourg, Munich.

Von Halle, B. and Goldberg, L. (2009): The Decision Model, Auerbach, Boca Raton.

Von Neumann, J. and Morgenstern, O. (1944): Theory of Games and Economic Behavior, Princeton University Press, Princeton.

Ward, W. and Jenkins, H. (1965): The Display of Information and the Judgment of Contingency, Canadian Journal of Psychology, Vol. 19, pp. 231-241.

Wärneryd, K. (2001): Stock-Market Psychology: how People value and trade Stocks, Edward Elgar Publishing, Cheltenham

Watson, D. and Head, A. (2007): Corporate Finance: Principles & Practice, 4th edition, Pearson Education, Harlow.

Webster, T. (2003): Managerial Economics: Theory and Practice, Elsevier, San Diego.

Weiten, W. (2007): Psychology: Themes and Variations, 8th edition, Wadsworth Cengage Learning, Belmont.

Weitzman, M. (1976): The New Soviet Incentive Model, The Bell Journal of Economics, Vol. 7, pp. 251-257.

Wheaton, K. and Chido, D. (2006): Structured Analysis of Competing Hypotheses: Improving a tested Intelligence Method, Competitive Intelligence Magazine, Vol. 9, pp. 12-15.

Wilson, T., Houston, C., Etling, K. and Brekke, N. (1996): A new Look at Anchoring Effects: Basic Anchoring and its Antecedents, Journal of Experimental Psychology: General, Vol. 125, pp. 387-402.

Wisniewski, M. (2006): Quantitative Methods for Decision Makers, 4th edition, Pearson Education, Harlow.

Yoon, K. and Hwang, C. (1995): Multiple Attribute Decision Making: An Introduction, Sage Publications, Thousand Oaks.

MIX
Papier aus verantwortungsvollen Quellen
Paper from responsible sources
FSC® C105338

If you have any concerns about our products,
you can contact us on
ProductSafety@springernature.com

In case Publisher is established outside the EU,
the EU authorized representative is:
Springer Nature Customer Service Center GmbH
Europaplatz 3, 69115 Heidelberg, Germany

Printed by Libri Plureos GmbH
in Hamburg, Germany